Redefining
Global
Strategy

Redefining Global Strategy

Crossing Borders in a World Where Differences Still Matter

Pankaj Ghemawat

HARVARD BUSINESS SCHOOL PRESS
BOSTON, MASSACHUSETTS

Copyright 2007 Harvard Business School Publishing Corporation
All rights reserved

Printed in the United States of America

11 10 09 08 07   5 4 3 2 1

No part of this publication may be reproduced, stored in or introduced into a retrieval system, or transmitted, in any form, or by any means (electronic, mechanical, photocopying, recording, or otherwise), without the prior permission of the publisher. Requests for permission should be directed to permissions@hbsp.harvard.edu, or mailed to Permissions, Harvard Business School Publishing, 60 Harvard Way, Boston, Massachusetts 02163.

Library of Congress Cataloging-in-Publication Data

Ghemawat, Pankaj.
   Redefining global strategy: crossing borders in a world where differences still matter / Pankaj Ghemawat.
      p. cm.
   Includes bibliographical references and index.
   ISBN-13: 978-1-59139-866-0 (hardcover: alk. paper)
   1. International business enterprises—Management. 2. Strategic planning.
3. Intercultural communication. I. Title.
   HD62.4.G474 2007
   658.4'012—dc22

                                                                    2007009124

The paper used in this publication meets the requirements of the American National Standard for Permanence of Paper for Publications and Documents in Libraries and Archives Z39.48–1992

To Anuradha

Who has helped me understand that globalization
does not mean forgetting where I'm from

Contents

Foreword

I FIRST MET Pankaj Ghemawat in September 1978, when I was looking for a very talented undergraduate to help develop a course for the then-nascent Harvard Negotiation Project. Ghemawat stood out on account of his international orientation as well as his intellectual gifts and curiosity. Working with him for a year confirmed my initial sense that he would go on to do great things.

I watched with interest as Ghemawat sped through his undergraduate and PhD degrees at Harvard in a total of six years. I was pleased when he decided to go consult after receiving his PhD. And I was delighted when he was recruited by Michael Porter to join the Harvard Business School faculty at age twenty-three. He went on to become the youngest professor ever granted tenure at Harvard Business School, on the strength of a body of distinguished work on sustainability and competitive dynamics, particularly *Commitment*, which is my favorite book of his. Or was, until this one.

Redefining Global Strategy is based on a decade of immersion in the strategies of global enterprises. This research has already resulted in a stream of articles in the *Harvard Business Review*, of which the two most recent are "Regional Strategies for Global Leadership" (December 2005), which received HBR's award for the best article published that year, and "Managing Differences: The Central Challenge in Global Strategy," which was published as the lead article in March 2007. But it is only in this book that Ghemawat fully elaborates and explores the implications of his core proposition: that frontiers matter. Our age, he says, is not one of complete—or even near-complete—globalization. Rather, the state of the world is more appropriately characterized as "semiglobalization."

Ghemawat's notion of semiglobalization contradicts the current fanfare about frontiers subsiding and creating a flat world in which people find both work and opportunity without being constrained by their location. For Thomas Friedman, the most prominent purveyor of this view, "flatness" is forced primarily by technology. For Ted Levitt, writing more than twenty years before Friedman, it was the result of a demand-side force, the convergence of tastes. And then there are other variants on this broad vision. But they all naturally lead to an emphasis on size, and on one-size-fits-all strategies.

Ghemawat is not persuaded. I imagine him, like Galileo Galilei before the Inquisition, unable to keep from saying, "But it *does* move around the sun!" In other words, a flat world may be rhetorically appealing to some, but extensive empirical observation and analysis suggest that cultural, political, and geographic barriers between countries still loom large—and have a major influence on global strategy.

If Ghemawat stopped there, he would simply have reminded us that the world is a complex place and that strategic leadership is difficult. But he is interested in providing *actionable knowledge* about global strategies that actually work. So *Redefining Global Strategy* gives the reader coherent, powerful frameworks for thinking about the ways in which borders matter and for evaluating cross-border moves. And perhaps even more importantly, it develops an array of strategies for dealing with such differences—strategies that go well beyond one-size-fits-all.

This array of strategies is particularly appealing to me because in twenty years as a strategy consultant, I have seen many companies fail precisely because they forgot the distinction between size and strategy. However, strategy, which was invented both as a word and as a discipline in the battles of Marathon and Salamis between the Persians and the Greeks, is the art and science of overcoming the advantage of size. Strategy is meant to allow for victory of the small over the large, and the few over the many, at least sometimes.

Ghemawat's concept of semiglobalization not only fits with this broad view of strategy, it also gives us the tools to advance successful globalization. As the founder of the consulting firm Panthea, and as the senior executive adviser on strategic leadership to Booz Allen Hamilton, I am proud that my two firms have recognized the value of these ideas. Their initial reception by Booz Allen clients has been enthusiastic, and we expect that they will help us better understand the world—and change it for the better.

—Nikos Mourkogiannis

Acknowledgments

BEHIND THIS BOOK is a personal journey from a small city in India, to Indiana, back to India, then to Cambridge, Massachusetts, and recently to Barcelona. Professionally, I began to work on the ideas in this book in the mid-1980s, soon after I had joined the Harvard Business School faculty, when I wrote an early analytical piece on global strategy with Mike Spence, one of my thesis advisers.

My interest in imbuing my work on strategy with a cross-border perspective was whetted further by a study on India's competitiveness that Mike Porter and I undertook in the mid-1990s for the Confederation of Indian Industry. Shortly after, I was fortunate enough to take over Mike Yoshino's Global Strategy and Management course at HBS, which provided an opportunity to synchronize research, course development, and writings for practitioners on this topic. I have now been focused on issues related to globalization and global strategy more or less full time for the better part of a decade. This phase of the journey has yielded about fifty case studies and papers, this book, and sundry supporting materials such as a CD on globalization, my Web site (which also lists most of my work to date), and material for several ongoing projects.

I am particularly grateful to the Harvard Business School, which, under Deans Kim Clark and Jay Light, has generously supported this program of study for almost a decade. IESE Business School, under Dean Jordi Canals, has been a wonderful place to put the finishing touches on this book. I am also deeply indebted to the *Harvard Business Review*, where Tom Stewart, David Champion, and others have helped shape and support my attempts to communicate with practitioners. And, of course, thanks to Harvard Business School Press for its work on this book, with particular gratitude to Melinda Merino and Brian Surette for their counsel. Thanks also to my agent, Helen Rees, for guiding me, and to my editor, Jeff Cruikshank, for helping shape a jumble of complex ideas into a book.

My other, mostly content-related, debts are too numerous to acknowledge, including, as they do, learning from scores of colleagues, from the hundreds of executives I've interviewed, and from the thousand-odd students with whom I've worked through the concepts discussed here—as well as from many excellent writings, not all of which can be cited here. Still, I must specifically thank people who have generously read and provided comments on recent drafts of part or all of this book: Steve Altman, Amar Bhide, Dick Caves, Tom Hout, Don Lessard, Anita McGahan, Nikos Mourkogiannis, Jan Oosterveld, Richard Rawlinson, Denise Rehberg, Jordan Siegel, and Lori Spivey. My long-time assistant at Harvard, Sharilyn Steketee, did some of the research for the chapters, read through them, and managed the multiple incarnations of the manuscript. I am also indebted to Ken Mark and Beulah D'Souza for able research assistance. And last but most important, thank you to my wife, Anuradha Mitra Ghemawat, for the reason explained in the dedication—and for many more.

Introduction

MY FIRST INTERNATIONAL case-writing experience, in the early 1990s, had me visit a Pepsi plant in the strife-torn Indian state of Punjab. Given the political environment—a low-grade civil war—many workers were militants who arrived at the plant each day toting their AK-47s. Pepsi had set up a system whereby these could be checked in and then retrieved at the end of a shift. *Absolutely no AK-47s inside the building,* the HR director explained forcefully—introducing me to the large differences with which international business must contend.

This sense of differences has been sharpened by the years I have spent since then working on globalization and global strategy. As a result, instead of focusing on market size and the illusion of a borderless world, this book reminds managers that if their businesses want to cross borders successfully, they need to pay serious attention to the sustained differences between countries in developing and evaluating strategies. And it provides them with the insights and tools necessary to do so.

To illustrate this perspective on globalization—or what I call *semiglobalization*—I'll use football as a metaphor.[1] U.S. readers may be disappointed that the kind of football that I have in mind is what they refer to as soccer, but that itself makes a useful point about the differences between countries. Although football is supposed to be a global phenomenon—former UN secretary general Kofi Annan noted enviously that more countries belong to FIFA, football's governing body, than to the United Nations—its hold on sports fans is very uneven, and the United States constitutes the single largest exception to its general appeal.[2]

That said, the game has come a long way since English villagers began kicking around pigs' bladders in the Middle Ages. Football began to spread internationally during the heyday of the British Empire, but the sport's globalization went into reverse in the interlude between World Wars I and II, as authorities restricted the international transfer of players.

The years after World War II saw escalating international rivalry, particularly around the World Cup. In the late 1950s and early 1960s, Real Madrid emerged as the first great European club, with players from a number of countries.[3] But until the late 1980s, West European leagues continued to limit the number of foreign players to between one and three per team. East European countries, meanwhile, restricted the "export" of their players. And increasing international rivalry did not supersede intense local competition. Thus, matches between Real Madrid and FC Barcelona reenacted the Spanish Civil War—and continue to do so to this day, as I can testify from living in Barcelona and going to watch them play.

The barriers to labor mobility largely disappeared—for club play but not country play—in the 1990s. Economic pressures in East Europe and other poorer parts of the world led to the abandonment of restrictions and the adoption of export-oriented strategies by many local clubs, as well as by football academies established for that purpose. And on the demand side, a ruling by the European Court of Justice in 1995 lifted restrictions on the number of foreign players allowed in European club play. In 1999, Chelsea F.C. became the first club in the history of the English Premiership to start a game without a single English player on the field.[4] By 2004–2005, an estimated 45 percent of the players in that league's starting lineups consisted of foreigners.[5] Similar internationalization is evident in other European clubs. But for World Cup play between countries, FIFA continues to restrict players to representing their countries of origin or citizenship.

Different degrees of cross-border labor mobility have led to very different outcomes. More or less free cross-border movement of players at the club level has concentrated quality and success at the national and regional levels among the richest clubs.[6] In the European Champions League, for example, the number of different teams that qualified for the top eight slots has decreased significantly in the last twenty years. And a recent report by the accounting firm Deloitte & Touche indicates that the concentration of revenues among the top twenty clubs—all European—is increasing as well, as richer clubs with better players secure proportionately more valuable broadcast rights.[7] Interestingly, the club with the most revenues in 2005–2006, Real Madrid with $373 million, thrived financially not just by building local identity but also by targeting global sales of merchandise featuring an all-star cast of *galácticos*, including David Beckham and Ronaldo. (This seems, however, to have exacted a cost on the playing field: as of this writing, Real Madrid has begun to rebuild its lineup with younger players after a spell of embarrassingly bad performance.)

This story of ever-more-concentrated success is not mirrored, however, at the World Cup level. With players' skills sharpened by European club experience, an increasing number of poorer countries have become globally competitive. Thus, the last five World Cups have each featured in the quarterfinals, on average, two teams that had never advanced that far before. And the arrival of these newcomers has *not* led to more blowouts: the average goal differential, from quarterfinals onward, in the last five World Cups has been one goal, versus an average differential of two goals in the first five postwar cups. Clearly, the lack of cross-border labor mobility has led to very different outcomes from club play.

Increased parity at the country level does not, however, mean that all international differences have been ironed out. Detailed statistical analysis of the determinants of the official FIFA rankings sheds some light on the matter. Generally speaking, large countries with Latin cultural origins rank highly, as do countries with temperate climates and high per-capita incomes (up to a point).[8]

Cross-border movements of capital as well as labor merit consideration. Recent years have seen several English Premiership clubs bought out by foreign investors (e.g., Chelsea by Roman Abramovitch). But attempts at foreign investment in Brazilian clubs, for example, have clearly not worked well. Consider the sad tale of Dallas-based buyout firm Hicks, Muse, Tate & Furst and its 1999 decision to invest in Brazilian football. As a company partner put it at the time: "It's hard to imagine a better sector in which to invest in Brazil. If you add up all the fans of professional baseball, basketball, football and hockey in the United States, that number is lower than the number of Brazilians who are soccer fans."[9] Based on this crude arithmetic, Hicks, Muse, assumed control of business dealings for Corinthians, São Paulo's leading club. And it invested more than $60 million in the team in the first year of a ten-year contract.

Unfortunately for Hicks, Muse, the Brazilian club circuit was as politicized and corrupt as the Brazilian style of play was captivating. Corinthians won the World Club championship in 2000, but its performance subsequently slumped, and fans began to protest bitterly against trades of key players, changes in the colors of jerseys, and the addition of advertising. In 2003, amid a row with its local partners, whom it accused of misappropriating funds, Hicks, Muse exited—as did two other foreign groups that had invested in Brazilian football at roughly the same time.

What does this brief discussion of football tell us about globalization—and about global strategy, which is the focus of this book?

- Football's global progress mirrors that of many economic indicators of globalization: there was a peak before World War I, followed by a reversal during and between the two world wars, and then a revival after World War II. The revival has, along a number of dimensions, led to new records being set. At the same time, football's failure to gain traction in the United States, by far the world's largest sports market, reminds us that despite the new records, globalization remains, in many respects, uneven and incomplete. Chapter 1 applies these themes from football to the broader context of globalization.

- Football's failure, so far, in the United States is just one indicator of the continued importance of the differences across countries. Others include the roles that Latin cultures, reasonable temperatures, and threshold levels of economic development play in explaining various countries' success in the FIFA rankings. And restrictions on cross-border labor mobility in World Cup play but not club play highlight the continuing importance of administrative and institutional factors, as does the more favorable record of foreign investment in English clubs than in Brazilian ones. These factors prefigure a framework for thinking about cross-border differences: the CAGE framework, developed in chapter 2, that highlights the cultural, administrative, geographic, and economic differences between countries.

- The story of Hicks, Muse, Tate & Furst's investing in Brazil also illustrates what is probably the most common bias in evaluating cross-border strategies: an emphasis on "size-ism," which fails to appreciate the persistence of differences between countries. Chapter 3 discusses a general structure for evaluating the cross-border effects of strategic moves—the ADDING Value scorecard—that goes beyond a focus on size and economies of size.

- The strategies followed by football clubs exhibit a range of approaches for dealing with the differences between locations. I refer to these approaches as AAA (adaptation, aggregation, and arbitrage) strategies. Many clubs have focused on forging a local identity, that is, *adapting* to particular locations. But there are also clubs that have *aggregated* across borders (e.g., Real Madrid's global merchandise sales). And some clubs in poor countries feed talent to richer counterparts; that is, the poorer clubs assist in *arbitrage*. Arbitrage is also prominent in at least some cross-border investments and in the manufacture of a specialized input, footballs: the Pakistani city of Sialkot has been a famous production hub for close to one hundred years and still accounts for the bulk of world production.[10] The strategies of adaptation to adjust to differences, aggregation to overcome differences, and arbitrage to exploit differences are the topics of chapters 4, 5, and 6, respectively. Chapter 7 is integrative: it examines the extent to which it is possible to mix and match across these AAA strategies for dealing with differences, given their different requirements.

- Finally, the description of football has focused on the state of play as of the end of 2006. But changes cannot be ruled out. For example, FIFA president Sepp Blatter has railed against the dominance of the richest European clubs and, relatedly, the free transfer of players across clubs, comparing the latter to slavery.[11] Analogously, there are always negative portents about globalization to fuel debates about whether it will stall or go into reverse. Chapter 8 uses the insights developed in the earlier chapters to discuss how you should think about such debates—and what your company can do *now* to build a path to a better future.

To recap, what is different about this book about global strategy is its focus on the differences across countries. The idea is to help businesses cross borders profitably by seeing the world as it really is, rather than in idealized terms. To achieve this objective, the book embodies what might be called the three Rs. First, the book is *readable* because of its unified point of view, its concision, the provision of boxed summaries for each chapter, and its use of numerous examples. (Additional examples and discussion can be found on my Web site, http://www.ghemawat.org.) Second, the book is *relevant* for business policymakers because I have written it around their needs (although it may also interest public policymakers or others seeking to understand cross-border business) and have kept the discussion grounded in reality by focusing on value creation and capture. Also important in this regard is the ease with which companies from different parts of the world can customize the frameworks presented—which suggests some obvious follow-on exercises. And third, the book is *rigorous* in the sense of drawing on research in a variety of fields—including international economics, industrial organization, business strategy, and international business—as well as extensive interactions with practitioners.

PART 1

Value in a World of Differences

CHAPTER 1 SUMMARIZES evidence that the current state of the world is one of *semiglobalization*: levels of cross-border integration are generally increasing and, in many instances, setting new records, but fall far short of complete integration and will continue to do so for decades. The chapter goes on to explain why semiglobalization is essential for cross-border strategies to have distinctive content—as well as why failing to keep it in view can be a recipe for poor performance.

Chapter 2 collects the reasons that borders still matter and classifies them in terms of the cultural, administrative, geographic, and economic (CAGE) distances between countries. This framework is usually best applied at the industry level because different types of distance vary greatly in importance from industry to industry. But in most industries, countries of origin *do* have important implications for destinations—a point that mostly eludes more established frameworks for country analysis.

Chapter 3 discusses *why*—if at all—firms should globalize in a world in which distance still matters. It presents a scorecard for tracking value creation that includes but goes beyond the familiar components of size and economies of size. It also supplies a set of analytical guidelines and a list of specific questions to ask—and answer. The aim is to foster more realism about how cross-border strategies will add value in the face of large cross-border differences. Such strategies themselves are the topic of part 2 of this book.

1

Semiglobalization and Strategy

The globalization of markets is at hand. With that, the multinational commercial world nears its end, and so does the multinational corporation . . . The multinational corporation operates in a number of countries, and adjusts its products and processes in each, at high relative cost. The global corporation operates with resolute constancy . . . it sells the same things in the same way everywhere.

—Ted Levitt, "The Globalization of Markets," 1983

A QUARTER OF A CENTURY after Ted Levitt's bold pronouncements, excitement about the globalization of markets has given way to excitement about the globalization of production.[1] But what has remained constant is the vision of a globalization apocalypse, sweeping all before it. And this apocalyptic vision leads to a focus on strategies for a post-apocalyptic, integrated world—strategies that inevitably have a one-size-fits-all character. That is why Levitt's definition of global strategy as a strategy for an integrated world still reigns.[2]

And, with apologies to my late colleague at the Harvard Business School, that definition is still as wrongheaded. In this book, I redefine global strategy to describe a broader set of strategic possibilities. I argue that differences between countries are larger than generally acknowledged. As a result, strategies that presume complete global integration tend to place far too much emphasis on international standardization and scalar expansion.

While it is, of course, important to take advantage of similarities across borders, it is also critical to address differences. In the near and medium term, effective cross-border strategies will reckon with both, that is, with the reality that I call *semiglobalization*. The primary goal of this book is to stretch our thinking about cross-border strategies for a semiglobalized world.

This chapter begins by establishing that semiglobalization is, in fact, the real state of the world today—and tomorrow. It does so by taking some data on board, because, as the late Daniel Patrick Moynihan observed, we are all entitled to our own opinions, but not our own facts. The chapter then starts to address the implications for company strategy, using the example of one of the great border-crossing companies, Coca-Cola. Around the time that Levitt's article appeared, Coke embarked on a global strategy of the sort that he recommended. The problems with that strategy took a while to surface, but by the millennium, Coke was adrift in a sea of troubles. Only recently has it started to regain its bearings. Other companies can either learn from Coke's experience or rediscover the same lessons about semiglobalization the hard way, through trial and error.

Apocalypse Now?

According to the Library of Congress catalog, we are positively awash in books on globalization. More than *five thousand* such books were published between 2000 and 2004, compared with fewer than five hundred in the whole of the 1990s. In fact, between the mid-1990s and 2003, the rate of increase in globalization-related titles—more than doubling every eighteen months—surpassed the celebrated Moore's Law!

Amid all this clutter, the books on globalization that *have* managed to attract significant attention have done so by painting visions of a "globalization apocalypse." These volumes tend to exhibit what scholars cite as general characteristics of apocalyptic argumentation: emotional rather than cerebral appeals, reliance on prophecy, semiotic arousal (i.e., treating everything as a sign), an emphasis on creating "new" people, and, perhaps above all, a clamor for attention.[3] The Flattening of the Earth is the globalization apocalypse that occupies center stage as of this writing.[4] Thus, during a recent TV interview, the first question I was asked—quite earnestly—was why I still thought the world was round![5] But other visions of the globalization apocalypse have been propounded as well: the Death of Distance, the End of History, or Levitt's own favorite, the Convergence of Tastes. Some writers in this vein view the apocalypse as a good thing—an escape from the ancient tribal rifts that have divided humans, or an opportunity to sell the same thing to everyone on earth.

Others see it as a bad thing: a process that will lead to everyone eating the same fast food. But they all tend to assume (or predict) nearly complete internationalization.

This is where I disagree strenuously, but on the basis of data rather than opinion. *Most types of economic activity that can be conducted either within or across borders are still quite localized by country.*

Ask yourself, for example, how large total foreign direct investment (FDI) flows are in relation to gross global fixed capital formation. (To put it another way, of all the capital being invested around the world, how much is being done by companies outside their home countries?) Maybe you've heard the rhetoric about "investment knowing no boundaries," and so on. The fact is, the ratio of FDI to overall fixed capital formation has been less than 10 percent for each of the last three years for which data are available (2003–2005). In other words, FDI accounts for less than a dime out of every capital dollar invested—or significantly less if one recognizes that much of FDI involves mergers and acquisitions, that is, investment that doesn't actually generate incremental capital expenditures. And although merger waves can push the ratio of FDI to gross fixed capital formation to higher than 10 percent, the ratio has never quite reached 20 percent.[6]

FDI isn't an isolated, unrepresentative example. Figure 1-1 summarizes data on internationalization along ten dimensions. As you can see, the levels of internationalization along these dimensions all cluster much closer to 10 percent—which also happens to be the average across the ten categories—than to 100 percent.[7] The biggest exception in absolute terms—the trade-to-GDP ratio shown at the bottom of the figure—probably recedes most of the way back toward 20 percent if you adjust for double-counting.[8] So if I had to guess the internationalization level of some activity about which I had no particular information, I would guess it to be much closer to 10 percent than to 100 percent! I call this the "10 percent presumption."

The 10 percent presumption notwithstanding, I prefer to talk of semiglobalization rather than "deciglobalization." One reason is that 10 percent is not meant to be any kind of global constant: my best guess is that the next few decades will witness increased internationalization of many of the categories in figure 1-1, and a (slow) upward drift in their average. Second, if internationalization levels *are* setting new records in many respects, international activity probably warrants a share of attention that exceeds its current share of total economic activity—it is increasingly important and its surge is taking it into uncharted territory. Third, business interest in internationalization may also exceed general internationalization levels because businesses have some distinct advantages—as well as disadvantages—compared with other channels for cross-border coordination. Thus, the largest companies are significantly more internationalized than

FIGURE 1-1

The 10 percent presumption

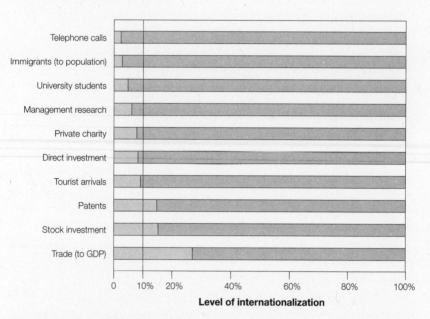

Level of internationalization

Note: The measures are defined as follows. **Telephone calls:** international component of total calling minutes; **immigrants (to population):** stock of long-term international immigrants as a percentage of global population; **university students:** foreign students as a percentage of total OECD university enrollment; **management research:** percentage of research papers with a cross-border component; **private charity:** international component of U.S. private giving; **direct investment:** foreign direct investment flows as a percentage of gross global fixed capital formation; **tourist arrivals:** international arrivals as percentage of total tourist arrivals; **patents:** patents of OECD residents involving international cooperation; **stock investment:** international component of U.S. investors' stock holdings; **trade (to GDP):** global exports of merchandise and nonfactor services as a percentage of global gross domestic product (GDP).

Sources: Data are presented for as close to 2004 as possible and are for that year unless noted otherwise. The figure for phone calls is based on data from the International Telecommunications Union's telecom database and is for 2001, although coverage drops off sharply, as of this writing, for more recent years. The estimate of the stock of long-term international immigrants is based on UNESCO, International Organization for Migration, *World Migration 2005: Costs and Benefits of International Migration* (Geneva: International Organization for Migration, June 2005). The data on foreigners among university students is from and for OECD (Organisation for Economic Co-operation and Development) countries and excludes Mexico and Luxembourg; see *OECD Education Online Database* (English) in OECD Statistics version 3.0. The figure for management research is drawn from Steve Werner, "Recent Developments in International Management Research: A Review of 20 Top Management Journals," *Journal of Management* 28 (2002): 277–305. The (generous) estimate for the international component of private charitable giving is for the United States only and was supplied by Geneva Global. The internationalization of direct investment is measured by dividing FDI flows by gross fixed capital formation; the internationalization of trade (merchandise and nonfactor services) is calculated by dividing FDI by gross domestic product (GDP), with all data taken from the *World Investment Report* issued annually by the U.N. Conference on Trade and Development (UNCTAD). The estimate for tourist arrivals is based on estimates by the World Tourism and Travel Council for 2000. The patent data are drawn from OECD, *Science, Technology and Industry Scoreboard 2005*. Data on portfolio investment are for U.S. investors' stockholdings, as reported and analyzed in Bong-Chan Kho, René M. Stulz, and Francis E. Warnock, "Financial Globalization, Governance, and the Evolution of the Home Bias," working paper (June 2006). Available at SSRN: http://ssrn.com/abstract=911595.

the 10 percent level: the one hundred largest nonfinancial corporations, for example, have, on average, one-half their sales, assets, and employment overseas.[9] And many smaller companies aspire to increase their internationalization levels.

So the point of the data presented in figure 1-1—and other data on cross-border market integration that I discuss at much greater length and more systematically in my published academic research—is not that we should neglect cross-border issues, but that we should see them from a semiglobalized perspective.[10] From this perspective, the most astonishing aspect of various announcements of the globalization apocalypse is the extent of exaggeration involved.

Apocalypse in the Near Term?

There is an obvious rejoinder available to apocalyptics: the assertion that even if the world isn't quite flat today, it will be tomorrow.[11]

To deal with such an assertion, we have to look at trends rather than at levels of integration at one point in time. The results are interesting. Along a few dimensions, integration reached its all-time high many years ago. For example, rough calculations suggest that the fraction of the world's population accounted for by long-term international immigrants was slightly higher in 1900—the high-water mark of an earlier era of migration—than in 2005.[12]

Along other dimensions, new records *are* being set. But this has happened only relatively recently, and only after long periods of stagnation and reversal. For example, FDI stocks as a ratio of GDP peaked before World War I and didn't return to that level until the 1990s. In fact, some economists have argued that the most remarkable development over the last few centuries was the *declining* level of internationalization between the two world wars, of which FDI is a particularly striking illustration.[13]

And finally, there *are* dimensions along which pre–World War I levels of integration were matched and surpassed relatively soon after World War II. International trade in relation to GDP is the leading example: it surpassed pre–World War I records during the 1960s, reached the 20 percent level for the first time in 1979, and, over the next twenty-five years, increased to 27 percent. Extrapolating this rate of increase would imply a trade-to-GDP ratio of less than 35 percent by 2030. Unprecedented yes, but hardly apocalyptic.[14]

It is useful to supplement such extrapolations with some consideration of the forces behind the trends. Consider the two drivers of cross-border integration that have been emphasized the most by apocalyptics:[15]

- Technological improvements, particularly in communications technologies
- Policy changes that have engaged more countries in the world economy

The question we have to ask is this: Do these two important forces really push us toward an integrated world in the near term?

Improving Communications Technologies

Technological improvements seem to be the most frequently cited drivers of the alleged globalization apocalypse.[16] Given their rate of improvement over the last century, transportation and, particularly, communications technologies have attracted the most attention. For example, the cost of a three-minute telephone call from New York to London fell from $350 in 1930 to about 40 cents in 1999 and is now approaching zero for voice-over-Internet telephony. And the Internet itself is just one of many newer forms of connectivity—enabled by digitalization and the convergence of communications and computing—that have progressed several times faster than plain old telephone service. This pace of improvement has inspired many apocalyptic announcements, including this one, from one of the better books of this sort, Frances Cairncross's *Death of Distance*:

> New ideas will spread faster, leaping borders. Poor countries will have immediate access to information that was once restricted to the industrial world and traveled only slowly, if at all, beyond it. Entire electorates will learn things that once only a few bureaucrats knew. Small companies will offer services that previously only giants could provide. In all these ways, the communications revolution is profoundly democratic and liberating, leveling the imbalance between large and small, rich and poor.[17]

There is a kernel of plausibility to some of Cairncross's ideas. Technologies and standards do enable connectivity and collaboration at a distance, and that is important. It is also likely that, as Cairncross asserts, the separation of where certain services can be *performed* from where they are *delivered* will matter a great deal.

Nevertheless, it's a gross exaggeration to jump from these kernels to proclaiming the "death of distance" based on improving communications technologies. Reconsider the Internet itself. The internationalization of Internet traffic is impossible to measure precisely, particularly because of problems sizing up domestic flows. But the best estimates I have been able to locate indicate an internationalization level a bit below 20 percent, that is, within a factor of two of 10 percent.[18] In terms of changes rather than levels, the international share and, particularly, the intercontinental share of total traffic is supposed to be decreasing rather than increasing, for reasons ranging from surging peer-to-peer traffic to the development of alternatives to the United States, which until recently was the hub for virtually all international switching.

Business-focused examples permit more definite statements based on better data. Look at information technology (IT) services, which are often cited as an illustration of technologically enabled globalization. A total of 2 percent or 11 percent of such work—depending on whether one looks at the total potential market or only the immediately addressable part of it—is currently offshored.[19] Or for an even more net-centric example that helps explain barriers at borders as well as exemplifying their effects, consider Google.

The company boasts of supporting more than one hundred languages and, partly as a result, has recently been rated *the* top global Web site. But Google's reach in Russia—cofounder Sergey Brin's country of origin—was only 28 percent in 2006, versus 64 percent for the market leader in search services, Yandex, and 53 percent for Rambler, two local competitors that account for 91 percent of the Russian market for ads linked to Web searches.[20] Google's problems reflect, in part, linguistic complexities: Russian nouns have three genders and up to six cases, verbs are very irregular, and the meaning of words can depend on their ending or the context. In addition, local competitors have adapted better to the local context by, for example, developing payment mechanisms through traditional banks to compensate for the dearth of credit cards and online payment infrastructure. And though Google *has* doubled its reach since 2003, this has required setting up a physical presence in Russia and hiring engineers there, underlining the continued importance of physical location.

Google's highly publicized travails with Chinese censors illustrate a different set of reasons that borders continue to matter: governments have become more adept at creating closed national networks and enforcing local laws (aided, in part, by Internet geographic identification technologies that continue to improve). Nor is it just totalitarian governments that flex their muscles in such ways. Many experts view the success of the French government's 2000 effort to restrict sales of Nazi memorabilia by Yahoo! as the key legal precedent in this regard. And the intervention that has probably had the biggest economic impact is the U.S. government's 2006 ban on online gambling.

The implications of all these barriers at the borders for the Internet are discussed at length in a book with the telling subtitle *Illusions of a Borderless*

World, which argues that: "What we once called a global network is becoming a collection of nation-state networks."[21] Chapter 2 looks more generally at barriers to cross-border economic activity and collects and classifies them in terms of the CAGE (cultural-administrative-geographic-economic) distance framework for thinking about the differences between countries.

Policy Openings

A second notable driver of cross-border integration is a constellation of policy changes that led many countries—particularly China, India, and the former Soviet Union—to come in from the cold and participate more extensively in the international economy. Economists Jeffrey Sachs and Andrew Warner provide one of the better-researched (although still apocalyptic) descriptions of these policy changes and their implications:

> The years between 1970 and 1995, and especially the last decade, have witnessed the most remarkable institutional harmonization and economic integration among nations in world history. While economic integration was increasing throughout the 1970s and 1980s, the extent of integration has come sharply into focus only since the collapse of communism in 1989. In 1995, one dominant global economic system is emerging.[22]

Yes, such policy openings are important. But to paint them as a sea change is inaccurate, at best. Remember that integration is still relatively limited. Meanwhile, the policies that we changeable humans enact are surprisingly reversible. Thus, Francis Fukuyama's *End of History,* in which liberal democracy and technologically driven capitalism were supposed to have triumphed over other ideologies, seems quite quaint today.[23] Especially in the wake of September 11, 2001, Samuel Huntington's *Clash of Civilizations* looks a bit more prescient.[24]

But even if you stay on the economic plane, as Sachs and Warner mostly do, you quickly see counterevidence to the supposed irreversibility of policy openings. The so-called Washington consensus around market-friendly, open policies ran up against the Asian currency crisis and has since frayed substantially—in the swing toward "neopopulism" across much of Latin America, for example—to the point where we are starting to see working papers with titles such as "Is the Washington Consensus Dead?" In terms of outcomes, the number of countries—in Latin America, coastal Africa, and the former Soviet Union—that have dropped out of the "convergence club" (defined in terms of narrowing productivity and structural gaps vis-à-vis the advanced industrialized countries) is at least as impressive as the number of countries that have joined the club.[25] At a multilateral level, the suspension of the Doha round of trade talks in the summer of 2006—prompting *The Economist* to run a cover titled "The Future of Globalization" and depicting a beached wreck—is not a good omen.[26] In addition, the recent wave of cross-border mergers and acquisitions seems to be encountering more protectionism in a broader range of countries than did the previous wave in the late 1990s.

Of course, given that sentiments in this regard have shifted more than once in recent decades, they may yet shift again in the future. Such possible inflection points are discussed further in chapter 8. The point here is not only that it is *possible* to turn the clock back on globalization-friendly policies, but also that we have a relatively recent example of that actually happening, during the interwar period. In particular, we have to consider the possibility that really deep international economic integration may not mix well with national sovereignty.[27]

So while the technological drivers of increased cross-border integration may be irreversible, we can't say the same about policy drivers. Policy drivers are, therefore, an even shakier basis for apocalyptic visions of complete cross-border integration—not to mention strategy making predicated on such visions!

It is interesting to speculate about why people's beliefs in globalization overshoot the reality of semiglobalization to the extent that they do. Jean de la Fontaine's aphorism "Everyone believes very easily what they fear or desire" subsumes at least some of the explanations: the paranoia of those who fear world domination by multinationals, the smug superiority of elites who have been variously characterized as Davos men and cosmocrats, the terminal insecurity of those trying to be "with it," the naive utopianism of internationalists, and so forth. But spending more time on this issue is a little bit like H. L. Mencken's characterization of going to the zoo: engaging, but not especially productive. So it's time to turn to the implications for companies and their global strategies, which we will pursue by looking at the rather amazing story of Coke.

The Case of Coke

Even companies with substantial global experience, presence, and success can fall prey to visions of the apocalypse—and thereby place themselves in great peril. A particularly cautionary case is that of Coca-Cola, which has a broader global presence than just about any other company in the world, owns what is reckoned to be the world's most valuable brand, and is much more profitable overseas than at home. Until the late 1990s,

Coke was also regarded as an exemplar of global management. But since then, it has experienced a fall from grace, from which it is still recovering. Consider Coke under successive CEOs.

Background

Founded in 1886, Coke made its first move outside the United States in 1902, when it entered Cuba—the same year that archrival Pepsi-Cola started up business. By 1929, five years before Pepsi set up its first foreign venture (in Canada), Coke was being sold in seventy-six countries around the world. Its international presence was greatly bolstered by World War II, when keeping U.S. troops overseas supplied with the soft drink became government policy. Coke, exempted from wartime sugar rationing, built sixty-three bottling plants around the world. Its global push continued after the war, under Robert Woodruff, who ran the company from the early 1920s to the beginning of the 1980s and was an avowed flag-planter: "In every country in the world, [Coca-]Cola dominates. We feel that we have to plant our flag everywhere, even before the Christians arrive. Cola's destiny is to inherit the earth."[28]

But despite this triumphalism (which one wit referred to as "Coca-Colonization"), Coke's strategy continued to be "multilocal" over this period. Its local operations were more or less independently managed. Their primary objective was to support a network of over one thousand bottlers, which employed more than fifty times as many people as did the mother ship and actually undertook most of the activities performed by the Coke system.

Roberto Goizueta: Exploiting Similarities

Roberto Goizueta, who took over as Coke's CEO in 1981, continued Woodruff's push into international markets but also set out to transform how they were managed. Over the course of his tenure, Coke came to *define* the aggressively globalized corporation: its strategy reflected Goizueta's sense that the only fundamental difference between markets in the United States and other countries was the lower average levels of market penetration overseas. As he put it in one speech, "At this point in time in the United States, people consume more soft drinks than any other liquid, including ordinary tap water. If we take full advantage of our opportunities, some day, not too many years into our second century, we will see the same wave catching on in market after market."[29]

This core belief in similarities across countries underpinned a global strategy that placed ever more emphasis on international growth, scale economies, statelessness, ubiquity, and centralization with standardization:

- *Growth fever:* Although U.S. volume growth slowed in the mid-1980s, Goizueta clung to historic targets and placed ever more emphasis on the non-U.S. operations as a way of meeting them. Given a belief in similarities across countries, the rest of the world seemed to be a blue ocean of growth opportunities: in Goizueta's last year as CEO, for example, Coke sold thirty gallons of soft drinks per capita in the United States (5 percent of the world's population), versus an average of three and one-half gallons per capita in the rest of the world. Room to grow!

- *Economies of scale:* Goizueta was also convinced of endless scale economies that would increasingly concentrate market share in Coke's hands. As he explained to Coke's bottlers in a speech shortly before his death, "We already have the most popular brand in the world. In fact, we have four of the top five soft drink brands . . . As I see it, that is a giant head start. I cannot think of one business that is in a better position to succeed than ours . . . in a time when trade barriers are tumbling."[30] Again, this element of Goizueta's strategy went hand in hand with a belief in similarities across countries.

- *Statelessness:* In 1996, Goizueta declared that "the labels *international* and *domestic*, which adequately described our business structure in the past, no longer apply. Today, our company, which just happens to be headquartered in the United States, is truly a *global company*."[31] And he acted on this assertion by officially embedding the U.S. organization in what used to be the international organization—although in practice, the U.S. operation continued to be an entity unto itself. The point is that such a move would make perfect conceptual sense, given a faith in cross-border similarities, because maintaining separate U.S. and international organizations would then be duplicative at best and probably dysfunctional (in the sense of creating unnecessary silos).

- *Ubiquity:* Goizueta inherited an enterprise that already operated in 160 countries; by the time he departed, that number had nearly reached 200. Some of this expansion—such as into East Europe as the Berlin Wall came down—made clear sense. But other market penetration efforts seem to have been justified on the basis of faith rather than market analysis. Thus, after the Soviet Union left Afghanistan—but as turmoil there continued—Coke successfully raced Pepsi to be the first to bring its soft drinks back to the Afghani market, in 1991.[32]

- *Centralization and standardization:* In pursuit of the objectives described above, Goizueta engaged in an unprecedented amount of centralization and standardization. Divisions were consolidated, and regional groups headquartered in Atlanta. Consumer research, creative services, TV commercials, and most promotions were put under the supervision of Edge Creative, Coke's internal ad agency, with the idea of standardizing these marketing activities—and the effect of further increasing the head count at headquarters. At the same time, the company designated so-called anchor bottlers, which would often operate in more than one country, and in which Coke would take equity stakes ranging from 20 to 49 percent— leading the company to become more involved internationally in decisions that it had previously delegated to (more) independent bottlers.

The emphasis on centralization and standardization obviously created a bias toward a one-size-fits-all strategy. But few were inclined to argue with it at the time. Coke had been rated *the* most admired U.S. corporation by *Fortune* in 1995 and 1996, and would be again in 1997. More objectively, its market value increased from $4 billion to $140 billion over Goizueta's sixteen-year tenure. Still, these impressive accomplishments reflected Coke's fundamental strengths and Goizueta's assiduity in exploiting them (as well as some creative accounting toward the end of this period in buying and selling bottlers), rather than the fundamental soundness of the one-size-fits-all approach. In light of his successors' travails, that approach turned out to have been grossly overrated.

Douglas Ivester: Staying the Course

When Goizueta died unexpectedly in 1997, he was succeeded by his chief financial officer, Douglas Ivester. The CFO had masterminded the strategy of buying bottlers and reselling them to Coke affiliates, with the gains booked as operating income; this practice helped mask pressures on concentrate profitability. Ivester shared Goizueta's vision of limitless international growth: his first letter to Coke's shareholders was titled "A Business in Its Infancy" and contained a section with the heading "Why is a billion [daily servings of Coke] just the beginning? A look at the other 47 billion."[33] Ivester clung to the other elements of Goizueta's global strategy as well: when a reporter asked him if Coke would change direction, his response was, "No left turns, no right turns."

But Ivester's strategy of staying the course quickly ran into roadblocks, many of them demand related. The world economy began to sag almost on the day he moved into the corner office, with Brazil and Japan—two of Coke's largest overseas markets—taking economic nosedives. The afore-mentioned Asian currency crisis intensified with a vengeance in 1998. By 1999, the Russian operations were limping along at 50 percent capacity.[34] The same analysts who had previously assigned high values to Coke's stock because of its global "presence" now marked it down for its global "exposure."

Ivester discounted the growth shortfalls as short-run setbacks and re-fused to cut the 7–8 percent volume growth target that had been set—and achieved—under Goizueta, although he did trim the earnings growth target. But by late 1999, Coke's stock valuation had declined by about *$70 billion* from its peak as a result of these problems and others, including fraying relationships with governments, particularly in Europe, and with bottlers. Regulators in the European Union resisted Coke's attempts—directed out of its headquarters—to acquire Orangina and Cadbury Schweppes, and lags in tackling contamination problems in France and Belgium caused fur-ther strains. Bottlers had begun to find Coke overbearing as well. They were under profit pressures in many geographies and were particularly embit-tered by Coke's attempts to stuff channels as its growth rate came under pressure. The last straw for them was Ivester's attempt to sustain perform-ance by imposing a 7.6 percent concentrate price increase. They put enor-mous pressure on Coke's board, to which they had always had a back channel, to fire Ivester. It did.

Douglas Daft: Succumbing to Differences

Ivester's successor was Douglas Daft, who had previously headed Coke's Middle and Far East Group. Daft's years in the field had imbued him with the belief that the way to win globally was to transfer strategic decision making to local executives. As he put it in January 2000, "No one drinks globally. Local people get thirsty and go to their retailer and buy a locally made Coke."[35] He elaborated on this theme in a March 2000 newspaper article titled "Think Local, Act Local":

> As the century was drawing to a close, the world had changed course, and we had not. The world was demanding greater flexibility, respon-siveness, and local sensitivity, while we were further centralizing decision-making and standardizing our practices, moving further away from our traditional multi-local approach . . . If our local colleagues develop an idea or strategy that is the right thing to do locally, and it fits within our fundamental values, policies, and standards of integrity and quality, then they have the authority and responsibility to make it happen.[36]

This was more than just rhetorical froth for locals to feel good about. Daft made an abrupt about-face in terms of how Coke was to be managed. He ordered six thousand layoffs—most of them at headquarters in Atlanta—and launched a massive reorganization that, among other things, aimed to relocate decision making closer to local markets. Perhaps the single most surprising announcement—which sparked an exodus of top marketing talent—was that no more global advertisements would be made. Instead, ad budgets and creative control were placed in the hands of local executives, who were understandably delighted—but also underprepared. As a result, quality suffered even more than scale economies. A flood of homegrown ads hit the airwaves, ranging from people streaking naked across a beach (in an Italian ad) to an angry grandmother in a wheelchair leaving a family reunion when her granddaughter couldn't come up with a Coke (in a U.S.-made spot). And the new umbrella themes proved short-lived as well: *Enjoy* lasted fifteen months, and *Life Tastes Good* five months (versus *Always,* which ran from 1993 to 2000).

Given this significant flailing around, it should come as no surprise that volume growth sagged. It averaged only 3.8 percent in 2000 and 2001, versus the 5.2 percent achieved in 1998 and 1999 under Ivester.

At a company that has traditionally cherished growth, this was unacceptable. In March 2002, the *Wall Street Journal* reported, "The 'think local, act local' mantra is gone. Oversight over marketing is returning to Atlanta." A hundred or so marketers in Atlanta had been reconstituted as the apex of a global marketing group that would set strategy for core brands and agency engagement, develop marketing talent, and help local markets share best practices. But efforts to rebuild headquarters capabilities in this and other functions lagged because hiring and integrating people required much more time than firing them had. Meanwhile, the advertising churn continued. As a result, Coke's volume growth rate recovered to only 4.7 percent over 2002–2003, well below the long-run target of 5–6 percent (to which Daft had lowered it in 2001), and its stock continued to stagnate. In February 2004, Coke announced Daft's retirement.

Neville Isdell: Managing Similarities and Differences

Coke looked outside as well as inside for a successor to Daft and ultimately tapped a retired Coke executive, E. Neville Isdell, who signed on in May 2004. The story of Coke under Isdell is still being written, but his moves in his first two years seem consistent with his publicly expressed viewpoint that under his immediate predecessors, the "pendulum swung too far over." Isdell has turned his back on the extreme localization that Daft initiated by continuing to rebuild headquarters capabilities and recentralize elements of marketing, with a particular emphasis on bigger, more universal advertising themes. Notably, however, this rejection of localization has *not* been accompanied by a reversion to Goizueta's and Ivester's one-size-fits-all approach with its emphasis on extreme standardization:

- *Growth fever* has receded as a result of Isdell's reduction of Coke's long-run volume growth target to 3–4 percent. Stock analysts, who no longer considered Daft's 5–6 percent target credible, actually reacted positively.

- *Economies of scale* and selling a few established soda brands are no longer Coke's primary focus: innovation, particularly in non-carbonated beverages, is.

- *Statelessness* is out. Early in 2006, Isdell reinstituted a position Goizueta dissolved a decade earlier: a head of all international operations outside North America. The intent was not just to improve possibilities for coordination overseas, but also to be realistic in recognizing the distinctive features and challenges of the home region. This is a far cry from the belief that for a company as global as Coke, there is no meaningful distinction left between home and abroad.

- *Ubiquity* has not been abandoned, but Isdell's emphasis on "looking at where we are most profitable and then expand[ing] our offerings there" does point toward more nuanced resource-allocation decisions.

- *Centralization and standardization* have been moderated. The regional heads have more authority than they did under Goizueta and Ivester, and Coke's strategies now exhibit more variation at the country level. In China and India, in particular, Coke has lowered price points, reduced costs by indigenizing inputs and modernizing bottling operations, and upgraded logistics and distribution, especially rurally. And as noted, there is more emphasis now on variety.

The last bullet point bears further discussion. What Coke headquarters seems to have realized, in the past few years, is that it *may not make sense to compete the same way in all markets.*

To be fair, this recognition really dates back to Daft: "I'm *not* saying that every market will turn into a mirror image of North America or Australia. What consumers in our most promising markets want from us may develop differently—maybe even *very* differently—than they have in our established markets."[37]

Unfortunately for Coke, Daft responded by letting a thousand flowers bloom. But such an approach naturally raises the question of why the whole is more than the sum of its parts. If there are no benefits to be derived from similarities across borders, why are the different country operations part of the same company in the first place?

Under Isdell, in contrast, Coke is trying to leverage ideas that have worked well in one market to rethink how to compete in others—in a way that *does* afford room for cross-border value addition. Particularly notable in this regard is Coke's reliance on what it has learned in Japan (see the box "Coke in Japan") to figure out how to become less cola driven in other markets. This is important in the United States, for example, because obesity has become a major concern, and also in China, where resistance to cola is compounded by an aversion to dark drinks. And in parallel, there is a newfound emphasis on globalizing noncola brands instead of simply treating them as localized add-ons.

In sum, Coke's strategy under Isdell should be seen as an attempt to find a new and improved way of competing across borders, instead of settling for some compromise between Goizueta's and Ivester's extreme centralization and standardization and Daft's extreme decentralization and localization—that would probably also compromise performance. How well this new strategy will work remains to be seen, but at least Coke is no longer seesawing between those two extremes. Instead, it is attempting to get off the seesaw altogether and compete in a way that neither ignores the differences across countries nor caves in to them entirely—that is, it recognizes the reality of semiglobalization.

Beyond Coke

It is time to extrapolate from the Coke case. This section begins by discussing why other companies may be subject to some of the same gravitational pull of one-size-fits-all strategies that Coke experienced under Goizueta and Ivester. The discussion then takes a cue from Coke's lurch toward localization under Daft to look at the possibility of protracted weakness after the selection of such strategy, instead of a quick recovery from it. It concludes by using Isdell's strategy as a springboard to a third way of competing across borders—a way that is more than a halfway house between the extremes of one-size-fits-all globalization and parochial local variation.

Broad Biases

The Coke story, although particularly colorful, is far from unique. Other examples of overstretch and retreat abound. Vodafone, in a faster-moving environment, managed to go through a similar cycle of overstretch-and-

Coke in Japan

Coke's dominance of the Japanese market can be traced back to the U.S. occupation of the country after World War II and the troops who stayed on there. As a result, Coke enjoys a crushing market-share lead in Japan, which is its most profitable major market and generates more profits than the rest of the countries in Asia and the Middle East combined. But this dominance is not due to Japan's being cola driven. Cola accounts for only a small share of Coke's sales there. The bulk of its Japanese sales and profits comes from selling canned coffees and two hundred other eclectic products, such as Real Gold, a hangover cure, and Love Body, a tea that some believe increases bust sizes.[a] The variety of products in the Japanese market reflects a limited appetite for colas, the need to offer multiple products to fill up vending machines, and a faddishness that has led Coke to introduce as many as a hundred new products there every year. Headquarters did not always welcome this level of variety; in fact, the leading Coke product in Japan, Georgia Coffee, was reportedly developed by bottlers over objections from headquarters and given its name as an ironic comment on how helpful headquarters had been. However, because the Japanese operations were so profitable, headquarters cut them some slack.

As a result, Coke Japan has developed its own product development capabilities and the ability to handle many more—and individually smaller—brands. Under Isdell, Coke has been deconstructing the "Total Beverage Company" model that it has worked out in Japan to figure out how to become less cola driven elsewhere.

a. Information on Coke's product offerings and introductions in Japan is based on Dean Foust, "Queen of Pop," *BusinessWeek*, 7 August 2006, 44–51.

retreat in a much shorter time span. While it built up a substantial presence in Japan and the United States as well as its home region of Europe, differences in mobile telephone standards invalidated its attempts to achieve interregional economies of scale. And in the tenth year of the DaimlerChrysler merger, speculation abounds about a demerger. Whatever the eventual outcome, the intended results have clearly not been achieved.

One way of deriving some insight into the incidence of such cases is to consider in a more general context the biases associated with Coke's failure, under Goizueta and Ivester, to take the differences across countries seriously.

- *Growth fever:* Even a company as internationalized as Coke averaged nearly *ten times* the penetration at home as it did overseas.
  For most companies, the differences between domestic and foreign
  penetration are even larger! A borderless frame applied to such
  differences in penetration levels runs an obvious risk of inducing
  growth fever about foreign markets, especially since most companies tend to cross borders after saturating their home market. To
  make matters worse, such biases can be exacerbated by advisers
  (e.g., investment bankers interested in doing deals).[38] As I write
  this, I'm looking at a slide from a major strategy consulting firm
  that superimposes offerings related to its "global strategy audit" on
  a stylized globe. On the North Pole is a label that summarizes the
  overarching objective of such audits: *Growth.*

- *Economies of scale:* Coke didn't pull its obsession with economies
  of scale out of thin air; it was the logical consequence of failing to
  take differences across countries seriously. As Bruce Kogut pointed
  out long ago, in the absence of such differences, the answer to the
  question of "what is different when we move from a domestic to
  an international context . . . [is] simply that the world is a bigger
  place, and hence all economies related to the size of operations
  are, therefore, affected."[39] There does, in fact, seem to be such an
  obsession with scale economies and, relatedly, increasing concentration. Thus, surveys that Fariborz Ghadar and I have conducted
  indicate that more than three-quarters of managers believe that
  increasing cross-border integration leads to increasing seller concentration—even though the eighteen global or globalizing industries for which we have compiled data show, on average, *no* such
  increase.[40] Incidentally, out of our sample, the soft drinks industry
  does exhibit the single largest increase in concentration. This suggests that a faith in scale economies would be even *more* misplaced
  in other contexts.

- *Statelessness:* Very few companies have gone as far as Coke did
  under Goizueta: proclaiming that they have no home base. Many
  managers do, however, seem to believe that a truly global company
  should strive to achieve such a state of statelessness. They run the
  risk of being severely disappointed since foreign companies don't
  seem to be able to shake their foreignness (see chapter 2 for more
  on the liability of foreignness). This is obviously true for such U.S.
  icons as Coke in parts of the world where the United States is
  widely hated. But even companies from countries that generally
  maintain lower international profiles can face problems: consider

the boycott of Danish products in the Middle East after a Danish paper ran cartoons of the Prophet Mohammed.

- *Ubiquity:* Very few companies are as ubiquitous as Coke, but many experience great angst because they are not—and would agree that a truly global company should compete everywhere. This logical consequence of believing in a borderless world seems to be reinforced empirically by an exaggerated conception of the number of countries in which the "typical" multinational operates. Thus, managers seem surprised to learn that U.S. multinationals typically operate in just one or two foreign countries and that for those that operate in just one, there is a 60 percent chance that this country is Canada.[41] And again, managers can get bad advice in this regard; thus, the "global strategy audit" of the leading strategy consulting firm cited above frames global expansion as a question of *when,* rather than *where.*

- *Centralization and standardization:* Finally, if you (as the leader of a company) become convinced that borders don't matter, you're most likely to compete internationally the same way that you do at home, for reasons ranging from economies of scale to the sheer difficulty of grasping how different the conditions in foreign countries truly are. The likelihood of such an overemphasis on similarities is reinforced by the observation that firms that are successful at home are disproportionately likely to be the ones that venture abroad and, presumably, to be overly enamored of their own domestic business models. Furthermore, even if such a bias runs up against an unfriendly reality, that may not be enough to overturn it. Coke continued to emphasize centralization and standardization under Goizueta and Ivester, despite pressures for market responsiveness that had forced it to increase its number of brands from a handful in the early 1960s to more than four hundred today, and despite the idiosyncrasy of its most profitable major foreign market, Japan, as described earlier.

So while Coke is clearly unusual along certain dimensions, other more "typical" companies may experience similar biases toward adopting one-size-fits-all strategies. In some cases, they may even be under greater pressure to do so!

Calamitous Consequences

Recall that after Coke got carried away with a one-size-fits-all strategy under Goizueta and Ivester, the pendulum swung too far in the opposite direction during Daft's first two years as CEO. In other words, not only does it take time to develop a strategy, detect problems with it, and devise an antidote, but all too often, the antidote is an overreaction.

One explanation for this kind of overshoot is emotional. If you get burned by an excessive faith in globalization, "globaloney"—Clare Booth Luce's original riposte to Wendell Wilkie's visions of One World more than half a century ago—is perhaps the natural, if irrational, reaction.

Another explanation is political. What happens in the wake of most revolutions? People settle old scores. After the peasants with pitchforks overrun headquarters—one characterization of what happened at Coke under Daft—it is easy to imagine headquarters' capabilities being dismantled, even if local or regional substitutes aren't yet in place.

For these reasons and others, many companies get their fingers burned by engaging first in misguided global standardization and then shifting abruptly to a localization strategy. Still other companies throw up their hands and terminate *all* their international operations. Why? For one reason, they don't enjoy Coke's huge border-crossing advantages. Some of these have already been cited: the world's most valuable brand, relatively standardizable major products, and a consolidating industry. Other advantages include international operations that are more profitable than domestic ones, a broad and balanced geographic presence—Coke is one of only a dozen or so *Fortune* 500 companies that derive at least 20 percent of their sales from each of the three triad regions of North America, Europe, and Asia-Pacific—and a powerful network of bottlers that provides some counterweight to tendencies toward standardization.

Without these safeguards or strengths, the average border-crossing company can make even bigger mistakes—and be less able to recover from them. To assess your company's proneness to such mistakes, answer the questions in the box, "Your Company's Beliefs About Globalization: A Diagnostic."

Rhetoric and Remedies

The challenges of beating the biased beliefs and avoiding the calamities just described are compounded by confused rhetoric. One vivid illustration is the slogan (mis)appropriated from the environmental movement, *"Think global, act local."* This tagline has come to mean such different things to different people that it stands for nothing in particular. Thus, Goizueta pressed it into service to describe the extremely standardized and centralized strategy he adopted at Coke, particularly in regard to marketing. But in "Think Globally, Market Locally," Orit Gadiesh, the chairman of Bain & Company, encouraged brand managers to "localize, localize, lo-

Your Company's Beliefs About Globalization: A Diagnostic

Which of the following beliefs underlie how your company thinks about globalization and global strategy? Check the more appropriate box in each case.

	Yes	No
1. Globalization is leading to a world of (nearly) complete cross-border integration.	☐	☐
2. Global expansion is an imperative rather than an option to be evaluated.	☐	☐
3. Globalization offers virtually limitless growth opportunities.	☐	☐
4. Globalization tends to make industries become more concentrated.	☐	☐
5. The truly global company has no home base.	☐	☐
6. The truly global company should aim to compete (nearly) everywhere.	☐	☐
7. Global strategy is primarily about exploiting the similarities across countries.	☐	☐

Scoring: Give your company a point for each "yes" answer, and then add the points up. The results can be interpreted as a simplification of the U.S. Homeland Security Administration's color-coded threat schema. With a score of 0 or 1, the threat of globalmania is low (code green); with a score of 2 to 4, it becomes elevated (code yellow); and with a score of 5 to 7, severe (code red). To further explain the scoring, I direct the reader to where these beliefs are discussed:

- Belief 1 was countered in the first part of this chapter and will receive further reconstructive work in chapter 2.

- Belief 2 will be discussed further and remedied in chapter 3.

- Beliefs 3 through 7 were, in that order, discussed in the context of Coke's global strategy in this chapter and will be dealt with further in chapters 2 and 3.

calize"—the exact opposite of Goizueta's strategy.[42] So one problem with the "Think global, act local" slogan is that it has been applied to strategic approaches ranging from the most localized to the most standardized, and has thereby been drained of specific content.

A second problem with "Think global, act local" is inherent to the basic idea of framing the challenge of global strategy as striking a balance between the extremes of local customization and global standardization. The problem is that these extremes do not so much span a strategy continuum as constitute two singularities in which cross-border complexities can be finessed and simple single-country approaches applied. To see this, note that if markets were totally segmented from each other, single-country approaches to strategy could presumably be applied country by country, and that if markets were totally integrated, there would be the equivalent of one very big country, and single-country approaches should, once again, suffice. These are not, therefore, the best reference points for a strategy that seeks to take cross-border complexities seriously.

Figure 1-2 reframes that point more positively, to emphasize that the intermediate levels of cross-border integration inherent in semiglobalization are what open up, over a very broad domain, the possibility of global strategy having content distinct from single-country strategy. In other words, the empirical diagnosis of semiglobalization in the first part of this chapter was more important than may have been apparent at the time. Semiglobalization is what enables the development of a distinctively global approach to strategy.

That opportunity, while enticing, isn't easy. This book takes a layered approach to it, starting out by laying new foundations. Thus, this chapter—on borders mattering for strategy—is followed by one that looks at the substrate in which cross-border economic activity is embedded to un-

FIGURE 1-2

Distinctive content for global strategy

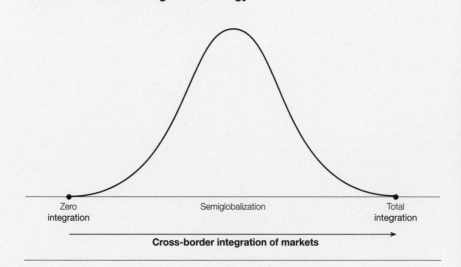

Cross-border integration of markets

derstand *why* borders still matter so much. But to convince possibly skeptical readers that more than abstractions will result—and also because I have critiqued "Think global, act local" for vagueness—here is a preview of some of the specific recommendations from the chapters that follow:

- Determine which of a range of international differences—cultural, administrative, geographic, and economic—are key in your industry, and look for differences in differences: categorize foreign countries into those that are close to your home base along the key dimensions versus those that are far. This is the topic of chapter 2.

- Analyze increasing returns to scale or scope instead of assuming them—or assuming that they are absent—but also go beyond volume, growth, and scale economies to look at *all* the components of economic value in assessing cross-border alternatives. This is the topic of chapter 3.

- Stretch the responses to differences beyond tweaking the domestic business model—and also consider ways to profit from differences, instead of treating them all as constraints on value creation. The objective, expanded on in chapters 4 through 8, is to foster creativity in thinking about how to compete across borders.

Conclusions

The conclusions from this chapter are summarized in the box "Global Generalizations." It should now be clear why semiglobalization is more than just a middle-of-the-road conclusion of middling—or even zero—interest about the state of the world. In particular, it is essential to the possibility of global strategy having content distinct from single-country strategy.

Global Generalizations

- The real state of the world is *semiglobalized.*
- The world will remain semiglobalized for decades to come.
- A semiglobalized perspective helps companies resist a variety of delusions derived from visions of the globalization apocalypse: growth fever, the norm of enormity, statelessness, ubiquity, and one-size-fits-all.
- Semiglobalization is what offers room for cross-border strategy to have content distinct from single-country strategy.

It is useful to conclude this chapter by beginning to shift attention from the importance of semiglobalization toward the implications of taking it seriously. Note, in particular, that semiglobalization involves integrated consideration of localized interactions and cross-border interactions—of the barriers and the bridges between countries—instead of a focus on just one or the other. In other words, to take semiglobalization seriously is to infer that business decisions cannot be made on either a country-by-country basis *or* on the one-size-fits-all-countries basis. What must be grasped, instead, is a business reality that lies in between "one (insular) country" and "one (integrated) world." This isn't easy, but the rewards include a richer sense of the strategic possibilities than afforded by the extreme perspectives of zero or complete integration. Semiglobalization can therefore be liberating as well as challenging.

2

Differences Across Countries

The CAGE Distance Framework

"There are no foreign lands. It is the traveler only who is foreign."

—Robert Louis Stevenson, *The Silverado Squatters*, 1883

CHAPTER 1 EMPHASIZED the semiglobalized state of the real world, in which borders continue to matter. This chapter digs deeper into the question of why. The more obvious part of the answer is that large differences arise at borders. The less obvious part concerns how to think about such differences. Instead of treating differences versus similarities in absolute terms, this chapter allows for degrees of difference. It does so by modeling differences in terms of the distances between countries along a variety of Cultural, Administrative/political, Geographic and Economic (CAGE) dimensions. As a result, the CAGE framework not only helps identify the key differences in particular settings; it also affords insights into differences in differences by providing a basis for distinguishing countries that are relatively close, along the key dimensions, from those that are relatively far.

This chapter begins with two vignettes involving Google and Wal-Mart that illustrate the effects of the CAGE dimensions of distance. It then summarizes systematic evidence that multiple dimensions of distance still matter a great deal. This systematic evidence is extended and elaborated into the CAGE framework for understanding the differences between countries, and illustrated with an analysis of China versus India as seen from the United States. The chapter goes on to discuss how the effects of different types of distance between countries are conditioned by industry characteristics, suggesting that the CAGE framework usually has to be applied at an industry rather than cross-industry level. The chapter concludes by reviewing several such applications. The CAGE framework also recurs in the discussion of strategies for globalization and specific strategy levers in part 2 of this book.

Double Trouble with Distance

The example of Google's difficulties in Russia and China, discussed in chapter 1, touches on all the components of the CAGE distance framework:

- *Cultural distance:* Google's biggest problem in Russia seems to have been associated with a relatively difficult language.

- *Administrative distance:* Google's difficulties in dealing with Chinese censorship reflect the difference between Chinese administrative and policy frameworks and those in its home country, the United States.

- *Geographic distance:* Although Google's products can be digitized, it had trouble adapting to Russia from afar and has had to set up offices there.

- *Economic distance:* The underdevelopment of payment infrastructure in Russia has been another handicap for Google relative to local rivals.

For a second example of a company that has been very successful overall but has run into a great deal of trouble with distance, consider the case of Wal-Mart, the world's largest enterprise in terms of sales. Despite its recent labor and nonmarket travails, Wal-Mart is lean and mean in its home base of the United States, where its $240 billion in revenue in 2005 accounted for close to *10 percent* of nonautomotive retail sales, according to U.S. Census Bureau data. Wal-Mart's international sales, while much smaller at $60 billion, have grown much faster and far outstrip those of any other international retailer. But the profitability of its international sales has been substantially less than that of its U.S. sales. Why?

While there are many contributing factors, the one I'll focus on in this chapter is that Wal-Mart failed to account for *distance,* broadly defined. Several years ago, CEO Lee Scott was asked about Wal-Mart's international prospects. His response: "People said we would struggle when we left Arkansas and got to places like Alabama, 600 miles from Arkansas. We even hired a person to work on the cultural differences between Arkansas and Alabama. Then we were told that in New Jersey or New York, our style wouldn't be successful."[1]

His implication was clear: *Our business model has performed well at home, despite the skeptics, so it should also perform well overseas.* The predictable consequence: Wal-Mart transferred its basic business model from the United States to overseas and did better in countries similar to the United States than in very different ones.

Consider Wal-Mart's profitability by major international market in 2004. The estimates in figure 2-1 suggest that only four out of nine countries generated accounting profits that year: Mexico, Canada, the United Kingdom, and Puerto Rico.[2] Even more interestingly, the profitable countries tend to resemble the United States along cultural, administrative, geographic, and economic dimensions whereas the unprofitable countries do not.

- Two of the profitable countries, Canada and the United Kingdom, share a *common language* with the United States, whereas none of the unprofitable ones do; the three are also linked by *colony-colonizer ties*.

- Unlike the unprofitable countries, two of the profitable countries, Canada and Mexico, partner with the United States in a regional *free trade agreement*, the North American Free Trade Agreement or NAFTA, whereas none of the unprofitable ones do. And a third profitable "country" as classified by Wal-Mart, Puerto Rico, is officially an *unincorporated territory* of the United States.

- The capital city of each of the four profitable countries is *geographically closer* to Wal-Mart's headquarters (international as well as corporate) in Bentonville, Arkansas, than the capital cities of the five unprofitable ones; in addition, Canada and Mexico share a *common land border* with the United States.

- *Economic differences* seem to matter as well: it seems a bit harder for Wal-Mart to do well in very poor countries—although the number of data points is very limited.

Having presented two examples of distance undermining performance, I should add that distance isn't always bad. Wal-Mart, for example, saves more money by procuring low-cost merchandise from China—that is, by exploiting economic distance—than it makes from its entire international store network. This example and, more broadly, arbitrage strategies that exploit distance instead of treating it as a constraint to be adjusted to or

FIGURE 2-1

Wal-Mart International's operating margin by country, 2004 (estimated)

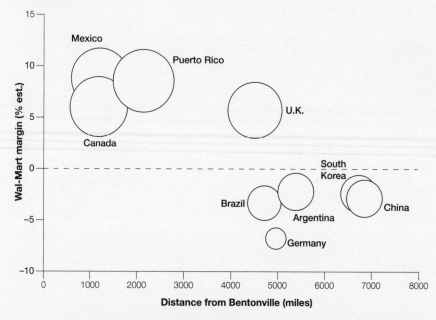

Sources: Compiled from filings by Wal-Mart and Wal-Mart de Mexico, China Commerce Ministry (11 February 2005), estimates by BBVA, Retail Forward, and Management Ventures, Inc., as well as analysis and estimates by Pankaj Ghemawat and Ken Mark, "Wal-Mart's International Expansion," Case 9-705-486 (Boston: Harvard Business School, 2005), exhibit 7. While the numbers are for just one year and involve some inferences, their relevance is shown by Wal-Mart's subsequent exit from two of the markets characterized as loss makers: South Korea and Germany.

Note: Areas of circles are proportional to Wal-Mart's revenues from different markets.

gotten around will be discussed at length in chapter 6. All that the discussion so far has meant to suggest is that distance *does* need to be taken seriously.

Taking Distance Seriously

The suggestion that distance can matter a great deal is borne out by more systematic data. The relevant evidence is potentially vast, encompassing as it does much of the literature on locational effects. A large amount of this literature is focused, however, on interactions over very short distances or at what is effectively a common location (e.g., the literature on agglomeration economies). This strand of work certainly demonstrates the general importance of location-specificity, but is just beginning to venture beyond the dichotomy of same location-different location. For finer-grained characterizations of how the intensity of economic interactions is affected by spatial (and other dimensions of) distance, the literature on so-called "gravity models" in international economics is a better starting point.

What Do the Numbers Tell Us?

International economists have adapted Newton's law of universal gravitation to describe international economic interactions.[3] Thus, the simplest gravity model of international trade predicts that the trade between two countries will be directly related to their economic sizes (a unilateral attribute of each) and inversely related to the physical distance between them (a bilateral attribute). In other words, bigger economies are predicted, as one would expect, to generate more trade in absolute terms, and greater distances between them should inhibit that trade. More sophisticated gravity models add in nongeographic dimensions of distance, as well as unilateral attributes other than the size of each economy. What do the attempts to fit such models to data on international economic interactions tell us about the world in which we live?

Let's begin by focusing on international trade. Fitted gravity models manage to explain one-half or even two-thirds of the variation in trade volumes by country-pair, which is remarkably good as economic models go. Looking across many such studies, we see that a 1 percent increase in the size of an economy is typically estimated to lead to a 0.7–0.8 percent increase in its total volume of trade. The effect of geographic distance goes in the opposite direction, and is somewhat larger: a 1 percent increase in the distance between (the capitals of) two countries is generally predicted to *decrease* trade between them by about 1 percent. In other words, the trade volume between countries one thousand miles apart is expected to be five times as large as it would be, other things being equal, if they were five thousand miles apart.[4]

The estimated sizes of the effects of other distance-related variables are even more impressive. Figure 2-2 summarizes the results of some statistical analysis (by Rajiv Mallick and me) of bilateral trade flows from this perspective.[5] Basically, it implies that two countries characterized by all five of the commonalities listed in the figure should be expected to trade 29 times as much with each other $(1.42 \times 1.47 \times 2.88 \times 2.14 \times 2.25)$ as an otherwise similar country-pair without any of these commonalities.

Such estimates are obviously meant to be indicative rather than exact, but the effects that they highlight do line up with actual cases. Canada, for example, is barely one of the world's ten largest economies, yet its bilateral trading relationship with the United States is by far the biggest in

FIGURE 2-2

Effects of similarities versus differences on bilateral trade

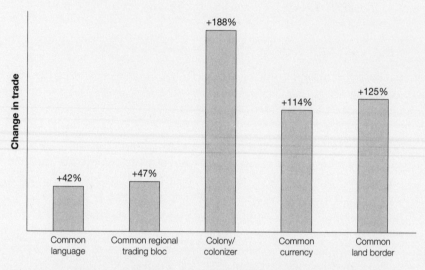

Source: Pankaj Ghemawat and Rajiv Mallick, "The Industry-Level Structure of International Trade Networks: A Gravity-Based Approach," working paper, Harvard Business School, Boston, February 2003.

the world. Geographic proximity is part of the answer, but so are the commonalities with the United States along four of the five dimensions listed in figure 2-2—more than any other country in the world can claim.[6]

But Canadian-U.S. trade data also remind us that economic integration is far from complete. In fact, the real mystery to economists about Canadian-U.S. trade is not why there's so much, but why there isn't much more. To see why, consider some more trade data. As of 1988, before NAFTA, merchandise trade levels between Canadian provinces—that is, within the country—were estimated to be *20 times as large* as their trade with similarly sized and similarly distant U.S. states. In other words, there was a built-in "home bias." NAFTA helped reduce this ratio of intranational to international trade—the home bias—from 20 to 1 to a ratio of 10 to 1 by the mid-1990s, and may have further shrunk it since, although it still exceeds 5 to 1. And these ratios are just for merchandise; for services, the ratio is still several times larger.[7]

So, international borders still loom very large, even if one looks at two countries that are very close to each other along most key dimensions. Once again, we're running into the reality of semiglobalization.

The evidence concerning forms of international economic interaction other than trade generally confirms the importance of distance—both geographic and nongeographic. Thus, significantly negative (overall) distance effects have been detected in foreign direct investment (FDI), equity trading, patent citations, and e-commerce transactions—although the strength of these effects does vary across forms of interaction.[8] Furthermore, a meta-analysis of nineteen separate statistical studies suggests that distance effects generally *haven't*—unlike in the Canadian-U.S. case discussed above—decreased significantly over the course of the twentieth century![9]

Frameworks for Country Analysis

The evidence just presented suggests that distance effects can be huge. So let's look at existing tools for "country analysis"—for example, the kinds of due diligence that a company would conduct before deciding to set up shop in a new country—and see how well they account for the effects of distance. The answer, basically, is that they don't!

Since this is not the place to undertake a detailed review of frameworks for country analysis, one example will have to suffice.[10] Consider the competitiveness indices published by the World Economic Forum. While this is a useful source of cross-country data, most of the categories covered—for example, finance, technology, labor, management, and institutions—focus on the *unilateral* attributes of countries. The category of openness, which covers tariffs, hidden import barriers, and the like, is *multilateral*: it measures the administrative distance between a country and the rest of the world. But that still misses out on differences in differences: for example, the idea, which Wal-Mart would have done well to pick up on, that Germany and South Korea—which it has had to exit since figure 2-1 was prepared—are much farther from the United States than are Canada or Mexico. Picking up on such effects requires *bilateral* measures of distance.

The competitiveness indices are not unrepresentative of other widely used frameworks for country analysis, which also tend to assume that countries can be assessed one by one—that is, unilaterally—against common yardsticks. The trouble with this yardstick approach, though, is that it treats countries as discrete structural objects when they really should be treated as nodes embedded in a network at varying distances from each other. Adding bilateral measures of distance that capture such differences to more familiar unilateral or multilateral attributes is *the* key contribution of the CAGE framework for country analysis.

Note that the bilateral measures are based on differences between the home country and the foreign country or countries being analyzed, that is, they are anchored in the focal company's home base. Chapter 1 provided part of the rationale for assuming a home base with its description and debunking of the fallacy of statelessness. Empirically, the clear identification of a company's home base is generally not difficult and may actually have become easier in recent decades, so the few cases where this is an issue should not be allowed to hold up the rest of the discussion.[11] And from a prescriptive perspective, a home base or some other established base of activities is essential to operationalizing the idea that where a company has come from should influence where it goes.

The CAGE Framework at the Country Level

The CAGE framework, as noted, is an acronym for four broad components of distance: cultural, administrative, geographic, and economic. These four components often intertwine: for example, it is hard to imagine countries being close to each other administratively—say, part of a free trade area—unless they also happen to be close culturally, geographically, or economically. Still, it is useful to distinguish between the four components, because they have different bases and, partly as a result, present very different challenges and opportunities. In addition, these four headings also provide a useful way of grouping unilateral influences on cross-border interactions that are specific to particular countries as well as bilateral ones that are specific to particular country-pairs (and multilateral ones too). These various types of influences, summarized in table 2-1, are all discussed below, although the focus falls primarily on bilateral influences, reflecting their novelty as well as the impact identified by gravity models.

The idea of going beyond physical distance in thinking about cross-border strategy is not new. Thus, the idea that would-be internationalizers should go first to countries that presented the least *psychic distance*—that is, the least "distance between the home market and a foreign market resulting from the perception and understanding of cultural and business differences"—was first proposed thirty years ago.[12] But the CAGE framework takes a much broader view of distance, and has a much more solid empirical base.

Cultural Distance

Culture as used here refers to the attributes of a society that are sustained mainly by interactions among people, rather than by the state (as lawgiver or enforcer). Cultural differences between countries generally tend to reduce economic interactions between them. Languages' effects in this

TABLE 2-1

The CAGE framework at the country level

	Cultural distance	Administrative distance	Geographic distance	Economic distance

Country-pairs (bilateral)	• Different languages
	• Different ethnicities; lack of connective ethnic or social networks
	• Different religions
	• Lack of trust
	• Different values, norms, and dispositions
		• Lack of colonial ties
		• Lack of shared regional trading bloc
		• Lack of common currency
		• Political hostility
			• Physical distance
			• Lack of land border
			• Differences in time zones
			• Differences in climates and disease environments
				• Rich-poor differences
				• Other differences in cost or quality of
				  ○ Natural resources
				  ○ Financial resources
				  ○ Human resources
				  ○ Infrastructure
				  ○ Information or knowledge

Countries (unilateral or multilateral)	• Insularity • Traditionalism	• Nonmarket or closed economy • Extent of home bias • Lack of membership in international organizations • Weak institutions; corruption	• Landlocked geography • Lack of internal navigability • Geographic size • Geographic remoteness • Weak transportation or communication links	• Economic size • Low per-capita income

regard are perhaps the most obvious: look at the first column of figure 2-2. Or for evidence of a different sort, consider classic cross-border faux pas such as the translation of Frank Perdue's advertising tagline, "It takes a tough man to make a tender chicken" into the Spanish equivalent of "It takes an aroused man to make a chicken affectionate." In fact, lists of marketing bloopers are usually dominated by such misadventures in foreign languages.[13]

Other aspects of cultural distance that can be measured systematically and have been shown to dampen economic exchange include differences in ethnicity and religion, a lack of trust, and variations in egalitarianism (defined as societal intolerance for abuses of market and political power).[14] Yet other cultural attributes are highly idiosyncratic (e.g., preferences for certain colors) or subtle in the sense of being nearly invisible even to those whose behavior they guide.

Take, for instance, the traditional Chinese tolerance of copyright infringement. Many people ascribe this social norm to China's recent communist past. But as William Alford argues in *To Steal a Book Is an Elegant Offense,* it probably reflects a Confucian principle that encourages replication of the results of past intellectual endeavors: "I transmit, rather than create; I believe in and love the Ancients."[15] Indeed, copyright infringement was a problem for Western publishers well before China's current growth thrust. Back in the 1920s, for example, Merriam-Webster, about to introduce a bilingual dictionary in China, found that a local publisher had already begun to distribute its own, unauthorized version.

In addition to bilateral attributes that take the form of cultural differences, cross-border economic activity may also be affected by unilateral cultural attributes. Thus, it is intuitively clear that nations with cultures that are insular or even traditional will tend to be relatively closed to international trade and investment, that is, more isolated than others.

Prolonged contact between countries is likely to blunt at least some of the effects of cultural differences between them. Such contact increases mutual familiarity, "seeds" the institutions and organizations required to support cross-border economic activity, and eases cultural adjustments. Broadly speaking, it seems as if many differences in values, norms, dispositions, and unilateral, isolating attributes are likely to prove more malleable, even in the medium run, than differences in language, ethnicity, and religion.

Administrative Distance

Administrative attributes encompass laws, policies, and institutions that typically emerge from a political process and are mandated or enforced by governments. International relationships between countries, including treaties and international organizations, are included as well, on the grounds that these relationships are sustained by the countries that create or support them.

The administrative or political attributes highlighted by gravity models as affecting cross-border economic activity include colonial ties, membership in the same regional trading bloc, and the use of a common currency. The statistical analysis reported in figure 2-2 indicates that colonizer-colony links can multiply trade nearly threefold, even if they have lapsed a long time ago—for reasons that presumably range from cultural familiarity to similarity in legal systems. On FDI, given the limitations of the systematic data, it is more efficient cite specific instances. Thus, between 1997 and 2001, nearly one-half of a huge surge in FDI from Spain was directed at Latin America—about ten times Latin America's share of world FDI—with Europe's much larger and physically much closer regional economy getting pushed into second place. This pattern clearly reflects administrative (and cultural) commonalities rooted in colonizer-colony relationships that were formally terminated in the nineteenth century rather than the effects of size or geographic distance.

Preferential trading arrangements and a common currency can also increase trade substantially—even more than colony-colonizer links, if combined (again, see figure 2-2). The integration of the European Union over the last half-century is probably the best example of deliberate efforts to reduce administrative distance among trading partners. Conversely, bad relationships can increase administrative distance. Although India and Pakistan share a colonial past, a land border, and linguistic ties, their long-standing mutual hostility means that official trade between them is less than one-tenth of what gravity models would predict it to be. And in the wake of tensions such as Dubai Ports World's forced relinquishment of the five U.S. port terminal facilities that it had acquired), various observers have noted a diversion of investments from the Middle East away from the United States.

As the last two examples suggest, administrative distance can be increased or decreased through unilateral measures. In fact, the policies of individual governments pose some of the most common barriers to cross-border trade. In some cases, the difficulties arise in a company's home country. Companies from member countries of the Organisation for Economic Co-operation and Development [OECD], for example, have to deal with domestic prohibitions on bribery and have to conform to relatively stringent health, safety, and environmental standards—all of which can hinder their global operations. More often, though, it is the target country's government that raises barriers to foreign investments—through trade quotas, restrictions on FDI, and preferences for domestic competitors in the form of subsidies and favoritism in regulation and procurement.

These are all examples in which a national government is powerful enough to affect outcomes. But a *weak* institutional infrastructure in a target country can also impede cross-border economic activity. For example, many companies shy away from doing business in countries known for corruption, unreliable legal systems, or social conflict. (Some research suggests that these negative local conditions, if left unchecked, can depress trade and investment far more than any explicit administrative constraint.) Conversely, when a country's institutional infrastructure is strong, the level of cross-border integration is likely to be higher.

Geographic Distance

The geographic attributes of countries that can affect cross-border economic activity mostly grow out of natural phenomena, although some human interventions may also be involved. This is the part of the CAGE framework that most people first think of when they hear the world *distance*. And they tend to focus on physical distance, which is in line with the empirical finding—and the commonsense notion—that other things being equal, the farther away a country is, the harder it will be to conduct business there.

But geographic distance is more than simply a matter of physical distance between, say, the capitals of two countries. Other geographic attributes that must be considered include the presence or absence of a common land border, differences in time zones and climates, and, in unilateral terms, access to the ocean, topography, and within-country distances to borders. (I am reminded of former Canadian Prime Minister William MacKenzie King's complaint, "We have too much geography.") In addition, man-made "geographic" attributes, such as a country's transportation and communication infrastructures, may also need to be taken into account—although they can also be treated as economic rather than geographic attributes.

The influence of physical distance deserves additional elaboration. The most obvious impact of longer physical distances is to raise the costs of physical transportation. These, of course, are more important for trade than for FDI, which is why we see a tilt toward FDI as distance increases. But gravity models indicate that FDI *also* tends to drop off as distance increases—reflecting the fact that physical distance raises communication costs as well as transportation costs. Remember the example of Google's having to set up offices in Russia to improve its local knowledge and responsiveness.

The broader lesson? Keep the "geography of information," as well as the geography of physical transportation, in mind when you're thinking through geographic influences on cross-border economic activity.

Economic Distance

Economic distance refers to differences that affect cross-border economic activity through economic mechanisms distinct from the cultural, administrative, or geographic ones already considered. In this regard, the gravity model flags not only economic size (which increases the absolute amount of trade but decreases trade as a percentage of GDP), but also per-capita incomes. Rich countries engage in more cross-border economic activity (relative to their economic size) than do their poorer cousins. And, as implied by the positive relation between per-capita GDP and trade and investment flows, most of this activity occurs with other rich countries.

Of course, high per-capita income goes hand in hand with higher labor costs. These can be looked at both directly and on a more disaggregated basis—in other words, in terms of different skill levels or types of training. Other factors of production whose cost or quality might be examined in this way include land, natural resources, capital, and more advanced man-made resources such as infrastructure and information.

Finally, it is worth noting that the rich-rich and rich-poor interactions tend to be associated, albeit imperfectly, with the performance of different economic functions. In particular, rich-poor interactions often involve arbitrage, in which a firm matches supply and demand across not within national markets but across them, by slicing up value chains internationally. While cultural, administrative, and geographic differences can also serve as bases of arbitrage, as discussed in chapter 6, economic arbitrage is particularly salient. It is, therefore, the best single reminder that while distance tends to have a dampening effect overall on cross-border economic activity, it may actually encourage such activity in specific situations.

A Country-Level Example: India Versus China from a U.S. Perspective

Let's use the CAGE framework to look at a specific topic that I'm frequently asked to talk about: *how India and China compare, from the perspective of U.S. companies.*[16] The comparison is summarized in table 2-2 and elaborated on in the following paragraphs.

Cultural factors. India's main source of cultural proximity to the United States is arguably its greater use of English. The pool of Indians who know

TABLE 2-2

India versus China from the perspective of U.S. companies

	Cultural attractions	Administrative attractions	Geographic attractions	Economic attractions
India	• English language • Westernized elites	• Common colonizer • Common law • Political friendship • Lower long-run risk?		• Specialized labor • Profitability • Firm strategy and upgrading • Soft infrastructure
China	• Linguistic and ethnic homogeneity • Diaspora	• Ease of doing business • Enclaves	• Closer to U.S. West Coast • Superior ports, other infrastructure • East Asian production network	• Larger markets • Higher income • Labor inputs and productivity • Capital availability • Supply chains • Foreign companies as export bridges

English is estimated to range from less than 100 million to more than 300 million—I'd go with the lower end of the range—but is generally agreed to be larger than China's. China is generally thought to have an advantage in terms of the size and commercial orientation of its diaspora—although the Indian diaspora in the United States, in particular, tends to be better educated, more recently arrived, and more likely to be involved in the technology sector.

Unilateral cultural characteristics of the two countries yield less clear-cut conclusions. China is more homogeneous linguistically and ethnically, but whether that smoothes progress or makes for too much insularity is a matter of debate. And while India's class- and caste-ridden social structure is deplorable on broader grounds, Westernized Indian elites may have reinforced Indo-U.S. economic ties.

Administrative factors. Colonization by Britain has created a number of commonalities between India and the United States. The most important of these is that the legal systems in both countries are based on English common law, with its emphasis on precedents and adaptation. China's legal system, by contrast, relies on civil law—the German version—with its emphasis on principles that are absolute and therefore don't need to be contextualized. In addition, the political relationships between the

United States and India are currently very close. While that situation is subject to change, what does seem fairly certain is that political tensions between the United States and China will persist for decades, if not longer.

The outlook for unilateral administrative and political indicators depends on the time frame adopted. In the short run, multinationals currently seem to see themselves as facing fewer administrative and political obstacles to doing business in China than in India, partly as a result of special economic zones and enclaves such as Hong Kong, and until recently enjoyed preferential tax rates in China. But in the long run, China faces greater challenges than India in establishing the rule of law, protecting private property, restructuring insolvent state-owned enterprises and banks, and dealing with political change.

Geographic factors. Chennai (in India) is 60 percent farther away from Long Beach, California—the busiest U.S. container port—than is Shanghai. But the greater shipping distance is only part of India's logistical problems: its ports are inefficient and slow, raising the estimated lead time in shipping to the United States to six to twelve weeks, versus two to three weeks from China, and exemplifying the relatively poor state of its infrastructure.

Another key geographic point is that China is the dynamo within a vibrant East Asian subregional economy, with regional partners that account for more than half of inbound FDI and three-quarters of imports. China's trading relationships with the United States are embedded in, and in some respects enhanced by, this broader network. India, by contrast, is located in a far less economically dynamic subregion, and trade with its South Asian neighbors amounts to less than 5 percent of its total trade.

Economic factors. Unilateral factors warrant particular attention under this heading. China's economy is reported to be more than twice as large as India's—although China's official statistics may overstate its actual economic growth rate by 2–4 percent![17] Moreover, the Chinese markets for many income-elastic products are more than five times as large as India's, reflecting the effects of higher per-capita GDP. China's labor productivity is also higher, in line with higher labor incomes, and its workers are generally better educated—although it trails India in a few higher-end categories (e.g., experienced managers and English-speaking graduates) and faces a somewhat worse demographic outlook, given its one-child policy. China has achieved better outcomes to date by reallocating labor from agriculture to manufacturing, and by mobilizing more domestic capital: its official savings rates—again, probably somewhat exaggerated—are 40–45 percent of GDP, versus 20–25 percent for India.[18]

The downside of China's capital abundance is that it has depressed returns and led to overinvestment, especially in construction and infrastructure, by companies not noted for their self-restraint. Indian companies have been consistently more profitable. In addition, the best Indian domestic companies have typically gotten less support from their home government than have the companies that the Chinese government is trying to build up into global companies. Part of the Indian companies' response has been a more disciplined, less investment-intensive approach.

Foreign companies account for about 20 percent of Chinese industrial production, and less of India's. Foreign invested companies *have* had a disproportionately large impact on Chinese exports, in which the foreigners have grown their shares to more than 50 percent overall and to 80 percent in the higher value-added categories. Since foreign companies account for less than 10 percent of total Indian exports, and since India's exports have recently run to one-tenth of China's, foreign companies' nominal exports out of China are about fifty times as large as those out of India. These figures also say something about the relative levels of development of supply chains in the two countries.

Summarizing very broadly, *China seems more attractive than India to general-purpose U.S. investors on many geographic and economic grounds, but less attractive on a number of cultural and administrative grounds.*

I'll add four elaborations to that bald summary. First, the choice of perspective is key. From West Europe, the comparison looks different: China is farther geographically, but on the other hand, India's English language capabilities are of narrower relevance. And East Europe and North Africa may be more attractive offshoring alternatives than either China or India.

Second, both China and India are very large countries with a great amount of internal variation. For example, both countries' coastal regions are significantly more vibrant than their hinterlands, suggesting that the CAGE framework can be applied intranationally as well as internationally. Thus, glass manufacturer Saint-Gobain has overtaken longer-established foreign competitors in India by focusing on the coastal south rather than north.

Third, many comparisons of China and India focus on the last column of table 2-2, particularly the points about larger markets and higher labor productivity in China. But the table reminds us of the need to take a broader perspective, the most unexpected conclusion from which is India's comparative cultural and administrative closeness to the United States. Not coincidentally, these are the two CAGE dimensions that most often get overlooked.

The fourth point is a logical extension of the third. Presumably, India should look more attractive than China as an investment destination *in industries that are more sensitive to cultural or administrative distance.* The software services industry provides a good example. Culturally, this is a business in which speaking English is particularly important and in which the Indian diaspora in the United States—variously reported to account for more than a third of the workforce of technology companies in Silicon Valley and to run 10 percent of new technology ventures there—has been directly helpful. In addition, geographic distance from the United States matters less and less, especially since the shift toward offshore development, and India has benefited economically from its much larger graduate talent pool. The result: India accounts for more than two-thirds of software services offshored from the United States, compared to roughly one-tenth for China.[19]

The software example leads directly to *industry-level* CAGE analysis, discussed in the next section.

The CAGE Framework at the Industry Level

An investment fund making portfolio investments might be satisfied with an answer to the question of how attractive China is *in general terms* relative to India. But most executives comparing the two countries are likely to want to do so from the perspective of a particular industry. In such situations, the impact of the differences between countries is conditioned by industry characteristics, which must be taken into account for most applications to company strategy. Table 2-3 summarizes the kinds of industries that are particularly sensitive to each component of distance and cites examples; the rest of this section elaborates.

Cultural Sensitivity

What kinds of products or services are most sensitive to cultural differences? Given our earlier discussion of language as one key determinant of cultural distance, linguistic sensitivity is one obvious indicator: differences in languages matter more in software or TV programming than they do, for instance, in cement. Similarly, one can think of products with a specifically ethnic appeal that are particularly sensitive to ethnic differences or products for which religious differences loom large. Thus, in cross-country statistical regression analyses, food products turn out to rank among the ones most sensitive to cultural distance partly for such ethnic and religious reasons, and partly because they trigger other associations related to the identity of a consumer as a member of a particular

50   VALUE IN A WORLD OF DIFFERENCES

TABLE 2-3

The CAGE framework at the industry level: correlates of sensitivity (with examples in parentheses)

Cultural distance	Administrative distance	Geographic distance	Economic distance
Cultural differences matter the most when	Government involvement is high in industries that are	Geography plays a more important role when	Economic differences have the biggest impact when

• Products have high linguistic content (TV programs)
• Products matter to cultural or national identity (foods)
• Product features vary in terms of
  ○ Size (cars)
  ○ Standards (electrical equipment)
• Products carry country-specific quality associations (wines)
	• Producers of staple goods (electricity)
	• Producers of other "entitlements" (drugs)
	• Large employers (farming)
	• Large suppliers to government (mass transportation)
	• National champions (aerospace)
	• Vital to national security (telecommunications)
	• Exploiters of natural resources (oil, mining)
	• Subject to high sunk costs (infrastructure)
		• Products have a low value-to-weight or value-to-bulk ratio (cement)
		• Products are fragile or perishable (glass, fruit)
		• Local supervision and operational requirements are high (many services)
			• The nature of demand varies with income level (cars)
			• The economics of standardization or scale are limited (cement)
			• Labor and other factor cost differences are salient (garments)
			• Distribution or business systems are different (insurance)
			• Companies need to be responsive and agile (home appliances)

community. For example, Americans think of rice as a commodity—like noodles or potatoes—but this foodstuff matters much, much more to the Japanese.

Other cultural differences at the industry level are partially derived from, and therefore blur into, economic differences. The Japanese, for example, prefer their cars to be small, reflecting social norms as well as considerations of economy and convenience in countries where space is limited and therefore treasured.

Finally, while the preceding country-level discussion of culture noted that such differences tend to reduce cross-border economic activity, this general tendency can be counteracted, to some extent, by industry-level considerations. The major countervailing force is strong *vertical differentiation* by country of origin that makes customers in different countries rank products from a particular country or particular countries as "best."

The leading French champagne houses, for example, have demonstrated that you can use local cachet to build up a global business. The purveyors of American pop culture, from Disney to denim, have made the same point, in a way that reminds us that strong country-of-origin effects need not always be associated with very high quality.

These two examples of vertical differentiation—champagne and Mickey Mouse—fit the adage that the two most global segments in consumer products are the luxury segment and the youth segment. There are two broader takeaways as well about analyzing cross-country variations in preferences:

- Distinguish vertical differentiation from horizontal differentiation, defined as a situation in which consumers in different countries rank the same products very differently (i.e., tastes are different rather than similar).

- Conduct the analysis at a micro level, for example, at the level of champagne rather than beverages, or in terms of bakery products (which are relatively sensitive to distance) versus protein products such as pork and poultry (which are not) instead of lumping both categories into "food."

Administrative Sensitivity

Administrative distance most often grows out of the desire to protect or regulate domestic industries: local governments see some reasons to intervene to shield industries from outside competition and erect barriers of one kind or another (e.g., tariffs, regulatory complications, local-content laws). In general, these kinds of barriers are most likely to be built if a domestic industry meets one or more of the following criteria:

- *It produces staples.* Governments are highly likely to interfere in local markets for goods that are perceived to be essential to their citizens' everyday lives. Food staples, fuel, and electricity, for example, fall into this category.

- *It produces an "entitlement" good or service.* Similarly, some industries, such as the health-care sector, produce goods or services to which people believe they are entitled as a basic human right. Governments often intervene to set quality standards and to control pricing in such industries as well.

- *It is a large employer.* Industries that represent large voting blocs often receive state support in the form of subsidies and import protection. Farmers and textile and garment workers are cases in point.

- *It is a large supplier to the government.* If governments are major buyers (e.g., for mass transit equipment), that obviously widens the scope for governmental intervention as well.

- *It is seen as a national champion.* Some industries or companies serve as symbols of a country's modernity and competitiveness. The shoot-out between Boeing and Airbus in the large-passenger-jet market, for example, has generated disproportionate passion on both sides of the Atlantic. This industry is about more than the jobs and dollars (or euros) directly involved.

- *It is, or is construed as, vital to national security.* Governments will intervene to protect those industries that they deem to be closely linked to national security. Thus, recent examples from the United States include the Dubai Ports World case cited above and the resistance to China National Offshore Oil Corporation's attempts to buy Unocal.

- *It controls natural resources.* Other cases from the oil and gas sector—for example, Bolivia's recent renationalization of its natural gas reserves—illustrate that a country's natural resources are often considered part of the national heritage and that foreign companies seeking to exploit them can be viewed as plunderers.

- *It involves high sunk costs.* Industries that require large, irreversible, geographically specific investments—including many of the heavy industries discussed above—are highly vulnerable to holdup by governments once those investments have been made.

An example of an industry that scores high on most of these dimensions—and feels the pain from ignoring them—is the electricity business, defined here to include generation, transmission, and distribution. One of the key "high-tech" fields of the late nineteenth century, this industry witnessed significant foreign investment early on, despite capital intensity of an order previously experienced only with steam railways. But because of the administrative pressures to which foreign ownership in this industry was particularly subject, a tide of "domestication" swept around the world, beginning with the Russian Revolution and running through the late 1970s and early 1980s.

This deglobalization was followed by a revival in interest in foreign direct investment as the electricity sector began to be deregulated around the world. The result has been a global investment bubble, particularly in electricity generation.[20] This bubble was fed by more than $400 billion in FDI between 1992 and 2002, and has resulted in more than $100 billion in value destruction, much of it—particularly in emerging markets—due to renegotiation and expropriation by local governments. But it would be even more surprising if this were the last example of a widely shared but wildly inaccurate sense of administrative security.

Geographic Sensitivity

What kinds of industries are most sensitive to geographic distance? The answers, as far as trade flows are concerned, are mostly intuitive: products that have low value-to-weight/bulk ratios (e.g., cement), products prone to hazards or high perishability in transport (e.g., fast foods), or products that present significant local-presence requirements.

Corresponding influences on cross-border investment are harder to specify cleanly, since such investment can serve as either a substitute for or a complement to trade. Thus, researchers have argued both that high local performance or supervision requirements tend to *decrease* FDI (by constraining trade) and that they tend to *increase* FDI (by causing investment to substitute for trade). Remember, however, that physical distance has been demonstrated to have a negative influence overall on FDI, as well as on trade. This increases the likelihood of trade and FDI moving hand in hand.

One corroborative example of geographic distance's having a powerful impact on FDI is provided by the case of Cemex, the Mexican cement company that will be discussed at much greater length in chapter 3. Cemex originally focused on expanding internationally through acquisitions in emerging markets and, after exhausting opportunities in Latin America, went as far afield as Indonesia (which is about as far as you can get from Mexico and still remain on planet Earth). But its more recent acquisitions—as well as an informed source—suggest that it has in fact refocused on the Western Hemisphere in an attempt to build a geographic fortress around itself.

Economic Sensitivity

To take a micro, industry-level perspective on economic distance, it is useful to decompose value for a representative firm in an industry into *costs* on the supply side, and *willingness to pay* on the demand side. This microeconomic perspective will be elaborated on further in chapter 3. What will be discussed here are the supply-side and demand-side determinants of sensitivity to economic distance.

On the supply side, economic distance is likely to have the greatest impact on products whose cost structures are dominated by factors with absolute costs that vary a lot internationally. While products with high labor-intensity stand out in this respect, the reality of semiglobalization reminds us that even the costs of factors such as capital are subject to some degree of location-specificity and associated variation.

On the demand side, large differences in willingness to pay—usually associated with per-capita incomes—create incentives to look beyond national borders. But income differences are likely to *hurt* rather than help international economic activity when they imply preferences for very different kinds of products. Industries that demand lots of variety, agility, or responsiveness are also likely to experience relatively low levels of cross-border international exchange because of the extra complexity costs.

Then there are other, less specific but still useful measures of economic sensitivity. For example, the extent to which economic distance leads to differences in customers, channels, or business systems—or, most broadly, industry structure—across countries is also relevant in assessing the impact of distance at the industry level. Thus, one study has suggested that domestic margins—the costs of domestic transportation, wholesaling, and retailing—play a bigger role in erecting barriers to imports into the United States than do international transportation costs and tariffs combined.[21]

To recap this section, the CAGE framework is usually most usefully applied at the industry level. The task, in other words, is not just to identify the differences between countries but to *understand which ones matter the most in the industry of interest to you*. This helps bring the analysis down from the macro level to the micro level.

Some Applications

The CAGE framework, once it is taken down to the industry level, lends itself to a very broad array of applications. Let's focus on five of the most important ones.

Making Differences Visible

One application of the CAGE framework is to make key differences visible. While this application may seem too obvious to be worth belaboring, a case study of Star TV helps show why it merits additional emphasis.[22]

Star was launched in 1991 as a satellite TV service for the top 5 percent of Asia's population. At that time, the use of satellites as gigantic transmission antennae was dissolving the constraints of geographic distance to which terrestrial broadcasters had traditionally been subject. Within its pan-Asian footprint, Star focused on a relatively cosmopolitan elite, which was expected to be able to afford the service, attract advertisers, and be willing to view recycled English-language programming. (This would spare Star the costs of creating new local-language programming.) Rupert Murdoch's News Corporation, which was betting on satellite instead of cable TV, was sufficiently taken with this business model and the idea of leveraging its English-language programming across Asia—particularly the 20th Century Fox movie and TV program library—to buy out Star's founder, Hong Kong billionaire Li Ka-Shing, for a total of $825 million by mid-1995.

By 2006, Star was finally making operating profits. Nevertheless, it seems to have been a poor investment for News Corp. The reasons are related to distance. Satellite TV *did* reduce geographic distance, but it did not address other aspects of distance that Star discounted initially—to its later regret:

- *Cultural distance:* Star initially assumed that Asian viewers would be satisfied with English-language programming, simply because many in the target demographic spoke English as a second language. The company paid no attention to evidence already available from continental Europe that given a choice, audiences strongly prefer local-language content, even if they do speak foreign languages.

- *Administrative distance:* News Corporation seemed administratively tone-deaf—especially in a business in which foreign ownership is always politically loaded, given TV's power to influence people. Shortly after acquiring Star, Rupert Murdoch pronounced satellite TV "an unambiguous threat to totalitarian regimes everywhere," because it permitted people to circumvent official news sources![23] The Chinese government reacted by banning the domestic reception of foreign satellite TV services. Much of Murdoch's China strategy has since involved digging out of this hole.

It is particularly surprising that Murdoch missed the last point, given his personal history—he had to become a U.S. citizen to buy the TV stations that anchored the Fox network—as well as his generally good political instincts. But his international experience and that of News Corp were confined to English-speaking democracies. As it turned out, this was poor preparation for dealing with China.

My broader point is that making key differences more visible—as the CAGE framework does—is important in part because in a very diverse world, many foreign contexts will be alien to many of the managers who must decide on cross-border issues. In such situations, personal experience is not enough. It might not occur to a U.S. speechwriter that there could be a problem with antiauthoritarian rhetoric. Such blind spots can be minimized by being careful to attend to all dimensions of the CAGE framework.

Understanding the Liability of Foreignness

A second application of the CAGE framework is as an antidote to the visions of triumphant multinational companies (MNCs) that often accompany the visions of the globalization apocalypse discussed in chapter 1. The application involves using the framework to pinpoint all the differences between countries that might handicap MNCs relative to local competitors—the so-called liability of foreignness—or more generally affect their relative positions.[24] This can be a useful exercise for MNCs, their local competitors or both.

To help stretch minds and overcome a bias toward believing in the inevitable triumph of MNCs, table 2-4 provides a fairly comprehensive list of all the disadvantages that MNCs might suffer relative to local competitors. Consider, as a specific example, the case of beauty products, in which a handful of MNCs, led by L'Oréal of France and Procter & Gamble of the United States, have orchestrated a significant increase in global concentration over the last few decades and now lead in most major markets around the world. One of the biggest exceptions is South Korea, where "local beauty" AmorePacific accounts for more than 30 percent of the market for cosmetics—versus 8 percent for its leading local competitor and 5 percent for L'Oréal, the leading multinational competitor—and has posted operating margins that are among the highest in its industry worldwide. Why has Korea proved such a tough market for MNCs?

The CAGE framework suggests a number of answers to that question. First of all, beauty care products must represent the absolute peak in terms of ego-expressive products subject to cultural biases. Korea, in particular, is obsessed with skin care and makeup, product areas that permit horizontal differentiation around distinct Asian skins and conceptions of beauty—especially white skin in East Asian markets. These influences have combined to limit the cultural appeal of MNCs' global product lines. In addition, MNCs face extra administrative hurdles that include tariffs, discriminatory product regulations, and initiatives such as the Korean Cosmetics Industry Association's "Made in Korea products are good for Koreans" campaign. And economically, MNCs have lacked access to door-to-door sales, a very important distribution channel in Korea, which has confined MNCs to the small, high-priced department store channel and denied them scale economies. These are all critically important considerations for a beauty care MNC thinking of entering or expanding in the Korean market—or rethinking its presence there.

Probably the most obvious expedient for trying to overcome the liability of foreignness is to acquire a local competitor. But whether buying a

TABLE 2-4

The possible disadvantages of multinational competitors versus local ones: A CAGE analysis

Cultural disadvantages	Administrative disadvantages	Geographic disadvantages*	Economic disadvantages
Disadvantages in achieving a local face: language, tradition, identity (TV programming versus cement)	Host government discrimination against foreign products/firms. Generally most likely with	High transport costs. Generally most likely with	Cost disadvantages (costs of labor, managers, restructuring, or adaptation)
Disadvantages in catering to preference heterogeneity (horizontal distance)	• High government involvement ○ Regulation (health care) ○ Procurement/ funding (construction) ○ Political salience (TV broadcasting) ○ State ownership (infrastructure) ○ Anointed national champions (aerospace) ○ National security concerns	• Low value-to-weight/bulk • Hazards/difficulties in transport • Perishability Lack or required transportation/ communications infrastructure Intense local supervision requirements Other local performance requirements for value activities (many services)	Know-how disadvantage if differences in suppliers, channels, business systems, or regulations
• Idiosyncratic tastes (fish sausage, boxer shorts) • Different designs (home appliances) • Different standards (electrical equipment) • Different sizes/ packages (processed foods) • Differences in target segments (portable radio and cassette players in U.S. versus Japan)			Disadvantages in providing variety/ agility/responsiveness Susceptibility to global pricing squeezed (home shareholders unfamiliar with local markets)
Entrenched tastes for local products	• Organized domestic resistance to displacement (agriculture, textiles) • National patrimony effects (national resources) • Size/salience/ strategic character (automobiles) • Asset specificity and the scope for holdup problems (infrastructure)		Efficiency of local competition from tough selection environments; dilution of profitability by expanding there
Local biases in demand ("buy local" campaigns)			Late-mover disadvantages
Lack of social connectivity or networks	Negotiations with host government hindered by activities elsewhere in the world (Disney and China regarding the Dalai Lama)		Less perceived commitment to a particular market
	Constraints imposed by home government (bribery)		

*Such geographic disadvantages affect international trade more than they do international investment.

(continued)

TABLE 2-4 (continued)

The possible disadvantages of multinational competitors versus local ones: A CAGE analysis

Cultural disadvantages	Administrative disadvantages	Geographic disadvantages	Economic disadvantages
	Multiple regulatory requirements		
	Hostages to home-host relationships (Motorola in China)		
Susceptibility to home-country norms—or, more broadly, social influences—regarding health, safety, and environmental issues (U.S. footwear and apparel companies in Asia)			

local competitor makes you one depends on the circumstances. Many think that Star TV might have fared better in China if Murdoch had maintained his initial partnership with Li Ka-Shing—and access to Li's deep relationships with the Chinese government—instead of buying him out completely.

Assessing Natural Owners and Comparing Foreign Competitors

Even if MNCs can be confident that they are going to win out over local players in a particular market, the CAGE framework can be used at a finer level of resolution to shed light on the relative position of MNCs from different countries. Consider, for example, the interesting question of what will happen in Cuba after Fidel Castro's passage from the scene. Assuming that the country opens up further, will European or U.S. companies win out there?

Cuba's political relationships with Europe are currently much better, and the nation also has linguistic and colonial ties to one European country, Spain. But the United States is much closer to Cuba along most other dimensions. Its geographic proximity is quite obvious: on a clear night, the violet glow of Miami's lights is visible from Havana's harbor. And then there is proximity along at least some cultural dimensions: Cuba is part of the baseball zone rather than the soccer zone, for example. Spain's language advantage is at least partially offset by the use of Spanish as a second language in the United States, particularly around Miami, which has become a regional hub for Latin business, despite the fact that it is outside the region. Miami is also the hub for the very large Cuban diaspora in the United States, potentially widening the channels of contact between the two countries, even if the channels are not put to good use currently.

In addition, although Cuba was never a U.S. colony (despite repeated U.S. attempts to purchase the island), U.S. big business, including organized crime, dominated the Cuban economy in the decades before Castro's revolution. Most likely, the large claims that these business interests and the Cuban diaspora in the United States still have pending against Castro's government will result in significant transfers of assets in any post-Castro normalization. For this reason, I would bet on U.S. companies winning out over European ones except in industries where first-mover advantages can be secured by European companies before U.S. ones move in.

In line with the theme of the previous section, such analysis can also be pushed down to the industry level. Some success has recently been reported with broader efforts to predict which countries' firms will win out at the industry level in which markets. For example, U.S. firms are somewhat more successful as a group in achieving market leadership in India than in China—and are much more successful in Mexico, where they outperform even Spanish firms in terms of their rate and scope of success.[25] But having noted such "natural ownership" advantages, we must understand that they can easily be trumped by other factors—for example, particularly good or bad international strategies.

Comparing Markets

The CAGE framework can also be used to compare markets from the perspective of a particular company. Since I've already laid out the basic ideas on this subject, here I'll present an application that brings together a company and a pair of countries already considered earlier: AmorePacific looking at China versus India.

From the perspective of a Korean company, China has several attractions over India. Perhaps most obviously, New Delhi is nearly three thousand miles away from Seoul, versus less than six hundred miles for Beijing. Reinforcement is provided by an array of historical links between Korea and China: ethnic commonalities that reflect, in part, significant cross-migration; the influence of Confucianism and Buddhism; the ancient kingdom of Kogoryo, which stretched from northeast China to North Korea; and Korean use of Chinese script for a millennium. More recently, Korean movies, TV programs, and musicians have enjoyed such popularity in China that the media in both countries refer to this infatuation as the "Korean Wave."

These country-level commonalities were reinforced at the industry level by the great influence of the Chinese herbal medicine system on the Korean one—Korea had historically been a transshipment point for herbal medicine from China to Japan—and at the company level, by Amore-Pacific's focus on ginseng, green tea, and bamboo sap as proprietary ingredients, which also resonated with Chinese traditions. India wasn't as close to South Korea along any of these dimensions and therefore seemed much more of a challenge.

Discounting by Distance

The examples discussed above are qualitative, but it's also possible to take a more *quantitative* approach to assessing the effects of distance. Consider the most common tool that companies use in deciding where to compete: country portfolio analysis (CPA), which includes some measure of market size as one of its principal components. Unfortunately, this is a recipe for exactly the sort of "size-ism" that I described and decried in chapter 1. One remedy is to discount (specifically, divide) raw measures of market size or potential with measures of distance, broadly defined. While such discounting involves numerous approximations, making some adjustments for distance is a better idea, given how much it matters, than refraining from making any adjustments at all.

Consider the case of Yum! Brands, the parent of the Pizza Hut, Taco Bell, and KFC fast-food chains, which was spun off from Pepsi in 1997. At that time, its international operations were very dispersed, with restaurants in twenty-seven countries (although two-thirds of international revenues, and an even higher proportion of profits, came from just seven markets). Furthermore, its debt-service obligations and limited international profitability left it with less than one-tenth as much money as archrival McDonald's to invest outside the United States. As a result, the head of international operations at Yum! Brands, Pete Bassi, decided to cut the number of its primary equity markets to just ten. But *which* ten?

Figure 2-3 maps twenty major international markets for Yum! in terms of per-capita income, per-capita fast-food consumption, and total fast-food market size (the areas of the bubbles in the figure). The logic of such country portfolio grids would tend to steer the company toward the larger bubbles to the center and right of the chart in picking its ten primary markets. But note that this would entirely miss out on the effects of distance!

To get a sense of how much difference accounting for distance might make, consider the case of Mexico, which is labeled in the figure, and

FIGURE 2-3

Major international fast-food markets: per-capita consumption versus per-capita income

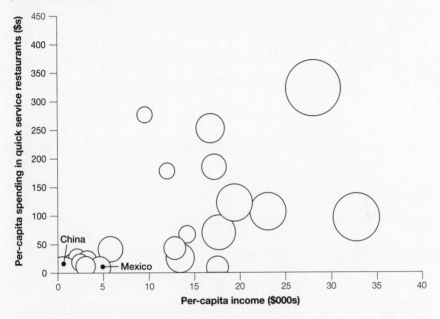

Source: Pankaj Ghemawat, "Distance Still Matters: The Hard Reality of Global Expansion," *Harvard Business Review*, September 2001, 146.

ranked as the sixteenth of the twenty major markets in terms of total fast-food consumption.[26] When this ranking is combined with estimates of low per-capita income and consumption, it appears that Yum! should bail out of Mexico. But when the market size numbers for each country are adjusted for their geographic distance from Dallas—the company's home base—Mexico jumps to sixth place in terms of market opportunity. And when one further adjusts the numbers to reflect a common land border (the absence of which is assumed to halve the business opportunity) and Mexico's membership in NAFTA along with the United States (the absence of which is again assumed to halve the opportunity), Mexico climbs all the way into second place—behind only Canada. Of course, not all the obvious adjustments are positive—Mexico's lack of a common language with the United States pushes it down a bit in the rankings, although it still remains in the top three, along with Canada and the United Kingdom. But the overall message is clear: reasonable attempts to account for distance imply that the market opportunity in Mexico is relatively large.[27] In contrast, country portfolio analysis unadjusted for distance might have suggested to Yum! that it pull its equity out of Mexico!

Bassi's perspective? "Mexico is one of our top two or three priorities."

In addition to my warning about the procedure being approximate, I should add two other caveats. First, the efficacy of distance discounting depends on the parameters of the situation. It works best when *distances between the home base and the various foreign markets being considered vary greatly*—a condition satisfied in the Yum! case.

Second and more important, market analysis is only part—and sometimes only a *small* part—of success. Big successes often require creative thinking about competitive positioning or other dimensions along which new-and-improved strategies might be devised, rather than just mechanical resizing of market potential.

The evolution of Yum! since the time Bassi was deciding how to restructure the non-U.S. operations provides a good example. China, which accounted for 263 units in 1998, has grown to 1,800 units in 2005 and generates more operating income than all the company's international operations did in 1998. Returns on invested capital in China exceed 30 percent, versus a corporate cost of capital of 9 percent, and Yum! now describes building dominant China brands as its key *corporate* strategy. It also claims that KFC in China is on track to be "as big as McDonald's [in the United States] some day."[28] What lies behind this stunning performance?

Very briefly, Yum! repositioned KFC in China to offer extended menus, full table service, and better facilities, reckoning that while China had developed very rapidly, there was a dearth of affordable, casual dining options, particularly ones with assured quality. Yum! China still faces no serious challenger in this booming category.

Note the divergence between this outcome and the predictions of a pure distance-discounted analysis of the market as it was in 1998—which, if performed as described earlier, would have led to China's barely making the top ten. To make the same point more broadly, attempts to adjust for distance are usually warranted. But they have to *complement,* rather than substitute for, thoughtful competitive positioning and other elements of strategy—which are explored at greater length in chapter 3 and beyond.

Conclusions

The box "Global Generalizations" summarizes the specific conclusions from this chapter. To provide a broader recap, while the previous chapter, on semiglobalization, argued the importance of the distinction between

Global Generalizations

1. In a semiglobalized world, both the differences and the similarities between countries must be taken into account.

2. The effects of differences versus similarities on cross-border economic activity are enormous—and do not seem to be vanishing.

3. Distance suggests a good set of metrics for capturing the degree of difference versus similarity between countries.

4. Distance should be thought of as a multidimensional construct with four types of components, cultural, administrative, geographic, and economic, which are summarized in the CAGE framework.

5. The CAGE framework is typically most fruitfully applied at the industry level, that is, with some sense of how the importance of distance between countries is conditioned by or varies with industry characteristics.

6. Applications of the CAGE framework include making differences visible, understanding the liability of foreignness, comparing foreign competitors, comparing markets, and discounting market sizes by distance.

home and abroad, this chapter pushed farther by recognizing not only this distinction but also the finer-grained one that countries differ greatly in the extent to which they are different from each other. The key innovation in this chapter has been the presentation of a framework, the CAGE framework, that captures such "differences in differences" in terms of bilateral measures of distance along various dimensions. The addition of bilateral measures of distance to traditional models for country analysis permits countries to be represented as the nodes—embedded at varying distances from each other—in a global network.

Having explored the CAGE distance framework and its possible applications, it is worth concluding by noting that distance is *not* a sufficient basis for setting international strategy, which is why this book doesn't stop here. The CAGE framework helps us map the global landscape. But to decide how to move across that landscape, we need a more granular understanding of the costs and benefits from crossing borders. For an example, reconsider Wal-Mart's market entry decisions. While it is striking that the profitability of its store operations declines with distance from

Bentonville (figure 2-1), it is more useful to unbundle that relationship and determine that Wal-Mart accounts for 5 percent-plus of retail sales in the non-U.S. markets where it is profitable, versus less than 2 percent in its unprofitable markets. Clearly, its approach to procurement and logistics requires relatively large local market shares to work. The question then becomes this: in light of distance, but also given the company's strategy, mind-set, and so forth, does the required share seem attainable in a particular target market? Finer-grained analysis along these lines of value creation and its drivers is the topic of chapter 3.

3

Global Value Creation

The ADDING Value Scorecard

"I conceive that the great part of the miseries of mankind are brought upon them by false estimates they have made of the value of things."

—Benjamin Franklin, "The Whistle," 1779

CHAPTER 2 DISCUSSED the similarities versus differences between countries and worked through the CAGE distance framework as a way of understanding how much they matter at the country and industry levels. This chapter discusses *why*—if at all—firms should globalize in a world in which distance still matters.

The chapter begins with a brief review of how global strategy often addresses—or fails to address—the question "Why globalize?" It then illustrates—using the example of Cemex, the Mexico-based cement company that has built itself into a global leader since the early 1990s—the ADDING Value scorecard, which adapts and extends the logic of value addition developed in a single-country context to a cross-border context. The chapter considers this scorecard and its elements in some detail, along with analytical guidelines to follow and specific questions to address in applying it. Finally, the chapter briefly discusses how to extend the analysis to address issues of sustainability, how to triangulate on the analysis by using judgment, and how to go beyond analyzing which strategic option is better for generating advantageous strategic options.

Why Globalize?

Writers on the globalization of business rarely examine the question of why, if at all, business should globalize. Although there are several reasons for this omission, perhaps the most important is the widespread tendency to believe in the globalization apocalypse. This naturally renders the question moot.

Second, there may have been some crowding out. Much of what has been written about globalization from a business perspective since the late 1980s has been dominated by concerns related to how, and not why: how to link far-flung units, build global networks, find and train global managers, create truly global corporate cultures.[1] Furthermore, to the extent that the literature *does* deal with global strategy as opposed to global organization, it focuses primarily on achieving global presence: entering the right global markets, making the right acquisitions, or choosing the right global alliance partners.[2] This addresses important questions related to where and who, but still doesn't have much to say about why.

Third—and from a more practical perspective—there is a sense that global strategic moves are so complex and so subject to uncertainty that they essentially become a matter of faith. This can be seen as a metastasis of the traditional tendency in single-country strategy to do detailed cost-benefit analyses of relatively small decisions, and to simply throw up one's hands and surrender to animal spirits in making large ones—a tendency first noted by the late C. Northcote Parkinson in one of his less famous laws.[3]

Whatever the precise mix of reasons, executives in global or would-be global companies, when asked their reasons for globalizing, often spout slogans rather than substance. Paul Verdin and Nick Van Heck have compiled a list of these that would be funny if it didn't strike so frighteningly close to home (figure 3-1).

Furthermore, such slogans aren't just siren songs for the unsophisticated or unwary. Recall the discussion in chapter 2 of the massive wave of foreign direct investment in electricity that began in the early 1990s, and that proved extremely unprofitable. Analysis of 264 foreign investment projects undertaken by 24 U.S. utilities between 1993 and 2002 indicates that:

- "High-status" firms (e.g., ones with current or former directors or top managers of *Fortune* 500 firms on their boards) were particularly prone to large-scale FDI.
- Stock analysts continued to pay more attention to high-FDI firms and to recommend purchase of their stocks through 2001.

FIGURE 3-1

A web of internationalization slogans

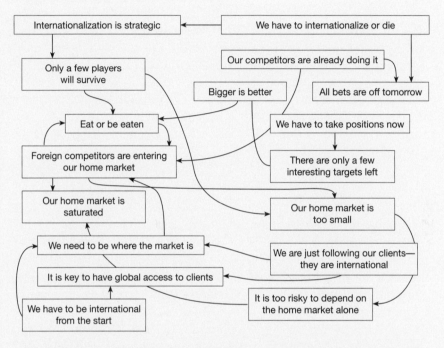

Source: Paul Verdin and Nick Van Heck, *From Local Champions to Global Masters* (London: Palgrave, 2001).

- Stock-market reactions to FDI continued to be positive through 1998, and the investment wave itself crested over 1998–2001—*after* the negative impact of FDI on reported financial results had started to become clear.[4]

Of course, managers and the financial markets aren't the only groups whose enthusiasm may get misplaced when it comes to cross-border moves—people who write about international business are also prone to such problems. To make this point, let me simply cite three examples. Wal-Mart was, despite the considerations discussed in chapter 2, widely acclaimed as an international retailing juggernaut because of its international size and growth—until it recently started to exit some of its less successful markets. Cemex is characterized—in a widely used textbook on international business, as well as in many business school cases—as a leader in using information technology and catering to its distributors, even though, as we shall see in this chapter, those are far from the most important reasons for its superior profitability. And Philips, whose evolution is explored in chapter 4, continued to be written about as a reasonably well-functioning example of various modish organizational models while it teetered at the edge of bankruptcy.

The common thread in all these examples is insufficient attention to the creation of economic value. What we see instead, in these and other cases, is value being ignored or analyzed superficially, survival being treated as a proxy for value creation, or a focus on trailing indicators of performance. The obvious antidote is to adapt and extend the rigorous focus on value creation that has been proven to work in single-country strategy. Although this will be accomplished with some rigor later in this chapter, it will begin by illustrating the importance of a value-focused perspective.

Cemex: Creating Value Through Cross-Border Expansion in Cement

Cement seems like a very unlikely setting for globalization. R&D-to-sales and advertising-to-sales ratios, the two leading indicators of propensity to engage in FDI, are very low. So is the product's value-to-weight ratio, which amplifies the effects of geographic distance. Furthermore, if the product gets wet during waterborne transportation—the only cost-effective way of shipping it over long distances—it becomes unusable.

Yet, despite these apparently unpromising basic conditions, global concentration in cement has increased greatly since the 1980s, when the top five competitors controlled only about 11 percent of the world market. Thanks to cross-border acquisitions, that number is now close to 25 percent, meaning that cement has experienced one of the greatest absolute increases in global concentration of any of the major industries for which I have compiled data! The cement majors, which have continued to be profitable over this period, seem to have found ways of benefiting from cross-border expansion. Of particular interest is Cemex, which had all its capacity located in Mexico through the late 1980s and didn't even figure in the top five then, but has since grown to be the third-largest competitor while maintaining the highest profitability levels of any of the majors. How has Cemex achieved superior performance, and in particular, what role has globalization played?

Volume

The most common rationale cited for crossing borders—adding volume and grabbing market share—certainly seems applicable to the Cemex case. Compare the company with another cement company headquartered in Latin America, Votorantim of Brazil. In 1988, Votorantim was slightly larger than Cemex and was the sixth-largest player in the world. Just fifteen years later, Cemex was the third-largest player, and Votorantim had slipped to tenth place. What happened in the interim? Simply put, Votorantim diversified horizontally, going into industries such as pulp and paper, aluminum, and other metals. By contrast, Cemex diversified geographically. To some extent, Cemex *had* to cross borders to grow because its home market in Mexico was small—significantly smaller than Votorantim's home market in Brazil—and because, by 1989, Cemex already controlled two-thirds of Mexican capacity. There was little room for growth at home.

However, simply adding volume doesn't explain how Cemex was able to sustain superior margins—or, more broadly, to create value through an expansion strategy that relied on acquisitions of existing capacity in other countries. A purely scalar strategy of acquisitions does nothing, as foreign investors in the electricity sector discovered, to address the most fundamental test of value creation in international business, the so-called *better-off test*: does combining and coordinating activities across multiple geographies enable the units to create and claim more value than they could as independent stand-alone operations? Unless the answer is yes, the prospects of superior value creation through acquisitions depend on value transfer: on being able to buy assets for less than they are truly worth. This is nice business if you can get it, but it is often infeasible, especially in light of takeover premiums and transaction costs.

Margins

The discussion of volume suggests that in order to apply the better-off test, we need to assess how Cemex's margins have been affected by global expansion. A comparative picture of margins and their two components, prices and costs, is a useful starting point. And here is where many, perhaps most, analyses of Cemex go astray—by making the simple but serious mistake of expressing costs and margins as percentages of prices. This results in something like figure 3-2, which compares Cemex with its largest global competitor, Holcim, at a time when they were largely undiversified. Such analysis not only confirms that Cemex's average margins are better than Holcim's, but also suggests that Cemex has lower costs.

The trouble with the approach taken in figure 3-2 is that by expressing costs and margins as a percentage of revenues, it mixes up cost differences and price differences. To see how important it can be to separate them out, compare Cemex's economics with Holcim's *on a per-ton basis* (figure 3-3). The big difference: figure 3-3 makes it clear that Cemex's advantage stems from higher average prices rather than lower average costs!

FIGURE 3-2

Cemex versus Holcim: percentage of revenues

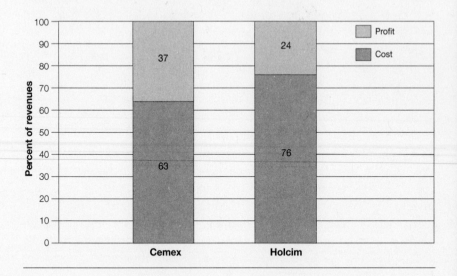

FIGURE 3-3

Cemex versus Holcim: $/ton

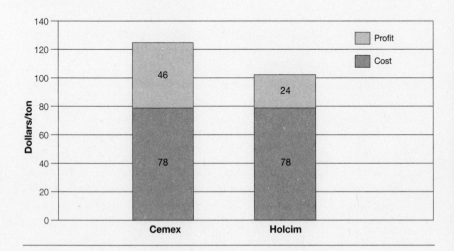

Costs

One might think that the parity between Cemex and Holcim in terms of operating costs per ton means that there is nothing interesting happening on the cost side at Cemex. But, again, not so fast. For one thing, Cemex has achieved parity despite much faster growth, which typically increases complexity and operating costs, particularly in the wake of major acquisitions. (In other words, adding volume can raise costs in the short to medium run.) Particularly remarkable in this regard is the company's postmerger integration process, which has become quicker and more thorough over time. Thus, it took Cemex approximately twenty-four months to integrate the Spanish acquisitions in the early 1990s in terms of standardization of operations platforms; eight years later, a comparably sized acquisition in the United States took just four months.

Second, the operating costs comparisons do not include capital or financing costs, which loom very large in the capital-intensive cement business. These costs can, in turn, be decomposed into the weighted average cost of capital (WACC) times the amount invested per ton of capacity. Cemex's investment and acquisition costs seem to have been comparable to those of its competitors. However, figure 3-4 shows a fairly steady decline in the cost of capital that Cemex paid between 1992 and early 2003.

FIGURE 3-4

Cemex's capital costs

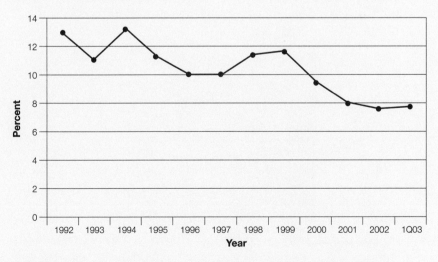

Source: "Cemex Financial Strategy," Rodrigo Treviño, CFO, July 3, 2003, presentation accessed from www.cemex.com.

Many factors contribute to the downward slope in figure 3-4, probably including the close relationship between Cemex and a Mexican bank privatized in the early 1990s, in which the company acquired a partial interest. But I want to focus here on the globalization-related factors, two of which appear to underlie the reductions in WACC. First, pooling across product markets has reduced the volatility of Cemex's cash flows (discussed below, in "Risk"). In addition, as CEO Lorenzo Zambrano has observed, product market globalization was accompanied by (and at least partly enabled) capital market globalization. When it was still a local company, Cemex essentially relied on local sources of finance. But after its big Spanish acquisitions, Cemex financed new acquisitions through its Spanish operations, benefiting from the tax-deductibility of interest in Spain (but not in Mexico), Spanish investment incentives, and the collateral value of assets in a developed country exempt from "Mexico risk." While many Mexican companies tried to tap foreign sources of capital after the country opened up throughout the 1980s, Cemex was unusual for its early reliance on European (rather than U.S.) capital, its use of real assets acquired overseas as collateral, and the apparent sophistication of its corporate finance team.

Of course, Cemex's recourse to European sources of finance probably does *not* help create an advantage vis-à-vis its major rivals, all of which are headquartered in Europe. But it does help mitigate what would otherwise be a major disadvantage associated with higher capital costs. Particularly given the capital intensity of cement, even a small capital cost disadvantage might be fatal to a strategy of cross-border expansion. Thus, a rough sensitivity analysis based on assumptions set out in analysts' reports suggested that a 0.5 percent decrease in Cemex's WACC would increase its market value by 5 percent. By way of comparison, note that Cemex estimated that the shift to financing acquisitions in Spain reduced its WACC by 2.5 percent!

Prices and Willingness-to-Pay

The truly startling difference between Cemex and its leading global competitors is in the much higher average prices Cemex commands. The international Cemex brand that the company has begun introducing in parallel with its acquired local brands may play a role here, particularly on sales in bags to small buyers rather than in bulk to large buyers. And in selling to bulk buyers, the company's guaranteed delivery within fifteen minutes of a stipulated time—inspired by Domino's Pizza—has contributed to buyer value and willingness-to-pay by reducing expensive downtime.

Observers have cited these and other programs as illustrations of the power of differentiation even in an industry as commoditized as cement. But common sense suggests that they go only part of the way toward explaining prices that are, on average, 20 percent higher than Holcim's. Advertising intensity in cement is, as noted, very low; the retention of local brands presumably further limits the power of global branding; and key programs such as the delivery guarantee were, until recently, confined to Cemex's home base in Mexico. What *does* seem to be a big driver on the price side is bargaining and market power, as discussed next.

Prices and Leverage

Different prices without differences in costs or willingness-to-pay are generally thought to reflect the effects of differences in leverage or bargaining power. That certainly seems to be an important factor in the case of Cemex. Cemex is very disciplined in the way in which it conducts its acquisitions. It buys capacity in countries or regions where it can (1) reduce the number of competitors, (2) wind up with the largest market share among those competitors, and (3) own a controlling interest in its acquired companies. Figure 3-5 summarizes the results.

Note the clear correlation between Cemex's operating profit by major market versus its share of that market. The idea that this correlation is based on bargaining power rather than on efficiency is corroborated by the fact that when Cemex "cleans up a country"—in the sense of consolidating a market—the other players there tend also to benefit. Cemex's smaller rivals in Mexico, for example, are enormously profitable.

Such domestic consolidation wouldn't help profitability much if imports could flood in whenever domestic prices rose above a certain level. But Cemex also controls what military strategists would call "strategic narrows" that allow it to influence the levels of imports into its key markets. Particularly important is Cemex's network of sixty marine terminals worldwide. On the Spanish coast alone, it controls nine such terminals, effectively sheltering its market there from lowballing invaders—and implicitly threatening foreign markets. You can get the stuff *out*, and they can't necessarily get it *in*. This control is complemented by Cemex's role as the world's largest cement trader—with much of that cement produced by third parties. This is not a very lucrative business in and of itself. But trading other people's products is a good way to divert low-priced imports away from your own key markets, as well as to gain experience in other markets before you decide whether to acquire local capacity.

Ironically, it was a threat along exactly this dimension that helped spur Cemex's globalization. Specifically, Holcim's investments in Mexico in

FIGURE 3-5

Cemex profitability by country or region, 1998–2002

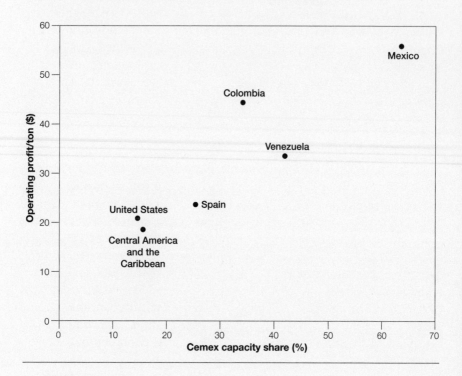

1989 prompted Cemex to begin investing heavily in Spain in 1992, where Holcim already had significant investments in place. The clear implication was that if a price war erupted in Mexico, another might well erupt in Spain. As it turned out, *no* price wars erupted. The caveat, of course, is that such dominance and recognition of mutual dependence with, in particular, other global competitors has triggered antitrust investigations and legal challenges, some of which are ongoing.

Risk

Globalization has also helped Cemex manage risk (and thereby contributing to the reduction in its cost of capital, as described above). The construction business, which drives the cement industry, is characterized by deep local and regional cycles. Pooling across markets with different construction cycles helped reduce the standard deviation in Cemex's quarterly cash flow margins from an average of 22 percent over the 1978–1992 period (in the run-up to its acquisitions in Spain) to 12 percent over the 1992–1997 period. It also helped the company weather Mexico's currency crisis of the mid-1990s—the so-called tequila shock—that might otherwise have forced Cemex to sell out to a global competitor. And having globalized, Cemex, like other global competitors, now buys capacity at a fraction of its replacement cost when local competitors come under pressure from local economic cycles (e.g., in Asia in the wake of the Asian currency crisis of the late 1990s).

Knowledge

The final broad area to be discussed here concerns the impact of globalization on knowledge generation and transfer. Once you go outside Mexico to make cement and sell it to other people, you get the opportunity to learn all kinds of useful new things. Figure 3-6 summarizes the origins of some of the best practices that Cemex has implanted across its global operations in the 1990s and early 2000s. Some of this cross-border learning was serendipitous. But some resulted from a purposeful quest for information and a determination to deploy it worldwide.[5] This determination is reflected in the company's range of organizational mechanisms summarized under the rubric "The Cemex Way": the adoption of a common language (English rather than Spanish) worldwide, the rotation of managers on a global basis, the use of international consultants, and sustained investments in technology, including information technology, to realize the potential unlocked by learning.

Table 3-1 summarizes the discussion in this section. The shaded cells are particularly important in explaining why globalization hasn't, in this case, simply become an excuse for using profitable operations at home to cross-subsidize unprofitable ones abroad.

The ADDING Value Scorecard

Table 3-1 parses value addition at Cemex into six components: adding volume, decreasing costs, differentiating, improving industry attractiveness, normalizing risks, and generating and deploying knowledge (and other resources). These components form what we will call the ADDING Value scorecard. While the acronym will help you remember the components of the scorecard, the deeper point is that they add up to a way of thinking about value creation that is general rather than specific to the Cemex case. The components into which value is parsed are meant to be commensurable, and to add up to determine overall value addition—or subtraction.

FIGURE 3-6

Knowledge transfer at Cemex

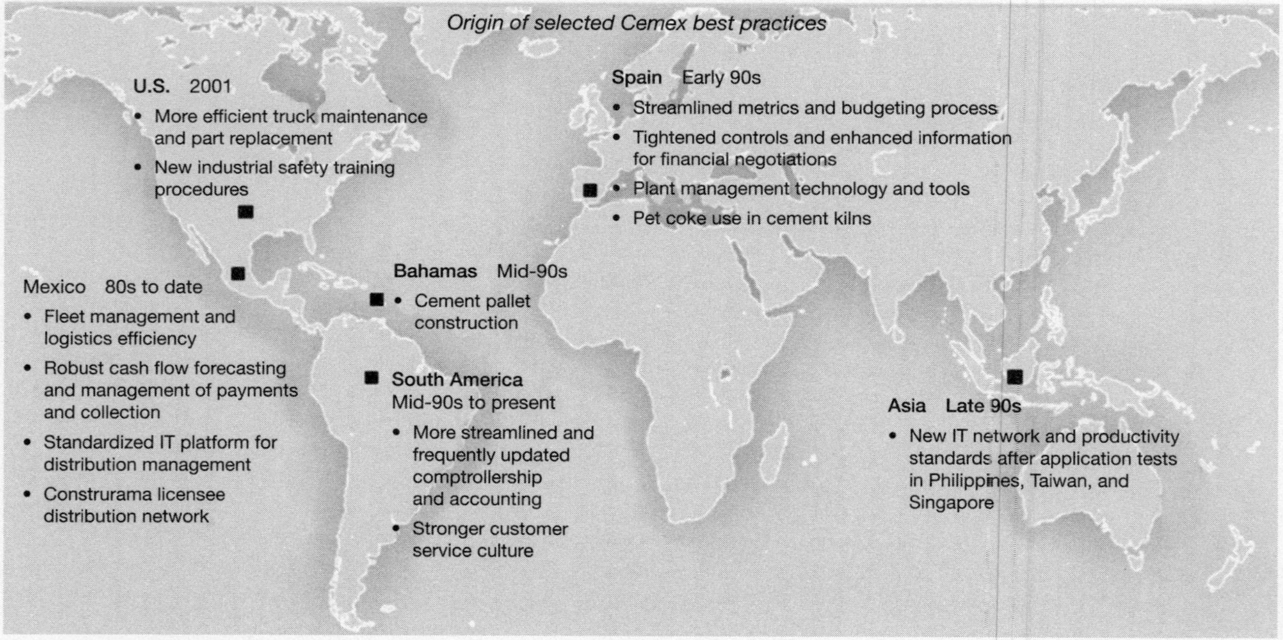

Origin of selected Cemex best practices

Spain Early 90s
- Streamlined metrics and budgeting process
- Tightened controls and enhanced information for financial negotiations
- Plant management technology and tools
- Pet coke use in cement kilns

Asia Late 90s
- New IT network and productivity standards after application tests in Philippines, Taiwan, and Singapore

U.S. 2001
- More efficient truck maintenance and part replacement
- New industrial safety training procedures

Bahamas Mid-90s
- Cement pallet construction

South America Mid-90s to present
- More streamlined and frequently updated comptrollership and accounting
- Stronger customer service culture

Mexico 80s to date
- Fleet management and logistics efficiency
- Robust cash flow forecasting and management of payments and collection
- Standardized IT platform for distribution management
- Construrama licensee distribution network

Source: Cemex Annual Report, 2002.

TABLE 3-1

ADDING Value through global expansion: the case of Cemex

Components of value	Cemex achievements, attempts, or intent		Effect, and comments
Adding volume, or growth	Growth into a member of the Big Six and then the Big Three	×	Performance related not to global scale (or else number three would not be most profitable) but to national or local scale
Decreasing costs	Absolute reductions in operating costs	+?	Probably limited since Cemex acquires competitors with large local shares rather than restructuring cases; operating costs *per ton* no lower than, e.g., Holcim
	Postmerger integration (PMI) costs	+?	PMI process upgraded and compressed from 2 years (Spain in 1992) to 100 days, reducing disruption and post-acquisition integration costs
	Acquisition costs	×	Bottom-feeding key to success through acquisition, but no effect on size of pie to be split between buyer and acquirer
	Capital cost reduced through collateralization, tax arbitrage, risk reduction, etc.	+	Probably not a source of advantage versus rich country rivals but avoids big disadvantage. Critically dependent on moving beyond Mexico
Differentiating or increasing willingness-to-pay	Brand-building	×	Branding mostly local; advertising-to-sales and R&D-to-sales ratios for industry fall in bottom decile for manufacturing
	Construction products retailing	×	Complements generally available on more competitive terms, limiting potential for bundling
	15-minute delivery guarantees	+	Only offered in Mexico (although could be rolled out elsewhere) but generated much buzz worldwide
		+	Avoid reductions in willingness-to-pay due to limited cross-country heterogeneity
Improving industry attractiveness or bargaining power	High local share or increases in concentration targeted	+	Plays on local or national scale or concentration; has yielded very high prices and profitability in concentrated local markets (three-firm concentration ratio greater than 90% in Mexico, Colombia, and Venezuela)
	Diversion of imports from key markets (biggest trader)	+	Reinforces and reinforced by control of local competition: trade softens up takeover targets
		–	Antitrust cases: Mexico, Colombia, Venezuela

(continued)

TABLE 3-1 *(continued)*

ADDING Value through global expansion: the case of Cemex

Components of value	Cemex achievements, attempts, or intent		Effect, and comments
Normalizing (or optimizing) risk	Reduction in standard deviation of quarterly cash flow margins: 22% (1978–1992) to 12% (1992–1997)	+	Important, given size of reduction, capital intensity; family exposure; based on limited correlation of cement prices across national borders (if company stayed Mexican, "tequila shock" would probably be fatal)
	Reduction in competitive risk	+	Important: other local players picked off by MNCs
		+	Creatively increased risk and created growth options as well: swapped Spanish capacity for Southeast Asian capacity
Generating knowledge (and other resources and capabilities)	Incorporation of best practices into Cemex way, dissemination	+	Knowledge transfer eased by industry homogeneity, standardization of technology, measurability of output
	Global mind-set: rotation, use of English, U.S. consultants, systems	+	Focus on global rather than horizontal expansion plus intensive control and intervention (supported by centralization and standardization)

Note: (x) no effect, (+) positive effect, (–) negative effect, (?) particularly uncertain. Shading denotes particularly important effects.

To elaborate, the ADDING Value scorecard adapts and extends the rigorous focus on value creation that has been well tested—in companies, by consultants, and in the classroom—in single-country strategy. Note that value is the product of volume and margin. The two components into which margin itself has been unbundled in single-country strategy are the average attractiveness of the environment in which a business operates and the competitive advantage or disadvantage of a business relative to its average competitor within that environment.[6] In loose terms, these quantities are linked by what might be called the fundamental equation of business strategy:

Your margin = industry margin + your competitive advantage

Michael Porter's famous five-forces framework for the structural analysis of industries has explored the strategic determinants of industry margin or profitability, the first term on the right-hand side of the equation.[7] And Porter and other strategists, notably Adam Brandenburger and Gus

Stuart, have probed the determinants of competitive advantage, the second term on the right-hand side, and emphasized characterizing it in terms of willingness-to-pay and (opportunity) costs:[8]

Your competitive advantage = [willingness-to-pay – cost] for your company – [willingness-to-pay – cost] for your competitor = your relative willingness-to-pay – your relative cost

In other words, in single-country strategy, an appreciation of the importance of a competitive edge has evolved into an understanding of the economics of what might be called "the competitive wedge." A firm is said to have created a competitive advantage over its rivals if it has driven a wider wedge between willingness-to-pay and costs than its competitors have done.

The ADDING Value scorecard follows single-country strategy in four of its six value components: adding volume (or, with a more dynamic frame, growth), decreasing costs, differentiating or increasing willingness-to-pay, and increasing industry attractiveness. Its other two components—normalizing risk and the generation of knowledge and other resources—reflect the large differences across countries, discussed in chapter 2. These are customary add-ons in international strategy, and their potential significance is illustrated by the case of Cemex. I prefer to take knowledge generation and broaden it to encompass other resources that might also be generated (or depleted) by globalization. This helps avoid overemphasis on learning—which, although important, has become a bit of a fetish in international strategy—by also bringing into the picture other resource stocks that affect a firm's future opportunity set, even if they don't show up directly and immediately in its cash flows.

That should explain the logic of the boxes in figure 3-7, which are also the ones that the scorecard in table 3-1 covers. Moreover, this logic, involving commensurability and adding up, distinguishes the ADDING Value scorecard from others widely used in business that simply list an assortment of more or less arbitrary items.

Before discussing how to analyze each of the boxes in figure 3-7, it is worth mentioning several broad analytical guidelines: the importance of thinking comprehensively about value creation, of unbundling of various sorts, of simple quantification, and of making comparisons.

Comprehensiveness

The strategic intent behind the scorecard is to look more broadly at cross-border value creation than is implied by the standard sort of size-ism: *The*

FIGURE 3-7

Components of ADDING Value

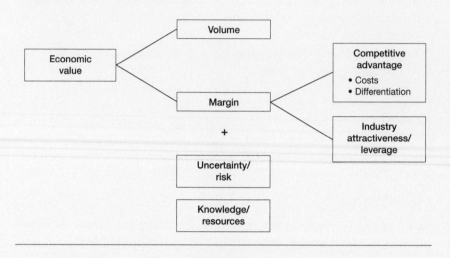

world is a big place, with lots of volume out there or on the way, and we need to scoop up our share! And the common corollary to such size-ism: *We'll cut our costs by chasing volume across borders.* Those two notions may or may not hold water, depending on circumstances. But as table 3-1 and figure 3-7 emphasize, they are only a subset of the components of the ADDING Value scorecard. You'll come closer to maximizing your potential if you have a suitably broad conception of how crossing borders might add value.

Of course, that isn't to say that all components are equally important in all industries or for all companies. Furthermore, different value components can become more or less important at different points in a company's history. For example, Citibank supposedly started taking country risk seriously in making market entry decisions only after it had entered its first one hundred countries. Thus, the examples discussed in the chapters that follow won't try to check off all the boxes in figure 3-7, just the most relevant ones. But in any real analysis, it is important to start off by being comprehensive: by at least *considering* all six value components, although some may warrant less attention than others.

Unbundling

This emphasis on comprehensiveness must be complemented by an appreciation of the importance of unbundling, or disaggregation. The very structure of the scorecard highlights the importance of unbundling value into its components. Other kinds of unbundling can also be very useful in analyzing value creation. Thus, it often makes sense to break firms down into discrete activities or processes and then analyze how each contributes to the components of the ADDING Value scorecard. And the components of value themselves may be worth unbundling: compare the distinction between operating costs and capital costs in the Cemex case.

Of course, you must also remember the strategic intent behind applying the scorecard: building a comprehensive picture of value-addition possibilities. As a result, any component-by-component analysis you conduct must be followed up by work to build or rebuild a vision of the whole—as depicted in table 3-1 in the case of Cemex.

Quantification

Some quantification is often essential to turbocharge the analysis. Thus, most groups with which I discuss the Cemex case register the company's attempts to both reduce costs and raise prices. But some calculations are required to get a sense of the relative magnitudes—with big implications for such issues as future market selection. (For example, if Cemex were earning superior profits based on cost advantages, considerations of market attractiveness would not loom as large in its market selection decisions.)

Most of the value added by quantification, I should stress, comes from simple, back-of-the envelope calculations, many of them illustrated by the Cemex case analysis: figuring out the relative magnitudes of various kinds of effects; understanding where a company is making most of its money; probing the big differences between its economics and those of its competitors; and doing breakeven analyses. Thus, if I were advising a client on whether to make an acquisition, I'd probably recommend a discounted cash flow analysis at some point—but I'd be likely to spend most of my time on the kinds of analyses listed above to shed light on the cash flows that should be plugged into such an analysis.

Of course, even for simple analyses, you need to make assumptions, analyze how sensitive the conclusions are to the assumptions, and, if necessary, iterate. Also worth mentioning is the caveat that not everything of interest can be quantified. One approach is to quantify as best as you can the expected value from doing one thing as opposed to another, and then to weigh the results of that analysis against the qualitative considerations that are left out of the calculations. This process gives a rough sense of how much qualitative considerations would have to matter in order to overrule the numbers.

You can apply a somewhat similar approach to values other than economic value. Even if you would prefer to do something in spite of, rather than because of, economic value, it is useful to understand how much your preferred option is going to cost your company in economic terms before you decide whether to pursue it.

Comparisons

For the analysis to have bite, you generally have to undertake comparisons. Possible types of comparisons include the following:

- *Option A versus B, C, and so forth:* This kind of comparison is particularly useful for decision making. It usually makes sense to compare all the options against each other rather than examine them one by one, against the alternative of doing nothing. Part of the reason is that such joint evaluation may make it easier to take hard-to-evaluate considerations (e.g., qualitative ones, as discussed above) into account.[9]

- *Position at one point in time versus another:* This kind of comparison tends to be particularly helpful for monitoring and diagnostic purposes. Thus, it is useful to go beyond checking for improvement to assessing whether the *rate* of improvement is satisfactory (e.g., whether it exceeds some target rate or will suffice to achieve some target level of performance). Such trajectories will be discussed further later in the chapter, in the context of sustainability.

- *Comparisons with competitors:* This kind of comparison tends to be directly helpful for diagnostic purposes—although, of course, the asymmetries that it highlights can also help suggest remedial or reinforcing actions. The appropriate choice of benchmark competitors is critical to deriving value from such analyses.

- *Comparisons with market contracting:* The question here is whether combining and coordinating activities across multiple geographies enables units to create and claim more value than they could as independent, stand-alone operations—already introduced as the better-off test. This kind of comparison is particularly helpful at assessing mergers and stretching strategic thinking by forcing a company to rethink what it does in-house.

Note that the analysis of Cemex ended up embodying all these kinds of comparisons, even though it was motivated by the attempt to understand how Cemex had outperformed its competitors.

Let us turn now to a general discussion of each of the six components of the ADDING Value scorecard.

The Components of the ADDING Value Scorecard

You've been introduced to the six components of the ADDING Value scorecard in the specific context of Cemex. But to make the scorecard more valuable, we need to discuss each of the six value components from a more general perspective. The discussion is organized around a number of recommendations for analyzing each of the six value components, as summarized in Table 3-2.

Adding Volume, or Growth

Probably the most cited reason for globalization, as noted in chapter 1, is that a company has run out of room in its home market. But if that's the only reason on offer, it is probably better to go on a diet. Thus, as noted in the Cemex discussion, without an increase in the size of the pie, the only way to create value through acquisitions is by buying companies for less than they are truly worth—a laudable objective, but not one that can be achieved unilaterally.

For an example of a global icon that has recently figured this out for itself, consider McDonald's. According to CEO Jim Skinner: "We proved that we were getting bigger but not better. And we have to be better . . . We had contributed $4 billion or $5 billion to capital expenditures and building new stores over four years, and yet we didn't have any corresponding incremental operating-income growth. So we decided to focus on our existing operations."[10]

But for every company that figures out that incremental volume may not be profitable, there are probably several that do not. What might help them perform better?

Look at economic profits, that is, accounting profits minus capital recovery costs. Subtracting capital costs from accounting profits helps focus attention on true value creation—a focus that seems to be lacking given the number of countries in the portfolio of the typical large multinational that generate negative economic value over long periods (see chapter 8)! Making these negative outcomes visible encourages a discussion of whether they reflect deliberate investments or undesirable operating outcomes.

Understand the level at which economies of scale or scope really matter. Economies of scale are the most direct link between volume and the other components of the ADDING Value scorecard. But their strategic implications depend on the level, if any, at which additional scale or scope matters:

TABLE 3-2

Applying the ADDING Value scorecard

Components of value	Guidelines
Adding volume, or growth	• Look at the true economic profitability of incremental volume. • Probe the level at which additional volume yields economies of scale (or scope): globally, nationally, at the plant or customer level. • Calibrate the strength of scale effects (slope, percentage of costs or revenues affected). • Assess the other effects of volume.
Decreasing costs	• Unbundle cost effects and price effects. • Unbundle costs into subcategories. • Consider cost increases (e.g., due to complexity, adaptation) as well as decreases, and net them out. • Look at cost drivers other than scale or scope. • Look at labor costs-to-sales ratios for your industry (or company).
Differentiating or increasing willingness-to-pay	• Look at the R&D-to-sales and advertising-to-sales ratios for your industry. • Focus on willingness-to-pay rather than prices paid. • Think through how globality affects willingness-to-pay. • Analyze, in particular, how cross-border (CAGE) heterogeneity in preferences affects willingness-to-pay for products on offer. • Segment the market appropriately.
Improving industry attractiveness or bargaining power	• Account for international differences in industry profitability. • Understand the concentration dynamics of your industry. • Look broadly at the impact of changes in industry structure. • In particular, think through how you can deescalate or escalate rivalry. • Recognize the implications of what you do for rivals' costs or willingness-to-pay for their products. (Worsening their positions can do as much for added value as improving one's own.) • Attend to regulatory and other nonmarket restraints—and ethics.
Normalizing (or optimizing) risk	• Characterize the extent and key sources of risk in your business (e.g., capital intensity, other correlates of irreversibility, demand volatility). • Assess how much cross-border operations reduce or increase risk. • Recognize any benefits that might accrue from increasing risk. • Consider multiple modes of managing exposure to risk or the exploitation of optionality.
Generating knowledge (and other resources and capabilities)	• Assess the location-specificity versus mobility of knowledge. • Consider multiple modes of generating (and diffusing) knowledge. • Think of other resources or capabilities in similar terms. • Avoid double-counting.

global scale, national scale, plant scale, share of customer wallet, and so on. Thus, International Paint underperformed internationally for a long time because—unlike Cemex—it focused on global scale in a business in which key scale economies operated at the national level. Or to cite a positive example, Goldman Sachs seems to have done well by focusing on its share of the investment banking business of a select list of global clients. Also note that firms can try to deliberately engineer extra economies of scale through strategies of aggregation in particular (see chapter 5).

Calibrate the strength of economies of scale or scope. Obviously, the strength as well as the locus of economies of scale or scope matters a great deal. Thus, in the late 1990s, Whirlpool, the market leader in home appliances (see chapter 4), tried, and quickly abandoned, a strategy of halving the number of product platforms that it offered worldwide. Given the limited scale economies in the home appliance industry, this move was projected to reduce costs by only 2 percent of revenues—not enough to overcome the other distance-related impediments to successful implementation of Whirlpool's strategy. In contrast, automakers (which Whirlpool was trying to emulate) have done much better with such strategies because of the greater scale sensitivity of their industry.

Assess the other effects of incremental volume. The preceding discussion focused on scale economies, particularly on the cost side. But incremental volume can have other effects—not all of them positive—on a company's economics. Additional volume may, for instance, raise rather than lower costs if a key input is in short supply—or because of adjustment costs such as those associated with post-merger integration. And it can clearly affect the other components of the ADDING Value scorecard, which we will discuss later.

Decreasing Costs

Companies contemplating cross-border moves often do consider cost reduction when making such decisions. But here, too, there is much room for improvement, especially since managers are often dissatisfied with their ability to achieve the cost reductions targeted through cross-border expansion.[11]

Unbundle cost effects and price effects. From the Cemex case, we saw that instead of looking at margins as a percentage of sales, it was better to separate out cost effects and price effects. Single-country strategy recognizes the importance of such unbundling for products that aren't true commodities. But in a semiglobalized cross-border context, such unbundling can be important even for commodities such as cement.

Since separating out cost effects and price effects rules out the expression of costs as a fraction of revenues, it opens up the question of which other basis of normalization to use. The analysis of the Cemex case relied on expressing revenues, costs, and profits on a per-ton basis. In other situations, it may make sense to normalize by unit of resource input rather than by unit of output. And while capital is the most common resource in this context, other kinds of resources may make sense, depending on industry characteristics. Thus, because capital-intensity is very low in software services and skilled labor-intensity very high, the quantification of costs and revenues in per-employee terms often makes more sense, as we shall see in chapter 6.

Unbundle costs into subcategories. Once again, the Cemex case illustrated this point by highlighting the usefulness of distinguishing between operating costs and capital costs. Fixed costs and variable costs represent another key distinction, particularly for purposes such as breakeven analyses. Other essential distinctions are more specific to the cases being studied. In the home appliances industry, for example, the problem of complexity particularly affects selling, general, and administrative costs, so that this subcategory of costs is worth tracking separately.

Consider cost increases as well as decreases. This point, already made briefly, is important enough to reiterate. Consider, for example, a cross-border merger that is generally thought to have been a failure rather than a success: DaimlerChrysler. While there were many problems with this merger, one important one—especially from the perspective of shareholders in the old Daimler-Benz—concerned added costs: the 28 percent premium effectively paid to Chrysler's shareholders; hundreds of millions of dollars in investment bankers' fees and transaction costs; and, on an ongoing basis, hundreds of millions of dollars in extra compensation for German managers to bring their pay packages in line with those of their U.S. counterparts. These numbers loomed large in comparison with the merger's targeted cost savings, which were mostly confined to procurement and back-end activities such as finance, control, IT, and logistics.

Look at cost drivers other than scale and scope. While the preceding discussion focused on scale and scope, strategists know that there are many other potential drivers of costs: location, which is of particular importance, in a cross-border context; capacity utilization; vertical integration; timing (e.g., early-mover advantages); functional policies; and institutional factors such as unionization and governmental regulations such as tariffs. Looking at the full range of cost drivers increases a company's ability to reduce, or at least contain, the costs that result from cross-border expansion.

Relate the potential for absolute cost reductions to labor- or talent-intensity. The intensity of labor or talent is just one dimension of the possibilities for economic arbitrage, but has attracted special attention. You might, therefore, want to compare your businesses to cross-industry averages (for U.S. manufacturing), where personnel expenses equal to 17 percent of revenues mark off the bottom quartile, 23 percent the median, and 31 percent the top quartile. High values for your company relative to these benchmarks increase the potential for absolute cost reductions through labor arbitrage.

These are just some of the cost-related issues to consider in applying the ADDING Value scorecard. Others will be mentioned even more briefly. When opportunity costs differ greatly from actual costs (e.g., when cheap inputs are in short supply), it is important to focus explicitly on the former. And even where this isn't a problem, many companies have grossly inadequate costing systems—this tends to be particularly true of overhead costs—that must be cleaned up before costing can be a useful input into strategic analysis. Analysts sometimes also confuse differences in firms' costs with differences in their product mixes instead of looking at comparable products. Another set of problems that concerns cross-border volatility (e.g., fluctuations in currency exchange rates) will be discussed in the section on normalizing risks. And, finally, a focus on costs should not crowd out consideration of differentiation, or customer willingness-to-pay, as discussed next.

Differentiating or Increasing Willingness-to-Pay

If companies are often sloppy in doing their cross-border cost analyses, they are often even worse when it comes to differentiation or willingness-to-pay. They may assume that what worked at home will, with some tinkering, work as well (or better) abroad. But such an assumption is no substitute for serious analysis of this value component. Here are some helpful guidelines.

Relate the potential for differentiation to R&D-to-sales and advertising-to-sales ratios for your company or industry. Expenditures on R&D

and on advertising in relation to sales are the two longest-established and most robust indicators of multinationalization, which is why product differentiation is considered the hallmark of (horizontal) multinationals.[12] R&D expenditures equal to 0.9 percent of sales revenues define the bottom quartile for U.S. manufacturing, 2.0 percent of revenues the median, and 3.5 percent the top quartile. The corresponding cutoff points for advertising-to-sales ratios are 0.8 percent, 1.7 percent, and 3.5 percent. The Cemex case supplies useful perspective. Note that cement falls within or close to the bottom decile of U.S. manufacturing industries on both advertising intensity and R&D intensity. This doesn't mean that opportunities for differentiation are entirely absent: Cemex has devised delivery innovations for bulk buyers and displayed creativity in branding bagged cement for individual buyers, and in financing their purchases. Rather, the implication is that the room for differentiation is simply more limited in this industry than in, say, detergents, soft drinks, or pharmaceuticals, and that it is important to be realistic about that point.

Focus on willingness-to-pay rather than prices paid. There are at least two problems with using prices as proxies for the benefits for which buyers are willing to pay. First, prices mix in a number of other influences related to industry attractiveness and bargaining power, as we saw in the Cemex case. Second, a focus on willingness-to-pay encourages envisioning things as they might be rather than as they actually are. These and other kinds of game-changing strategies are discussed more systematically in the subsection, later in this chapter, on creativity.

Think through how globality affects willingness-to-pay. There is a lot of talk about cravings to belong to a global community, as well as a few possible examples, such as Zara, the Spanish fashion retailer: one can imagine fashionistas in one country caring to some extent about what their counterparts in other fashion-forward countries are wearing. However, examples of globality per se increasing willingness-to-pay are relatively rare, especially in consumer products. (For business-to-business products and services, buyers may themselves be globalizing, making such increases more likely.) Of seemingly comparable importance but often underemphasized are country-of-origin advantages—associated with specific countries or regions, rather than with globality in general—that can, to some extent, be influenced through strategy.[13] Häagen-Dazs is a good example: the name was devised by the Bronx-based company's U.S. founders to give a faux-Scandinavian appeal to their ice cream.

Against these kinds of possible advantages from cross-border operation, one has to weigh all the liabilities of foreignness that apply broadly to foreigners, and country-of-origin disadvantages attached to specific countries. For every Häagen-Dazs, there seems to be an Arla, the truly Danish dairy products company that was badly hurt by the Middle Eastern outcry against cartoons insulting Islam published in a Danish newspaper. Note that country-of-origin disadvantages—for example, being Danish, for Arla—need not be confined to countries that are generally prominent or widely disliked.

Analyze how cross-border (CAGE) heterogeneity in preferences affects willingness-to-pay for the products on offer. Chapter 2 covered this topic in depth, so all that will be added here is a reminder of the challenges in this regard. Even preference heterogeneity that seems relatively simple and obvious may require transformational changes if it is to be handled effectively. Thus, consider the trend selected as the most portentous for global business over the next five years, in a survey by the *McKinsey Quarterly* in early 2006: the growing number of consumers in emerging countries.[14] The income-related differences thereby spotlighted seem rather straightforward when compared with some of the other cross-country differences discussed in chapter 2. But actually adapting business models tuned to advanced markets to compete effectively in emerging markets is likely to require massive efforts, with uncertain odds of success. Adaptation is the topic of chapter 4.

Segment the market appropriately. Segmentation obviously picks up on differences in willingness-to-pay (and, sometimes, differences in costs). Typically, the number of segments to be considered increases with diversity in customer needs and ease in customizing the firm's products or services. Resegmentation can play a broader role as well, by shifting perspectives on a situation and thereby stretching strategic thinking. These benefits of segmentation are often more important in a cross-border context than in a single-country one because cross-border differences generally exceed within-country ones. But the benefits from better thinking across borders can also be helpful in a within-country context. As a European manager of a major U.S. consumer products multinational told me, "We're now reeducating headquarters in segmentation."

In conclusion, it may be harder to pin down the implication of a move for willingness-to-pay than for costs, especially when preferences have a significant subjective component. But that is no reason not to improve on generally bad practice in this area. The guidelines offered here help suggest how to do so.

Improving Industry Attractiveness and Bargaining Power

Our discussions of decreasing costs and differentiating, the two Ds in the ADDING Value scorecard, focused on efficiency. As the Cemex case illustrates, it is also important to bring considerations of industry attractiveness or bargaining power to bear. Here are some specific guidelines for doing so.

Account for international differences in industry profitability. The simplest way to illustrate international differences in industry profitability is to note the very large variation in average profitability across countries; see figure 3-8 for data on more than four thousand firms from forty-two countries. Such cross-industry differences in average profitability represent one source of cross-border variation; the other one to be picked up, of course, involves variation in the profitability of the same industry across different countries. Both types of systematic variation seem to be too large to ignore.

Understand concentration dynamics in your industry. Chapter 1 pointed out that managers overwhelmingly believe that increased global

FIGURE 3-8

Average profitability for 42 countries, 1993–2003

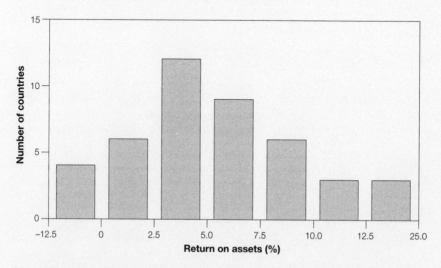

Source: Rogerio Victer and Anita McGahan, "The Effect of Industry and Location on Firm Profitability in the Global Market: Empirical Evidence That Firm Performance Depends on the Interaction Between Industry Affiliation and Country Identity," working paper, Boston University School of Management, Boston, February 2006.

integration increases global concentration—even though it doesn't. This isn't just a generalized misconception: managers are sometimes unaware of concentration dynamics in their own industries!

The auto industry is a case in point. The common belief, used to justify megamergers such as DaimlerChrsyler, is that this industry is getting progressively more concentrated.[15] Yet, the concentration data actually indicate that the big story since World War II has been a decline in global concentration, followed by a flattening-out at levels much lower than a few decades ago (figure 3-9).[16] In fact, the heyday of global concentration in the autos was eighty years ago, when Ford's Model T accounted by itself for more than one-half of the world's stock of cars! And the difference matters. Megamergers would make the most sense if rising economies of scale were actually raising global concentration, but the prevailing situation in autos is one of fragmentation and excess capacity. In such a fragmented situation, a megamerger takes on the flavor of paying privately for the costly good—spread across all the firms in an industry—of removing a major competitor from the scene. Nice for one's competitors, but not necessarily for one's shareholders.

Look broadly at (other) changes in industry structure. The point of the previous guideline was that instead of *assuming* that globalization is increasing industry concentration, you must look at the evidence. Along

FIGURE 3-9

Global concentration levels in automobiles

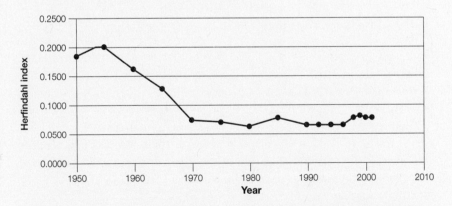

Note: The concentration measure used here, dictated by the need for harmonizing with the data reported for 1950–1970 by Raymond Vernon and his associates, is a modified Herfindahl index. The index is calculated by squaring the unit market shares of the top ten producers in a given year and summing them (although the shares themselves are based on the size of the total market, rather than the combined size of the top ten firms).

the same lines, it is also important look at whether other elements of industry structure—the factors highlighted by Michael Porter's five-forces framework, for instance—are changing. Examples include shifts in sales or production to emerging markets and the possibility of greater exposure to holdup by global buyers and suppliers as a result of increased cross-border activity.

Think through how you can de-escalate or escalate the degree of rivalry. It is common to assume (often without offering any rationales) that competitors will behave in one of several standard ways: by imitating moves (e.g., entry into new markets), backing off in the face of threat, running as hard as possible, and so on. But figuring out competitors' likely responses to a move is better undertaken on the basis of detailed structural and competitor analysis. Detailed analysis of this sort is needed to explain, for example, why multimarket contact appears to have raised prices in some industries, such as cement, but has led to price wars in others, such as tires.

Recognize the implications of your actions for rivals' costs or willingness-to-pay for their products. Raising your rivals' costs or reducing their willingness-to-pay can do as much for your company's margins as improving its own position in absolute terms. Thus, in order to cope with low-cost competitors in software services from India, Western firms such as IBM and Accenture have built up significant operations there. The intent is to raise their Indian competitors' labor costs and reduce their own.

Attend to regulatory, or nonmarket, restraints—and ethics. The legal status of the strategies listed under the two headings immediately above, in particular, varies across countries. This raises a broader issue related to regulatory or other nonmarket restraints on behavior, particularly behavior aimed at building up bargaining power of the sorts considered in this section. Not surprisingly, this was also the kind of behavior that raised legal and ethical questions as well as prices in the Cemex case.

I tell my MBA students several things about such cases. First, if they ever think about sitting down in a room with their rivals and agreeing to raise prices, they should probably think again: horizontal stripes look a lot worse than pinstripes. Second, I have them consider a list of behaviors like the following:

1. Recognizing that dominance or recognition of mutual dependence can help raise prices (e.g., through tacit coordination)
2. Exploiting local contacts (e.g., lobbying for protection)

3. Building market power indirectly to circumvent restrictions on concentration (e.g., through cross-holdings)

4. Renegotiating deals if opportunities present themselves (e.g., threatening to cut off service after establishing incumbency—most effective in natural monopolies)

5. Striking secret agreements with government officials (e.g., postprivatization "discovery" of valuable tax loopholes that effectively reduce privatization prices)

6. Figuring out (semi)legal ways of making payoffs to governmental officials (e.g., through intermediaries)

Only the first two elements of this list—which, to many of my students, are the least problematic—have been established in the Cemex case. But it is easy to come up with examples of the other, more problematic kinds of behavior as well. Students tend to vary greatly as to how far down the list they are willing to go. But the one caution I give them is that if none of the behavior on the list worries them, they probably have an underdeveloped sense of ethics. And that's also what I would tell you.

Normalizing Risk

This value component is deliberately framed in terms of normalizing rather than neutralizing risk so as to recognize the potentially large divergence between risk optimization and risk minimization. In addition, while finance theory has been very precise about how to calculate the risk-adjusted discount rates that go into the denominator of discounted cashflow analysis, the strategic perspective on risk emphasizes getting a better handle on the variability of the cashflows that go into the numerator of this analysis. This is a challenging task, but some general guidelines can be offered.

Characterize the extent and key sources of risk in your business (capital intensity, other irreversibility correlates, demand volatility, etc.). From a strategic perspective, a rough and ready way of unbundling risk is to classify it into the following categories:

- Supply- and demand-side risks
- Financial risks such as foreign exchange volatility and the systematic correlation between local returns and the world portfolio
- Competitive risks, including those associated with not investing, such as allowing a competitor a profit sanctuary in its home market
- Nonmarket risks

In applying this or some other classification scheme, it is important to avoid double-counting. Also note that relevant risks vary both by strategy and by industry: a company that emphasizes cross-border supply chains in its globalization strategy faces very different risks from those faced by a company that has set up self-contained operations in different geographies. A useful way of summarizing risks is in terms of the learn-to-burn rate: a ratio that looks at how quickly information resolving key uncertainties comes in versus the rate at which money is (irreversibly) being spent. The learn-to-burn ratio looks much higher for investments in fast-food outlets, say, than in electricity.

Assess how much cross-border operations reduce risk—or increase it. Cemex provides a good example of geographic pooling that reduces operating risk. But Coke supplies a counterexample: the volatility in demand growth that it has faced since the Asian crisis was almost entirely generated by Coke's less mature, non-U.S. operations. Broader global scope also increases the risk of multimarket contagion: Arthur Andersen's post-Enron problems in the United States wouldn't have affected the accounting firm in, say, France if the two had been separate entities. The importance of such counterexamples to risk-pooling is amplified by research suggesting that multinationals' returns from the diverse markets in which they operate often tend to be much more correlated than local competitors' returns across the same markets.

Recognize any benefits that might accrue from increasing risk. The idea of normalizing risk seems to suggest that risk is always to be minimized. Given optionality, however, risk can be valuable for the same reason that financial options are more valuable in the presence of greater (price) volatility. Cemex's swap in the late-1990s of capacity in the low-risk, low-growth Spanish market for higher-risk, higher-growth capacity in Asia exemplifies an appreciation of optionality shared by many multinationals from mature, developed markets—thinking of emerging markets as gigantic strategic options rather than just as risk traps.

Consider multiple modes of managing exposure to risk or exploitation of optionality. There are many ways of managing risk. Thus, a company might enter a foreign market with a fully owned greenfield operation, make an acquisition, work with a joint venture partner, or simply export there—which typically have very different implications for risks (and returns). Or, given widely diversified shareholders (unlike the case of Cemex, where a significant fraction of the controlling family's wealth was tied up in the company), it may make more sense to rely on shareholders to eliminate industry-specific risks and, on that basis, discount them in formulating company strategy. Registering a broad sense of the possibilities is likely to improve the risk-return trade-off that a company faces.

Generating Knowledge—and Other Resources and Capabilities

More than any other component of the ADDING Value scorecard, the generation of knowledge (and other resources and capabilities) addresses what can be thought of as a company's strategic balance sheet instead of its strategic income statement. It focuses on *developing* and *deploying* resources and capabilities over time, of which knowledge is probably the most widely studied example.

Assess how location-specific versus mobile knowledge is and what to do about it. Cemex exemplified successful knowledge transfer that was greatly simplified by environmental characteristics: cement is cement is cement, so ideas generated in one part of the world can be applied relatively easily (i.e., without much translation) in other parts of the world. Multidimensional distance between countries presents more of a challenge in many other environments, requiring explicit attention to knowledge decontextualization and recontextualization if knowledge transfer is to work well. Otherwise, knowledge transfer can make matters worse rather than better.

Consider multiple modes of managing the generation and diffusion of knowledge. Research on knowledge transfer tends to focus on formal transfer within multinationals in a way that excludes other modes of knowledge development and deployment across borders: through personal interactions; working with buyers, suppliers, or consultants; open innovation; imitation; contracting for the use of knowledge; and so forth.[17] And even the effectiveness of internal knowledge transfer can vary greatly, depending on how it is managed.

For example, while beauty company AmorePacific has done a good job of protecting its home base in Korea, it has had difficulties capturing and integrating knowledge from some of its non-Korean operations. Thus, while its French operation has enjoyed some success in launching new perfumes, particularly Lolita Lempicka, knowledge flowback has been limited by weak links with the parent organization. The efforts of Japanese cosmetics manufacturer Shiseido are more impressive in this regard: after its success in making and launching perfumes in France, the company has used its French facilities to start making "Shiseido lines" for Japan (where most of the concept development and final fragrance adjustment is done) and has transferred some French managerial techniques to Japan for other products.[18]

Think of other resources or capabilities in similar terms. Knowledge transfer still has a technical or technological tinge. Other types of information—such as management innovations, as in the case of Shiseido— can also usefully be transferred across borders (with information technology often supplying a boost). More broadly, there are many other kinds of resources and capabilities that might also be taken into account under this value component.

Relationships constitute one important example. What accounts for Cemex's success at weathering antitrust challenges at home and at blocking attempts to import cement into Mexico, as in the case of the *Mary Nour,* a ship that tried unsuccessfully for six months to unload its cargo of Russian cement at various Mexican ports before giving up? Part of the answer is probably to be found in CEO Lorenzo Zambrano's web of domestic relationships: kinship ties with other leading business families based in Monterrey, such as the Sadas and the Garzas; interlocking board memberships with their companies and other leading Mexican ones; membership in the powerful business association Consejo Mexicano de Hombres de Negocio; and close links to the political establishment.

And while this particular example is domestically focused and again raises some ethical questions, it is easy to think of cross-border relationships that do not. Thus, a time-honored reason for multinationals to partner with local firms, even when local regulation doesn't mandate it, is to tap into their local partners' domestic networks of relationships.

Avoid double-counting. While this is a generic problem in applying the ADDING Value scorecard, double-counting is particularly likely to arise in the context of this component of the scorecard. If you have already managed to account for the effects of generating (or depleting) a resource on costs, willingness-to-pay, and so on—which is what is generally recommended— avoid including them under this component of the scorecard as well.

Beyond the ADDING Value Scorecard

The ADDING Value scorecard provides a basis for assessing whether a particular strategic move makes sense. In addition, a full-fledged consideration of strategic alternatives should cover several auxiliary but important questions:

1. Is the selected strategic option likely to lead to sustained value creation and capture?

2. Does experience tend to confirm or contradict the results of the analysis?

3. Has enough attention been devoted to considering whether any better alternatives can be devised?

Each of these three additional considerations is something that I could write a separate chapter about—and actually have.[19] But considerations of space permit just a quick review here.

Sustainability

What's really important about a strategic option is not whether it will add value at a point in time, but whether it will continue to add value *over* time. And if it does succeed at adding value over time, how much of that added value will a firm get to appropriate or pocket, given competition from other players in its environment?

Recognize that superior performance is often short-lived. The first step in taking sustainability seriously is to recognize that you can't take it for granted. At the industry level, industries that are subject to rapid real price declines—3 percent declines per year are one suggested threshold— are *fast-cycle* industries in which superior performance tends to be short-lived unless a firm can innovate continuously. For example, price declines in consumer electronics exceed this threshold, whereas those in cement do not. And company-level indicators of unsustainability include earnings that are highly dependent on returns from resources with short half-lives.

Think through how your environment is likely to evolve. Although summary indicators of sustainability versus unsustainability are useful sensitization devices, they are no substitute for thinking through how a specific strategic move fits with trends in your environment, broadly conceived.

Reconsider News Corporation's acquisition of Star TV. This move was supposed to add value by letting News Corporation recycle English-language programming from its library, thereby decreasing programming costs. But at the time of the acquisition, News Corporation could have predicted that a host of changes were under way in Asian TV markets that would undercut the viability of this strategy. In particular, it was reasonable to expect that rapid growth in viewership would reduce the per-viewer importance of the country- and language-specific programming costs that News Corporation was seeking to avoid. Superimpose on these changes, in relative costs, the greater appeal of domestic programming—evident from either common sense or contemporaneous data (figure 3-10)—and you get a clear picture of the English-language strategy becoming less viable over time.

Anticipate how other players in your value system are likely to behave. In addition to thinking through broad changes in your environment, a useful test of sustainability is to put yourself in the shoes of other players with whom you interact. We have already talked about undertaking detailed analysis to figure out how direct rivals will behave. Similar analysis can be attempted for potential entrants, customers, suppliers, and companies that provide substitutes for, or complements to, your products. What could they do if they were trying to maximize value for themselves? What are they actually likely to do, given their predispositions? And what kinds of moves on your part are likely to elicit aggressive versus accommodating responses from them?

Look at the extent to which moves can be imitated (or neutralized). While the intent of detailed profiling of competitors or other players in your value system is to predict how they will behave, that quickly gets un-

FIGURE 3-10

Foreign TV programming and domestic market size

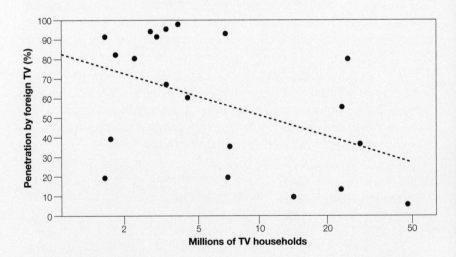

Source: Pankaj Ghemawat, "Global Standardization vs. Localization: A Case Study and Model," in *The Global Market: Developing a Strategy to Manage Across Borders,* ed. John A. Quelch and Rohit Deshpandé (San Francisco: Jossey-Bass, 2004) 123.

manageable as the number of players increases. It then makes sense to look directly at the extent to which a move that aims to create value can be imitated (or neutralized) on the grounds that if imitation is feasible, it will happen, eroding scarcity value.

Think through sequences of moves. Sustainability is often built up and, more broadly, opportunities unlocked, through sequences of moves. Given that, it is important to anticipate and account for such linkages among moves or projects before deciding whether to invest in the first one or not. While this requires a deep look into the future, which is often difficult, the basic logic should be clear enough: strategists should evaluate strategies overall, rather than individual projects or moves that are components of those strategies.

Remember that some moves are worth undertaking even if they do not afford sustainable advantages. If you do not undertake certain moves, your company will be at a sustained disadvantage. This is another way of reinforcing the point made earlier: while comparisons with competitors can be very useful, the ultimate objective is to create value for *your* company rather than to beat the competition per se.

Judgment

Most strategic decisions require judgment as well as analysis. Judgment involves recognizing that analysis is always potentially prone to error and that, therefore, you can improve the odds of making the right call by evaluating whether the recommendations that emerge from the analysis are *reasonable*.

While there are many ways of triangulating on the analysis, three kinds of judgments are considered crucial to strategic decision making:

- *Distinctive competence or capability:* The ratio of good opportunities to bad ones is likely to be higher inside your company's zone of distinctive competence than outside it.
- *Resource balance:* In making major strategic decisions, you should pay some attention to maintaining a rough balance between the supply of and the demand for key resources, including capital.
- *Structural context:* It is also important to consider how the strategic options being considered were surfaced and evaluated—often achieved, in part, by paying attention to who is championing them.

Consider, for example, Santander of Spain's 2004 acquisition of Abbey National of the United Kingdom for €12.5 billion to create what was then the world's tenth-largest bank by market capitalization. Santander's assessment of Abbey covered all the components of the ADDING Value scorecard. But from talking to Santander chairman, Emilio Botín, I realized that all three bases of judgment described above also factored into his decision. First, Santander thought it was well placed to be the acquirer: the company had significant experience at restructuring retail banking acquisitions; it had enjoyed a window on the United Kingdom since 1988 because of a strategic alliance with Royal Bank of Scotland (RBS) that had also let Santander closely observe RBS's absorption of a much larger bank, National Westminster; and bids by larger U.K. banks, including RBS, were likely to be blocked by regulators. Second, the acquisition helped boost topline growth that had begun to falter—while representing about the largest deal that Santander's balance sheet could handle. And finally, the Abbey opportunity had been vetted by Juan Rodríguez Inciarte, a confidant who had been responsible for several other successful initiatives and who, along with Botín, served as one of Santander's two representatives on RBS's board.

Creativity

So far, this chapter has focused on improving the evaluation of strategic options. But creativity in improving the set of considered options is a very important and complementary element of strategy development because multiplying tests without improving alternatives is a good recipe for analysis paralysis—that is, for inaction.

Creativity can never be completely systematized, but there are some obvious ways of enriching the set of strategic options considered. While this chapter has mentioned some in passing, here are five broad, complementary approaches to consider. Most of them are generic—that is, they could also be applied to single-country strategy—but they will be elaborated along lines particularly useful for global strategy.

Vary the options considered in terms of control, mode of development, scale, timing, and other factors. International business has noted many possible modes of product market participation: exports, supply agreements, licensing and franchising, strategic alliances, joint ventures, and fully owned operations, with the choice between the last two attracting the most attention. Proponents of ownership stress its advantages in terms of security and control. On the other hand, proponents of joint ventures point to their advantages in terms of accessing local capabilities and networks and reducing adaptation challenges, as discussed in the next chapter.

While this debate is bound to continue, I would argue that from a managerial perspective, the choices between different modes of market participation tend to be so situational that generic assessments are unlikely to help. Rather, managers need an understanding of the implications for each component of ADDING Value and for the share of the added value that can be pocketed on a sustained basis. Also note that similar arguments hold for modes of participation in input markets (e.g., captive versus noncaptive offshoring) and for internal development versus acquisitions.

Broaden the scope of the scanning effort. The discussion of sustainability touched on some such suggestions, including focusing on changes as a way of uncovering what's new; expanding the scope of external scanning efforts to include the entire value system in your industry, not just direct rivals; and putting yourself in other players' shoes. Of course, the most obvious way to broaden the scope of the scanning effort in a global context is to look at multiple geographies. Thus, even if your company has no direct interest in India or China, it may be worth looking at the strategies being developed by competitors there. For example, every wireless services operator should at least be aware of the radical outsourcing strategy pioneered by the leader in the Indian market, Bharti Airtel, which has helped Bharti reduce calling rates to less than two cents per minute, compared with twenty-cents-plus in many developed markets. And take my own line of work: many business schools, particularly in the United States, have a strongly domestic orientation. However, they could learn from looking at examples such as ICFAI Business School in India, which has—by emphasizing scalability, distance learning, and a focus on market requirements—expanded its MBA enrollment tenfold over ten years to become one of the largest business schools in the world. Of course, given distance, literal translation of such examples to other contexts probably wouldn't work: instead, explicit attention to knowledge decontextualization and recontextualization would seem to be required.

Shift the perspective. Looking at competitors from very different geographies is just one way of trying to achieve a radical shift in perspective. Many others have also been proposed, of which only a few can be mentioned here. Drop one assumption, a few, or even all (e.g., think about how one might solve a particular problem if starting afresh or if money were no object). Identify the unwritten rules that drive the industry and competitor behavior, and try to break them. Emphasize threats as well as opportunities as a way of increasing receptivity to change. Follow outside-in paths, from possible answers to the issues facing a business—threats and opportunities—that they might address, as well as inside-out paths, from issues to answers. Understand how to do the opposite of what you actually wish to achieve, and then do the opposite of *that*. Adopt a can-change attitude toward the current state of affairs by asking yourself, "Why not?" Think of other ways of flipping things around (e.g., by changing who pays whom). Use techniques developed to enhance lateral or parallel thinking. And take the idea of putting yourself in your competitors' shoes one step farther by analyzing your company as a competitor from *their* perspectives.

The mechanisms mentioned above might seem both abstract and diffuse, but examples help underline how valuable such radical shifts in perspective can be. Diamond producer De Beers initially opposed restrictions on trade in conflict diamonds, but then had the mental agility to realize that such restrictions could actually help it deal with oversupply and commoditization in the diamond market. Ryanair, Europe's low-fare airline, came up with a strategy of not only charging passengers for their flights to less popular airports, but also charging both these airports and tourist authorities a fee for bringing them many passengers. Zara, the Spanish fashion retailer, figured out that it could cut down on overstocks and enhance customer willingness-to-pay by speeding up its design-and-manufacturing cycle, thus making key items based on within-season trends instead of guessing ahead. And Lakshmi Mittal, who now controls Arcelor-Mittal, saw that much of the value of the integrated steel mills that he started to acquire in the mid-1990s in the former Eastern Bloc might reside in the associated mineral rights rather than in their steelmaking capacity per se.

Harness the creative powers of the whole organization. Yet another way to stretch thinking about strategic options involves moving beyond the "one big brain" model of strategic innovation and instead shaping organizational processes and structures to reflect what we know about creativity. Again, very briefly, recommendations include cultivating open-mindedness; fostering risk-taking and a commitment to learning; tolerating divergent thinking; developing suitable sensors; making strategic planning more discovery driven or more like an extended dialogue; emphasizing rich information flows and mastery of the details of the business; conducting data-driven analysis; countering known biases (e.g., the "not invented here" syndrome); relying on intrinsic commitment devices such as passion as well as extrinsic commitment devices such as incentives; and continuously revitalizing, challenging, and even unsettling the organization. Such organizational traits obviously affect the evaluation of new options as well as their generation.

While these mechanisms are, again, generic, harnessing the power of the whole organization across borders has a particular resonance in a semi-globalized context, as illustrated by the case of Coke. Thus, one of the changes that Neville Isdell has made since he took over as CEO of Coke is the reinstitution of internal trade fairs and other global get-togethers. There were reportedly no such gatherings under Douglas Daft, reflecting his "think local, act local" bias, and the ones that took place under Roberto Goizueta presumably had a "one big brain" bias—in other words, they simply served as a conduit for headquarters to tell the field what to do.

Read the rest of this book. A final approach to enhancing creativity in devising global strategies is the one that occupies the rest of this book. Given the conclusions drawn thus far—that we live in a semiglobalized world in which the differences across countries still matter a great deal— part 2 of this book looks at several broad strategies for dealing with differences. This systematic treatment of differences helps develop an approach to thinking about value creation that complements but is much more customized to global strategy than the other approaches to enhancing creativity discussed in this subsection.

Conclusions

The box "Global Generalizations" summarizes the specific conclusions from this chapter. More broadly, this chapter provided a comprehensive, rigorous basis for tracking value creation through cross-border moves. The intent was to provide you with a more realistic way to analyze such moves. Realism is not meant, however, to be a substitute for creativity; rather, it is blending the two that will optimize performance.

Global Generalizations

1. The diagnosis that we live in a semiglobalized world in which the differences across countries still matter a great deal makes it important to answer the question "Why globalize?" Answering this question requires serious analysis.

2. The ADDING Value scorecard provides a basis for such analysis by parsing value addition into six components: adding volume, decreasing costs, differentiating, improving industry attractiveness, normalizing risks, and generating and deploying knowledge (and other resources).

3. In applying the ADDING Value scorecard, it is important not just to keep all six value components in mind but also to unbundle, quantify (to the extent possible), and make comparisons.

4. It is useful to supplement analysis based on the ADDING Value scorecard with some attention to sustainability.

5. You can and should use judgment to evaluate the results of the analysis.

6. There is much to be gained by both enriching the set of options considered and improving the evaluation of that set.

Armed with the ADDING Value scorecard, part 2 of this book will consider broad strategies for dealing with the differences across countries—while, of course, also recognizing and exploiting similarities. The Cemex case, discussed in particular detail in this chapter, was relatively simple in this regard, given that cement is cement is cement—with the caveat that geographic distance does matter a great deal even in this industry. The chapters that follow will, among other things, expand on the practicalities of applying the concepts and tools developed in part 1 to situations where differences are more multidimensional—and more salient.

PART 2

Strategies for Global Value Creation

PART 2 FOCUSES ON STRATEGIES for adding value in the face of large cross-border differences. Chapters 4–6 introduce the AAA strategies for responding to differences: *a*daptation, *a*ggregation, and *a*rbitrage. Chapters 7 and 8 provide an integrative perspective.

- Chapter 4 focuses on *adaptation* strategies that *adjust* to differences across countries. Since this category of responses to differences will already be familiar, the chapter aims to stretch thinking by emphasizing the range of levers and sublevers available for adapting more effectively.

- Chapter 5 focuses on *aggregation* strategies that *overcome* some differences among countries by grouping them based on similarities. While there are many possible bases of aggregation, this chapter strives for depth rather than breadth by focusing on geographic aggregation by region.

- Chapter 6 focuses on *arbitrage* strategies that *exploit* selected differences across countries instead of treating them all as constraints. The chapter reviews arbitrage strategies based on the CAGE differences discussed in chapter 2, but covers economic arbitrage, especially labor arbitrage, in particular detail.

- Chapter 7 examines the trade-offs among the AAA strategies and the extent to which it is possible and advisable to pursue more than one of the As at the same time. It addresses, in other words, the development of integrated strategies for playing the differences.

- Chapter 8 concludes the book with a look at the future of globalization, about which both optimism and pessimism have been expressed. Insights developed in the earlier chapters are used to cut through such debates—and to suggest a step-by-step approach for companies to enhance global value creation.

4

Adaptation

Adjusting to Differences

"Everything should be made as simple as possible, but not simpler."

—attributed to Albert Einstein

PART 1 OF THIS BOOK established the context of semiglobalization and developed a framework for thinking about the differences across countries and a template for evaluating cross-border strategic options in light of such differences. Now we turn to what to *do* about differences, starting with the strategy of *adaptation,* or adjusting to differences.

Some degree of adaptation is essential for virtually all border-crossing enterprises. Consider just two of the examples discussed in part 1:

- Cement is close to a pure commodity produced with a mature technology, but Cemex must still adjust to international differences in energy prices, the mix of demand between bagged and bulk cement, etc.

- Wal-Mart has historically performed more poorly the farther it gets from Bentonville, Arkansas. Inflexibility and under-adaptation seem to be the most obvious reasons. Visible manifestations include such merchandising missteps as stocking U.S.-style footballs in soccer-mad Brazil. But the problems run much deeper: I estimate that of fifty policies and practices that distinguish the company domestically, thirty-five were historically carried over more or less completely, and twelve at least partially, to its international operations—an amazing degree of consistency in an industry subject to large cross-border differences.

The example of Wal-Mart, in particular, illustrates what seems to be a common bias toward under-adaptation in cross-border strategies.[1] Part of the solution, as suggested earlier, is to analyze the differences that still divide countries instead of ignoring them because of a belief that they are or will become insignificant. But it is also important for companies to think through the full array of levers available to adapt to those differences—tools that improve the terms on which they can actually achieve adaptation. To dig deeper into the challenge of adaptation and the variety of possible responses to it, this chapter will explore in some detail an industry that demands great variety—major home appliances—with a particular focus on the strategies of the ten largest competitors worldwide.[2] Then, using many additional examples, it will discuss levers for adaptation more broadly before turning to some of the organizational issues that arise around managing adaptation.

The Major Home Appliance Industry

Although the major home appliance industry has been consolidating within the United States and Western Europe since the 1960s, globalization across regions began in earnest in the mid-1980s, with a round of big acquisitions. In 1986, Electrolux, the leader in Europe, acquired White Consolidated, the third-largest U.S. producer. The major U.S. competitors responded over 1989–1990: Whirlpool, the largest, acquired Philips's major home appliance business, which was the second-largest in Europe but struggling; General Electric, the second-largest U.S. producer, bought a stake in the home appliance business of the United Kingdom's GEC; and Maytag, the fourth-largest, acquired Hoover, expanding its footprint to the United Kingdom and Australia. The 1990s saw international expansion by other competitors from Europe, particularly Bosch-Siemens of Germany, as well as from Asia: Japanese companies such as Matsushita were joined on the world stage by, among others, Korean companies LG and Samsung and China's Haier.

The case for global expansion was made most forcefully in a 1994 interview by David Whitwam, the CEO under whom Whirlpool acquired Philips's business: "Over time, our industry would become global, whether *we* chose to become global or not. With that said, we had three choices. We could ignore the inevitable—a decision that would have condemned Whirl-pool to a slow death. We could wait for globalization to begin and then try to react. Or we could control our own destiny and try to shape the very nature of globalization in our industry."[3]

But international expansion has failed to bolster performance. Figure 4-1 shows the recent profitability of the ten largest competitors world-wide.[4] In light of the profitability data, the firms that moved early to ex-pand across regions—Electrolux and the four U.S. majors—do not seem to have tapped into early-mover advantages. Nor have they managed to grow their home appliance businesses particularly rapidly: the early globalizers also fall into the bottom half of the top ten in terms of revenue growth rates between 2002 and 2004 (the numbers in parentheses in the figure). In the same vein, the biggest of the top ten—the firms that generally have broader geographic footprints—have not been the most profitable. So, while consolidation *has* taken place in this industry, it has generally dragged down the performance of the consolidators. Why haven't things played out the way they were supposed to?

FIGURE 4-1

Profitability versus size (and growth rates) for the top ten competitors in major home appliances

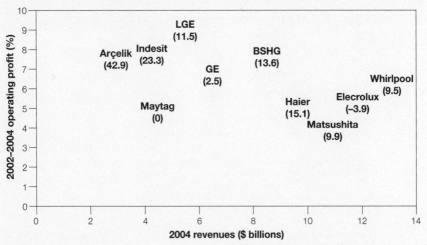

Sources: Annual reports of companies shown on chart; Freedonia Group, "World Major Household Appliances: World Industry Study with Forecasts to 2009 and 2014," Study 2015 (Cleveland: Freedonia Group, January 2006); Pankaj Ghemawat and Catherine Thomas, "Arçelik Home Appliances: International Expansion Strategy," Case 705-477 (Boston: Harvard Business School, 2005); Pankaj Ghemawat and Thomas M. Hout, "Haier's U.S. Refrigerator Strategy 2005," Case 705-475 (Boston: Harvard Business School, 2005); and Global Market Information Database. Matsushita profit margins are for 2002–2003; GE and Haier numbers are estimates.

Industry Context

Whirlpool made the most explicit case for adding value by expanding globally with a Ted Levitt–like faith in consumers' desire for the same products everywhere. As the company's annual report for 1987 stated, "Consumers in major industrialized countries are living increasingly similar lifestyles and have increasingly similar expectations of what consumer products must do for them."

The trouble with such reasoning, in major home appliances as in many other industries, is, as Charles Darwin once put it, that it seems to have been based on inner consciousness rather than observation. As of the early 2000s, the leading manufacturers of major home appliances still offered thousands of varieties—as many as fifteen thousand in the case of Electrolux. The CAGE framework from chapter 2 helps flush out the full range of cross-border differences that have prevented preference convergence, and the diagnostic tools from chapter 3 shed light on the extent to which these differences dilute (already weak) incentives for cross-border expansion (table 4-1).

Working through table 4-1 from left to right, the number of varieties required to compete effectively across multiple markets is swelled, first of all, by a range of *cultural* differences—some idiosyncratic, others derived from other, more fundamental differences. An example in the former category was provided by clothes washers, a category in which such diversity is often supposed to be relatively limited—but really isn't:

TABLE 4-1

Cross-border differences that increase requirements for variety in major home appliances

Cultural differences	Administrative differences	Geographic differences	Economic differences

• Idiosyncratic tastes
• Derived entrenchment
• Mostly mature products
• Lack of consumption externalities
	• Electrical standards:
	  ○ Plugs and outlets
	  ○ Voltages
	  ○ Cycles
	• Other regulations: environmental
	• Protectionism: up to 20% tariffs into U.S.
		• Climate
		  ○ Temperature
		  ○ Sunshine
		• Bulk or low value-to-weight ratios
			• Income levels: lower cost or willingness- to-pay
			• Growth: new household formation
			• Price or availability of substitutes or complements:
			  ○ Space
			  ○ Electricity

In France, top-loading machines accounted for about 70 percent of the market: front-loading machines typically sold at a small discount to top-loaders, despite the fact that the production costs were comparable. West German consumers preferred front-loaders with high spin-speeds of 800 rpm or more. Italian consumers preferred 600–800 rpm, front-loading machines. The British prefer 800 rpm front-loaders, but with a hot and cold water fill rather than cold-water-only supply.[5]

An even larger part of preference diversity seems to derive from other, more fundamental differences across countries. Thus, from a cultural standpoint, national cuisines have a significant impact on demand in a number of appliance categories. For example, compared with U.S. refrigerator buyers, Germans want more space for meat; Italians prefer special compartments for vegetables; and Indian families, with a mix of vegetarians and nonvegetarians, require internal seals to stop food smells from mingling. To hold Christmas turkeys, ovens are larger in England than in Germany, where geese are cooked. Germans also don't need self-cleaning ovens, since they bake at lower temperatures than the French do. And Indian households generally don't need ovens at all.

Furthermore, preferences concerning older categories of home appliances are relatively well formed. As one marketing expert explained, "The home is the most culture-bound part of one's life. Consumers in Paris don't care what kind of refrigerator they are using in New York."[6]

Administratively, requisite variety in home appliances is increased by variation in electric standards, with thirteen major types of plugs and wall outlets, as well as different voltages and frequencies, in use around the world.[7] Other kinds of regulations, particularly environmental ones, also vary significantly by country. And protectionism combines with high transport costs to make otherwise identical varieties produced in different locations imperfect substitutes for each other—in other words, these factors constrain intra-industry trade (one way of increasing the varieties on offer without necessarily increasing the number produced per location). Trade historically took place mostly within regions and has become even more regionalized in recent decades.[8]

Other relevant *geographic* factors include the climate. Thus, air conditioners aren't needed where (or when) it isn't hot, and clothes dryers have proven less successful in the Mediterranean sun.

In terms of strictly *economic* differences, probably the single most important driver of cross-country variation is the local income level. A refrigerator can account for the bulk of annual per-capita income in India, compared with a few percentage points in the United States. As a result, refrigerator penetration is still very limited in India, despite the heat, and the varieties sold there are much smaller, simpler, and cheaper than those in the United States. Other economic factors that matter greatly are variations in the availability and prices of substitutes or complements such as space and electricity. U.S. buyers generally have the most living space and, therefore, tend to buy larger varieties and tolerate higher noise levels. Electricity costs are often higher outside the United States, focusing more attention on energy efficiency. Unreliable electricity supply also creates niches, such as the Chinese interest in electronic controls that reset automatically after power failures.

All this cross-border variation is superimposed on significant domestic differences in preferences about characteristics such as color, material, size, energy efficiency, noisiness, other aspects of environmental friendliness, basic layout, the design of the door, the configuration of shelves, the position of the freezer, inclusion of a defroster, and controls. This compounds the challenges of dealing with variety and complexity. In addition, the discussion above focused on the cross-border differences that drive preference diversity rather than on *all* the differences that matter. Many of the additional differences discussed in chapter 2 continue to apply in this industry and make it even more difficult to manage across borders. Thus, linguistic limitations would seem to undercut Electrolux's infamous "Nothing sucks like an Electrolux" advertising campaign in the United States.

The one kind of cross-country difference that does have a significant effect in the opposite direction—that is, it encourages cross-border expansion—is the difference in labor costs, which can account for 20 to 30 percent of sales revenue for domestic production in high-cost countries. But, again, given relatively high transport costs, the product subcategories that this opens up to cross-border, particularly interregional, competition are limited. Thus, although Haier ships many under-the-counter refrigerators from China, the world's lowest-cost production platform, to the United States, transport costs preclude the profitable export of large refrigerators—even before U.S. tariffs are taken into account.

To look more systematically at industry economics, consider different categories of expenditures as a percentage of revenues. In terms of the intensity of advertising, R&D, and labor, the major home appliance industry ranks higher than the median manufacturing industry, but falls far short of the ninetieth percentile. It also lags the auto industry in terms of advertising intensity and, particularly, R&D intensity, suggesting weaker incentives for cross-border expansion—even though many managers in home appliances regard autos as a big cousin and bellwether. So, there is limited impetus to override the variety and complexity required to compete across borders.

From our perspective, unlike that of would-be consolidators, this is a help rather than a hindrance. Not only does the major home appliance industry pose an extreme adaptation challenge, but—since it lacks a dominant driver of value creation through global expansion—it has also afforded different competitors room to try out very different ways of responding to that challenge. In particular, the competitive strategies followed by the ten largest competitors, which I will outline next, span most of the levers for responding to adaptation challenges.

Competitive Strategies

Some of the top ten competitors in major home appliances follow the basic competitive strategies stressed in single-country strategy, low cost (e.g., Matsushita and Haier) or differentiation (e.g., Bosch-Siemens and LG). Obviously, a deep enough competitive advantage in terms of cost or differentiation can offset at least some of the pressures to adapt to different markets. But differences across countries have mandated significant modifications to such basic strategies. In response to pressures from competitors in other countries, Matsushita has had to retool its scale-based cost-leadership strategy of producing relatively standardized products in a few plants in Japan. Haier's exports to the United States under its "difficult first, easy second" approach have led not only to a focus on compact refrigerators and other easy-to-transport products, but also to an unusual partnership with an entrepreneur, Michael Jemal, president of Haier America. And Bosch-Siemens's and LG's product offerings vary substantially across emerging and developed markets. Understanding these and other responses to differences, and thereby maximizing the degrees of strategic freedom, requires going beyond characterizations in terms of low costs versus differentiation—or other components of the ADDING Value scorecard. Keeping score is not a substitute for thinking about strategy content.

Adopting this perspective, the strategies followed by the largest home appliance competitors span all of the main levers for responding to adaptation challenges that are illustrated in the shaded ovals in figure 4-2.

The first, most obvious approach to adapting to differences across countries is *variation*. Electrolux of Sweden—which represented the cumulation of the mergers of more than five hundred companies and which offered fifteen thousand varieties by the late 1990s—exemplified this approach to an extreme. In fact, at one point, Electrolux even experimented with individualization—allowing customers to mix and match using more than ten thousand combinations of colors and materials in refrigerators alone![9] But simple variation proved insufficient to cater to all the different requirements implied by the industry's broadest geographic presence

FIGURE 4-2

Adaptation levers

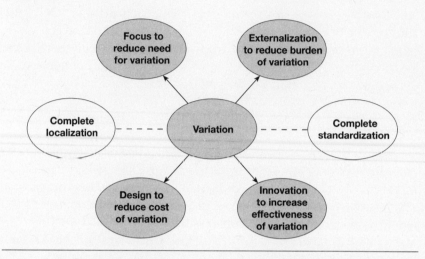

and, given poor performance, Electrolux has recently attempted some consolidation.

A second lever for dealing with adaptation challenges involves *focus* on particular geographies, products, vertical stages, and so forth as a way of reducing heterogeneity. Thus, smaller players in the top ten—companies such as Indesit of Italy, Arçelik of Turkey, and Maytag (prior to its acquisition by Whirlpool in 2005)—focus on particular regions instead of operating globally. Haier's focus on compact products has already been mentioned. And an example of focus on a vertical stage is provided by Brazilian compressor manufacturer Embraco, which holds nearly a quarter of the global market—nearly twice the market-leading share of Whirlpool in home appliances. Since Whirlpool also owns a major interest in Embraco, it seems that the difference between the extent of their global consolidation reflects product characteristics—for compressors, high R&D intensity, and particularly high value-to-weight ratios—rather than management approaches.

A third lever for adaptation involves *externalization*—through joint ventures, partnerships, and so forth—as a way of reducing its internal burden. An example is Haier's partnership with Michael Jemal as a way of adapting to the unfamiliar requirements of the U.S. market. A number of other top ten competitors also emphasized externalization. In particular, GE Appliances acquired a 50 percent stake in a large joint venture in the United Kingdom, GDA, tied up with a major retailer in Japan to access distribution and limited its investment in China by branding products from local manufacturers. (However, GE sold off its 50 percent stake in GDA to Indesit in 2002, reinforcing its regional focus on North America.)

A fourth lever for adaptation is *design* to reduce the cost of, rather than the need for, variation. Probably the clearest example of this lever in major home appliances is provided by Indesit, which has been quite successful with a strategy in which each plant produces one category of home appliance products using one basic product platform.

A final lever for adaptation is *innovation,* which, given its cross-cutting effects, can be characterized as improving the effectiveness of adaptation efforts. Market leader Whirlpool provides one of the best examples of this approach among the home appliance majors. After a relatively halfhearted attempt at platforming, Whirlpool has, since 2000, shifted its strategic emphasis to "brand focused value creation" involving "innovation from everyone and everywhere." The company has benefited from introducing the Duet front-loading washer, designed by its European arm, into the U.S. market, which had long favored top-loaders. But it has had less success with its more ambitious attempt to develop a "world washer."

This discussion of the top ten producers' competitive strategies has focused on adaptation as a response to the differences across countries. In addition, virtually all the competitors profiled paid some attention to two other strategies: aggregation at the regional level—either by focusing on a particular region or in terms of how they were organized across regions—and arbitrage, as a way of reducing costs in the face of continuing pressures on prices and margins. Strategies of aggregation and arbitrage are the focus of chapters 5 and 6, respectively.

Levers and Sublevers for Adaptation

The need to eschew the extremes of total localization and standardization in deciding how to adapt is not new. What *is* new is the assemblage of multiple levers for adaptation shown in figure 4-2: it provides a menu of possibilities that goes beyond vague injunctions to "get the balance right" or "glocalize." And since variety is the essence of adaptation, each of these levers can and will be articulated further, into an array of sublevers (table 4-2).

Note that this is not an exhaustive list of sublevers. It is easy to think of other sublevers that might serve as bases of adaptation, at least in specific industry or company contexts. For example, under externalization, one might add licensing and other forms of interfirm contracting.[10] But the twenty sublevers listed in table 4-2 constitute a large enough set to make the basic point that there are many ways to adapt.

TABLE 4-2

Levers and sublevers for adaptation

Variation	Focus: reduce need for variation	Externalization: reduce burden of variation	Design: reduce cost of variation	Innovation: improve effectiveness of variation
• Products	• Products	• Strategic alliances	• Flexibility	• Transfer
• Policies	• Geographies		• Partitioning	• Localization
• Repositioning	• Verticals	• Franchising	• Platforms	• Recombination
• Metrics	• Segments	• User adaptation	• Modularity	• Transformation
		• Networking		

Nor are the sublevers, and even the levers, mutually exclusive. That said, given their distinct requirements and ramifications, trying to achieve superior leverage along *all* the different levers or sublevers is probably a foolish pursuit. For one thing, excellence at any form of adaptation typically requires an aligned organization. A second reason that strategy requires choices to be made has to do with complexity, the bane of the competitors in the major home appliance industry. Note that complexity can be killer in terms of most of the value components identified in the ADDING Value scorecard: it can undercut scale economies; elevate costs; reduce differentiation or the ability to serve customers by blurring image or creating real conflicts—with channels, for example; exacerbate risk and inflexibility; and use up rather than augment (other) resources, particularly managerial bandwidth. And finally, the need to pick and choose is also related to the requirements for aggregation and arbitrage as well as for adaptation—requirements that we will take up in the following chapters.

In other words, the list of levers and sublevers in table 4-2 provides a menu from which to select items rather than a checklist of items to be ticked off: attempting the latter would typically lead to the corporate equivalent of indigestion. And while such a menu does not, in and of itself, solve the problem of strategic choice, it should, by expanding the set of possibilities, permit companies to improve the terms on which they achieve adaptation. For example, as discussed earlier, Douglas Daft had limited success trying to make Coke more adaptive by reconsidering which policies would be allowed to vary by country as opposed to being set at headquarters in Atlanta. Explicit attention to a broader array of levers and sublevers might have helped. So consider them in a bit more detail, illustrated with a range of examples.

Variation

Variation is the most obvious way of adapting to differences across countries. It is also ubiquitous. Variation encompasses changes in *products* but also in *policies*, business *positioning*, and even *metrics* (e.g., target rates of return). Social scientists, emulating biologists, have long stressed the critical role of variation in evolutionary improvements through the cycle of variation, selection, and retention or amplification. Seen from a distinctively strategic perspective, the variation should not be blind: rather, it needs to be guided, and strategy supplies that guidance while leaving room for incremental refinements.

Products

Even products that are supposedly standardized have to be varied a great deal. In adapting Windows and, more recently, Vista, Microsoft contended with languages such as Hebrew that flow from right to left and German, with words about 30 percent longer than English words (requiring changes in the user interface); icons and bitmaps that weren't universally acceptable; and disagreements about boundaries embedded in maps—not to mention variations in piracy rates and per-capita income levels. Unilever offers more than 100 variants of its global Lux brand of soaps around the world. And even Coke Classic varies in sweetness and other taste dimensions around the world. In fact, branding guru Martin Lindstrom reckons that Pringles potato chips is the *only* major consumer product that is widely available and totally standardized—and that Procter & Gamble (P&G) imposes significant penalties on itself by insisting on that much uniformity.[11]

The variations described above are relatively minor modifications to what might otherwise be described as global products. Other products—even at Coca-Cola, considered one of the world's most globally standardized companies—are often much more idiosyncratic to particular countries. Think of Coke's two-hundred-plus products in Japan, as described in the box "Coke in Japan" in chapter 1. Visitors (mainly American) to Coke's Tastes of the World exhibit in Atlanta are reported to often spit out many of the featured products from Japan and elsewhere, since the tastes are jarringly alien.[12]

Policies

The need to vary policies across countries can be somewhat less obvious than the need to vary products. Consider the case of Cleveland-based Lincoln

Electric, which produces both welding machines and consumable products for those machines.[13] Lincoln Electric has been one of the most frequently taught Harvard cases of all time because it outperformed its competitors—including much larger firms such as General Electric and Westinghouse—in its home market through industry-leading productivity levels. These, in turn, were achieved through the use of piecework and supporting human resource policies.

As Lincoln Electric has expanded abroad, it has focused on establishing a presence in the largest markets around the world. It might have done better to use the CAGE framework to select markets: it has done much better in countries that resemble the United States in allowing unrestricted use of piecework. In addition, the company is apparently starting to do better in other environments as well, where piecework *isn't* allowed. It manages this by thinking hard about mixing and matching policies in a way that strikes the best balance possible between internal consistency and fit with the external environment—rather than naively emphasizing one or the other.[14]

Repositioning

Changing the overall positioning of a business is somewhat distinct from, and broader than, changing products or even policies. As outlined in chapter 1, after Coke got serious about doing more than simply skimming the cream off big emerging markets such as India and China, it repositioned itself to a strategy of much lower margins and higher volumes, a strategy that involved lowering price points, reducing costs, and expanding availability.

Another, even more dramatic example of repositioning from the same broad category of beverages is provided by Jinro, which may be less familiar than Coke to most readers, but is the world's top-selling brand of spirits by volume. The bulk of its sales are accounted for by its domestic market in Korea, but Jinro has—despite a taste compared (by Westerners) to embalming fluid—expanded into several dozen countries, with a major focus on Japan, where it is the market leader.[15] In addition to taking more than two decades, the achievement of market leadership in Japan has required a reduction in sugar content to one-tenth the original level; a reformulation to allow the product to be drunk diluted with hot or cold water (instead of straight, as in Korea); very different packaging aimed, in part, at achieving more of a resemblance to whiskey; the adoption of a premium pricing position (unlike the one targeted in many of Jinro's other export markets); and the use of Caucasian models in its TV commercials, to the point that a majority of Japanese customers do not know that Jinro is from Korea.[16]

Metrics

A final sublever here concerns the adjustment of metrics and targets across countries. As described in chapter 3, average profitability varies greatly across the same industry in different countries, suggesting that profitability targets may have to be set at different levels for different countries if a company is serious about penetrating all of them. Thus, Arçelik accounts for more than 50 percent of the Turkish market for home appliances because of more than twenty-five hundred exclusive retail outlets—and earns double-digit margins there. It probably wouldn't expand overseas at all if it insisted on earning comparable margins, even though some such expansion probably does make sense for reasons including risk reduction: thus, an economic crisis that caused Turkish demand to decline by one-third in 2001 was the spur for its current internationalization drive.

Of course, having made this point, I should add that this logic should not be pursued to the point at which it leads to value destruction rather than value addition. Thus, Whirlpool has maintained a large European presence despite being much less profitable there than at home, partly as a way of increasing leverage vis-à-vis Electrolux by denying its competitor a "home sanctuary." But given the arithmetic of the situation—the $1 billion paid for Philips's European business, the estimates of subsequent losses there, and the time value of money combine to imply a net present cost more than one-half of Whirlpool's current market value—the company should probably have found a different, less costly mode of participating in the European market.

Focus to Reduce the Need for Variation

The trouble with relying exclusively on variation as a lever for adaptation is that it increases complexity. One, often complementary, lever for keeping complexity under control is to focus or purposefully narrow scope so as to bite off a manageable mouthful and thereby reduce the amount of adaptation required. I will elaborate on four specific sublevers: *product focus, geographic focus, vertical focus,* and *segment focus.*

Product Focus

Product focus is a potentially powerful sublever for dealing with adaptation challenges because there are often tremendous differences *within* broad product categories in the degree of variation required to compete effectively in local markets. Compare TV programs, where local offerings generally dominate in most large countries, with films, particularly action films, where Hollywood still dominates because of the more-compelling scale and scope economies associated with big-name stars and special effects. But analysis at the level of films or TV programs as a whole is too aggregated: finer-grained analysis is often required to expose particular challenges or opportunities.

For an example of an action film that traveled particularly poorly across borders, remember *The Alamo*—the 2004 movie, not the nineteenth-century battle between Mexican forces and Texan rebels. This film certainly met the big-budget criterion—it cost Disney nearly $100 million. It did not generate commensurate book office receipts in English. But what was really remarkable about it was Disney's attempts to create cross-over appeal for Latinos by, among other things, striving for a more balanced treatment of Anglos versus Mexicans, prominently featuring Tejano folk heroes in the film, running a separate Spanish-language marketing effort, and so on. The point is that no matter how well these tactics were executed, the effort was unlikely to work, because the Alamo is, in the words of one authority, "such an open wound among American Hispanics."[17]

Conversely, there *are* some TV programs that do cross borders rather successfully. Discovery Networks, which focuses on factual programs, particularly documentaries, provides an excellent example. As founder John Hendricks once commented, "Nature and science documentaries are one of the few programs that can be run in almost any country because there's no cultural or political bias to these programs."[18] In addition, dubbing or subtitling requirements are minimal, especially for nature documentaries. That is not to say that no variation is required: tastes do differ, even in documentaries, with East Asians, for instance, reported to have a predilection for "bloody animal shows" and Australians for forensics. As a result, about 20 percent of Discovery's programming is local. But compared with other kinds of TV programming, these are relatively minor problems, which is why Discovery and its affiliated networks (including the Learning Channel, Travel Channel, and Animal Planet) report reaching a cumulated total of 1.4 *billion* subscribers worldwide.

Geographic Focus

Geographic focus is another powerful sublever for reducing requisite variation. The deliberate restriction of geographic scope can permit a focus on countries where relatively little adaptation of the domestic value proposition is required—as well as raising the odds of success by permitting managers to concentrate their adaptation efforts on a particular part of the world. Focusing on the home region is a particularly popular expedient: the majority of the top ten competitors in major home appliances have a clear focus of this sort. Such a regional focus not only minimizes geographic distance and the problems of coordinating across time zones, but can also reduce administrative distance, given the large number of regional trade and investment pacts, and even cultural and economic distance, given greater homogeneity across these dimensions *within* rather than across regions in many cases.

The use of regions as building blocks of global strategy—with more of an emphasis on multiregional strategies—will be dealt with in detail in chapter 5. But two points do need to be mentioned in the interim. First, geographic focus aimed at tapping commonalities can also take forms other than focusing on one's home region. Thus, when the Spanish economy opened up in the 1980s, the Spanish focused on investing heavily in Spanish-speaking Latin America as a "soft target" rather than in their "home region" of Europe. Second, geographic focus can be helpful even when a company's international strategy emphasizes exploiting differences rather than similarities. Thus, Cognizant, a software services firm discussed in more detail in chapter 7, emphasizes India-based arbitrage like many others, but has sought to differentiate itself by cultivating more of a local face in going to market—an adaptive task aided greatly by its focus, until recently, on the United States.

Vertical Focus

In addition to adopting a product or geographic focus, companies can focus on particular vertical "value slivers" and thereby greatly simplify their cross-border operations. Thus Sadia, Brazil's largest pork and poultry processor and producer of convenience frozen foods, started off by exporting raw meat—eventually becoming the world's largest chicken exporter—before moving downstream into frozen and processed foods subject to more cultural variation.[19] And Brunswick, the U.S. leader in recreational boats and boat engines, tested the international waters, so to speak, with engines before starting to sell boats overseas, with a focus on the premium segment.

Segment Focus

Brunswick continues to focus on exporting premium boats as a way of overcoming geographic distance and associated shipping costs. Zara, the apparel retailing chain from Spain, provides another example of segment focus. Zara has managed to expand into 59 countries and routinely earns returns on capital employed in excess of 40 percent despite standardizing not only its product line, but also the look and feel of its stores, down to the level of window displays, store layouts, and in-store music and perfumes.

This reflects its focus on fashion-sensitive consumers, who are arguably more homogenous across countries than fashion-insensitive ones. (Also important, of course, is a strategy that can break even with a few tenths of a percentage point of the total local apparel market.) And companies as diverse as Indian packaged foods suppliers and Mexican media operations have penetrated the United States by focusing on their respective expatriate communities, thereby limiting the need for adaptation. While such "diasporic" communities tend to be small, they also tend to be richer than their counterparts at home, which can make them a profitable target.

Externalization to Reduce the Burden of Variation

The lever of externalization is related to the lever of focus. However, instead of simply narrowing scope, externalization purposefully splits activities across organizational boundaries to improve organizational effectiveness by reducing the *internal* burden of adaptation. Externalization subsumes multiple sublevers, of which we will focus on four: *strategic alliances, franchising, user adaptation*, and *networking*.

Strategic Alliances

Strategic alliances can provide access to local knowledge that would be hard to purchase, to links in the local value chain that would otherwise be inaccessible, or to local connections, including political ones, and associated benefits. Such alliances are used particularly in entering markets that are distant from one's home base.[20] In addition, they can reduce certain kinds of risks by permitting an acquisition in stages rather than all at once (as in the Whirlpool and Philips case), for example. Of course, strategic alliances also impose their own costs and risks, including financial insecurity, lack of control, and misuse of intellectual property.[21] For these reasons and because of their managerial complexity, alliances must be treated as a possible sublever for reducing the burden of adaptation and not, as enthusiasts would have it, as a panacea.

Given this complex of factors, many alliance successes—and failures—reflect the luck of the draw. But there *are* exceptions, of which perhaps one of the most notable is Eli Lilly's use of alliances to overcome technological as well as CAGE-related dimensions of distance.[22] In the late 1990s, as the pharmaceutical industry was engulfed by a wave of mergers and acquisitions, Lilly opted, instead, for an alliance-based strategy. The trouble was that external surveys placed the company's capabilities in this regard toward the bottom of its peer group. To become first-in-class, Lilly invested in creating an Office of Alliance Management alongside its five business units, setting up a standardized management structure for its hundred-plus alliances, developing a systematic training program and an alliance management toolkit (including a database that codified what it had learned from each alliance), and instituting an annual survey of the health of each of its alliances. One notable success has been the global strategic alliance with Takeda of Japan, which resulted in the rapid rise of the Japanese company's antidiabetes drug, Actos, to blockbuster status in the United States. The success of this alliance also resulted in a general shift in Lilly's reputation, toward partner of choice.[23] Furthermore, the alliance effort is now in its fourth generation of leadership, indicating that it has some staying power.

Franchising

A similar logic applies to other formal interfirm collaborations. Since I have already introduced the example of Yum! Brands, I'll use it here as an illustration. Like most other fast-food chains, Yum! has developed a sophisticated franchising operation that shares knowledge extensively in both directions—that is, to and from headquarters. This "plural" form of organization exhibits significant complementarities between franchised and company-owned units.[24] Franchising helps the chains relax their internal resource constraints on growth, increase local responsiveness, achieve innovation—it was franchisees that invented McDonald's Big Mac and Egg McMuffin, for instance—and inject, through voluntarism, some reality checks into their decision making. Company-owned units, in contrast, relax the constraints on growth due to the dearth of qualified franchisees, can be commanded instead of having to be coaxed at every juncture, and supply a basis for building franchisee confidence (e.g., by rapidly rolling out a new idea among company-owned units). Also, mutual learning between the franchised and company-owned units seems important but requires coordination through mechanisms such as cross-cutting career paths and ratcheting (the use of one type of operation to set standards for the other).

User Adaptation and Networking

Going even farther out on the spectrum of externalization, one can think of involving customers and other ostensibly independent third parties in the challenge of adaptation. Various recently emphasized approaches to doing so include lead-user development, "mashups," and "innovation jams."[25] Perhaps the ultimate example along these lines is provided by Linux, one of several initiatives to develop open-source software—in this case, a computer operating system. The brainchild of a Finnish programmer named Linus Torvalds, it has emerged as a powerful international challenger to the Microsoft operating system. But don't go looking for Linux's corporate equivalent of Microsoft's headquarters at Redmond: Linux is a loosely coupled network based on the efforts of individuals and companies around the world.[26]

How does something like this work? Roughly as follows: Torvalds sets broad guidelines for the next generation of improvements to Linux. Contributors, by several measures mostly non-American, send their proposed code refinements to Torvalds and his key lieutenants, who either approve or disapprove of their inclusion in the core of the operating system. Then, individual developers are free to embroider on that core to come up with distinctive software offerings. And, in addition to these user-innovators, Linux gets support around the world from a network of specialist firms—Red Hat (United States), Suse (Germany), TurboLinux (Japan and China), Conactive (Brazil), Mandrake (France), Red Flag (China)—as well as complementors such as IBM, which see Linux as a way of combating Microsoft.

Linux is an unusual model—not even a "business" in the traditional sense of the word—but it has yielded an operating system that, in many respects, is much more adaptable than Microsoft's proprietary code. In addition to being customizable by users, Linux's kernel (developed by Torvalds and based on Unix) is designed to be scalable so that it can drive devices ranging from wristwatches to computers. Furthermore, Linux does not arouse the same administrative concerns aroused by Microsoft's code (which the Chinese government, among others, fears is riddled with trapdoors permitting espionage) and, since it is free, is affordable by all.

Design to Reduce the Cost of Variation

The Linux example also hinted at the importance of design as a way of deliberately reducing the cost of variation rather than the need for, or the burden of, variation. Common, interrelated ways to reduce the cost of variation include *flexibility*, *partitioning*, *platforms*, and *modularization*.

Flexibility

Flexibility is the idea of deliberately designing business systems so as to reduce the fixed costs associated with producing different varieties. The major home appliance industry again provides a good example, as it encompasses two very different manufacturing paradigms: large, vertically integrated U.S. plants that concentrate on long runs for the relatively homogenous North American market, and smaller, less integrated plants that cater to European demands for greater variety. Large U.S. manufacturers typically strive for scales of 1 million units per product at their plants, a level up to which early studies suggested there might be significant economies of scale. In contrast, the more progressive European appliance manufacturers have traditionally placed more emphasis on absolute cost reductions rather than on scale, by designing plants to be comparatively more efficient at short run lengths with aggregate annual scales of one-half to one-third of the larger U.S. plants.

While this home appliance example focuses on production, the potential for flexibility has also been increased recently—for some industries and products—by changes that reduce the costs of inventory storage and distribution. Thus, it has been estimated that consumer benefits from the increased product variety in online bookstores are ten times larger than their benefit from access to lower prices online.[27] The Internet is, of course, what has unlocked these sources of value by providing access to a "long tail" of products.[28] Amazon, for example, stocks only a very small fraction of the 2.5 million titles that it purportedly offers, relying instead on orders from publishers and distributors to meet demand for the rest after consumers click in their orders. And note that available variety—and adaptability—might be further enhanced by e-books or print-on-demand publishing, in which storage costs are not just reduced, but virtually eliminated.

Partitioning

Partitioning can occur at multiple levels, but at its simplest, it involves clearly separating elements that can be varied across countries from elements that are integral parts of a complex system and that should therefore not be tampered with on a piecemeal basis. While this may sound rudimentary, it is a stumbling block for many organizations. Thus, it took Wal-Mart years, according to its vice chairman, John Menzer, to figure out "bandwidths of responsibility," namely, the zones within which local managers could make decisions without involving the corporate staff back in Bentonville.[29]

McDonald's is generally acknowledged to be a master at partitioning. Consumers, particularly in the United States, often think of McDonald's as a relentlessly consistent purveyor of Big Macs and the like. But if one has the appetite to visit the company's outlets around the world, it is obvious that its product offerings vary widely from country to country. To cite just a few Asian examples, McDonald's offers the Burger McDo (a sweeter burger) and McSpaghetti in the Philippines. (And no, McSpaghetti does *not* show up in its Italian outlets!) It sells a Teriyaki McBurger in Japan, as well as "lamb-burgers" in India to avoid offending Hindu sensibilities. In Taiwan, McDonald's launched a rice burger—involving two lightly toasted and flavored "rice patties" rather than conventional buns—in 2005, and started rolling it out in China in 2006.

Such one-off alterations to a system still known for extreme operating efficiency and consistency clearly require McDonald's to split choices into those where local adaptation is feasible and those where such adaptation would compromise system performance—following a roughly 20 percent local, 80 percent global rule in this regard. But such partitioning extends beyond the choice of products. Thus, although McDonald's runs global advertising campaigns, its mascot, Ronald McDonald, promotes McDonald's wine in France and McDonald's Filet-o-Fish in Australia—and celebrates Christmas in Northern Europe and the Chinese New Year in Hong Kong—but never appears in globally accessible media.[30] The idea is to weave the mascot's story into local cultures around the world.

Platforms

The next frontier for McDonald's, as of this writing, is to introduce a modular kitchen capable of preparing more than one type of meal in the same restaurant, based on a "combi oven" that can cook several varieties of dishes at once, in a way that will further expand variety at its restaurants.[31] (Look in various parts of the world for tilapia sandwiches, McRoaster potatoes, and flautas.)

The combi oven is one example of a platform that underlies cost-effective customization. Indesit, in the home appliance industry, offers another good example. Insiders attribute much of Indesit's superior performance to its ability to simplify its offerings to one or two basic platforms per product category that can be elaborated into hundreds of different SKUs. Indesit's discipline in this regard can be contrasted with Whirlpool's. Whirlpool also pursued platforms—but much more superficially—in a way that concentrated on procurement cost savings instead of making deeper changes to the organization. As a result, the savings that it identified from reducing its product platforms from roughly twenty times the number at Indesit to ten times came to just 2 percent of sales—insufficient to boost its performance up to desired levels and, therefore, deemphasized as the overarching strategic thrust in the early 2000s in favor of a focus on innovation.

Modularity

Modularity blurs into platform approaches but, conceptually, involves defining standardized interfaces between all choice elements, rather than just between a platform and the components that sit atop it, so that all choice elements can be mixed and matched.[32] This has been, for instance, the approach followed in the design of most computer systems since the IBM System 360 was introduced in the early 1960s—so that different parts of the computer could be worked on independently by separate, specialized groups. Ericsson's AXE digital switch, developed in the late 1970s at a cost of about $500 million—roughly equal to half the company's sales at the time—was a breakthrough in modularization that was explicitly designed to address cross-border variation. Since the size of the AXE's switching matrix could easily be varied, Ericsson sold it in more than one hundred countries around the world.[33] And modular products have also been shown to improve performance in the home appliance industry.[34]

Yahoo! provides an example of the uses and limits of modularity more broadly—in organizational design. The company set up a plug-and-play structure in which more than one hundred individual "properties" were able to pursue particular target sets of customers on a decentralized basis. What Yahoo! controlled centrally were the properties' interfaces with the external environment, particularly their "look and feel," the interface be-tween these services and the company's core directory search platform, and the contractual terms usable in signing content deals with partners. These arrangements led to rapid horizontal and geographic growth for a number of years, but also illustrate some of the risks of a modularization strategy. In a recently leaked memo, a senior executive described the problem in colorful terms: "I've heard our strategy described as spreading peanut butter across the myriad opportunities that continue to evolve in the online world [with the] result: a thin layer of investment spread across everything we do and thus we focus on nothing in particular."[35] Specific problems cited include a lack of a "cohesive vision," the separation of op-erations "into silos that far too frequently don't talk to each other," and a "massive redundancy that exists throughout the organization." More em-phasis on focus as opposed to modularization might have made sense in this case. More broadly, design for adaptability is often purchased at some cost in terms of efficiency.

Innovation to Improve the Effectiveness of Variation

Some of the levers and sublevers discussed above—such as repositioning and design for adaptability—could also be characterized as instances of the last broad lever for adaptation that will be considered in this chapter: in-novation. Innovation can sometimes have a global character. For instance, IKEA's flat-pack design, which has relaxed the constraints of geographic distance and the associated transportation costs, has helped that retailer expand into three dozen countries. But cross-border differences often imply innovation that is somewhat narrower in its scope, as illustrated in this section's discussion of progressively more radical sublevers: *transfer, localization, recombination,* and *transformation.*[36]

Transfer

One of the advantages of operating in multiple, varied contexts is that experience may yield innovations or insights in one context that can be transferred to others. The case of Cemex's transferring multiple innovations from one part of the world to another, discussed earlier, is one example. Whirlpool's introduction of the Duet, a European-designed front-loading washer, in the United States is another. A third example that reminds us that such innovations need not originate in the most advanced or otherwise significant geographies is provided by Disney. Thus, Disney Latin America—which accounts for less than 2 percent of Disney's total revenues—has, in recent years, been a major source of insights into improving Disney International's efficiency by sharing services and, more importantly, enhancing customer appeal through alignment of the Disney experience across major business segments. This is precisely because it has to deal with a challenging macroeconomic environment without the benefit of cash flow from a theme park.[37]

Localization

While transfer often has the flavor of serendipity, localization involves more explicit focus on innovation in a target geography. Take the examples of KFC in China, discussed in chapter 2, and the Indian arm of Unilever. Hindustan Lever is perhaps best known for its extensive distribution network, which penetrates deep into rural India. Other consumer packaged-goods multinationals have good networks as well, but they use them mainly to "skim" the (small) high end of the market. Hindustan Lever, by contrast, has created local innovative capabilities that leverage its network to great effect. Its product innovations include detergent bars for people who wash their clothes manually, toothpaste to be used with fingers instead of toothbrushes (traditional in India), a skin-lightening cream, and a unique shampoo-and-hair-oil product.

Other innovations have addressed the extreme price sensitivity of the Indian market. Examples include low-unit-price packs (e.g., sachets of shampoo), localization to cut manufacturing costs, and the use of advanced technology to coat one side of a soap bar with plastic (so that it will take longer to wear down). As a result of these innovations and many others, as well as the great reach of its distribution network, Hindustan Lever enjoys gross margins of close to 50 percent—return on capital employed has been reported to exceed 100 percent!—in a very price-sensitive market.

Recombination

Recombination involves melding elements of the parent business model with opportunities that arise in new contexts. As indicated at the outset of this chapter, adaptation goes well beyond simply tinkering with an existing product or service to achieve a better fit with a local market. Splicing in a few new "genes," while still respecting the host organism, can create an interesting new kind of beast.

News Corporation and Star TV came in for criticism in chapter 2, so I should also acknowledge one of their successes: an interesting example of recombination from the late 1990s that is largely responsible for India being the one major success in Star's portfolio. The example—*Kaun Banega Crorepati*—may not sound familiar, but it is the Hindi-language adaptation of the show *Who Wants to Be a Millionaire?* licensed from the British production house Celador. Star used the same basic set, music, and rules in the Hindi version as in the original, but decided that the participants, questions, and marketing had to be adapted to local conditions. In particular, it hired the dominant Hindi-language actor of the era, flew him to London to watch the British version of the show being taped, and worked with him to develop key catchphrases that might work in Hindi. Heavy investments were made in marketing as well, which ensured that the debut of the show was a major event in Hindi broadcasting. And while the success of *Kaun Banega Crorepati* inspired imitators, none fared very well, including erstwhile local leader Zee TV's attempt to succeed by offering ten times as much prize money. It's true that any foreign or local competitor could have licensed the show from Celador for the Hindi-language market—as James Murdoch, CEO of Star TV, told me, "We all go to the same fairs."[38] However, Star's specific knowledge of local viewers' preferences and News Corporation's production expertise (which included other game shows) gave it an edge at identifying and investing in what was, in many respects, more an attempt at recombination or hybridization than adaptation, conventionally construed.

Transformation

Transformation is a way in which firms may directly try to reduce the *need* for adaptation—by seeking to shape or transform the local environments in which they operate—instead of trying, as just discussed, to enhance their abilities to fit in. McDonald's, by developing markets around the systems that it had built up rather than the reverse, is often credited with being one of the first successful practitioners of this strategy on a global scale. Starbucks provides another interesting example. Although the Seattle-based coffee giant is frequently cited as being in the vanguard of American cultural imperialism, this accusation is a little misguided. Writing in his autobiography, CEO Howard Schultz paints a fascinating picture of his original attempt to recreate an Italian-espresso-bar experience in the United States—right down to recorded opera music and bow-tied waiters.[39] Although the opera music and bow ties soon disappeared—in a form of adaptation—Schultz had successfully called forth a clientele for a coffee-drinking experience that was substantially different from that of, say, Dunkin' Donuts. He had *transformed* U.S. coffee drinkers, who now expected easy chairs, hip music, and a smoke-free environment to enhance their coffee-drinking experience.

The transformation experience was even more dramatic when Starbucks moved to Japan. The company insisted on exporting the smoking ban that had helped distinguish its American outlets. Skeptics said that this would certainly doom the chain in Japan by alienating the hordes of chain-smoking Japanese businessmen who traditionally crowded Japanese coffee parlors, or *kissaten*. Instead, the no-smoking policy *helped* Starbucks Japan, by enticing a female clientele who didn't frequent the *kissaten*.

It bears repeating: because Starbucks was able to change local markets even while it was adapting to local conditions, it minimized the extent to which it ultimately had to adapt. Watch out, however, for a tendency to avoid other forms of adaptation by pretending that all situations can easily be transformed. Thus Microsoft, after a decade of making losses in China—where, the company now admits, it might wait another decade or two to make money—has given up on transformation. As one journalist put it, "It's clear that Microsoft is no longer trying to change China; China is changing Microsoft."[40]

Analyzing Adaptation

Many of the examples discussed in this chapter, particularly that of major home appliances, may have suggested that the principal objective of adaptation is to improve the demand curve that a company faces, that is, to enhance volume, willingness-to-pay, or both. But to think broadly about adaptation, it is important to remember the other components of the ADDING Value scorecard as well: influencing one or more of them may be an important objective, perhaps even the overriding one.

Some of the product indigenization efforts discussed in the subsection on localization provide examples of adaptation aimed at reducing costs.

On the process side, the Boston Consulting Group (BCG) has recently stressed that an interesting way of adapting manufacturing to an emerging market context is by building disposable factories, defined as labor-intensive, dedicated factories designed for temporary mass production.[41] Such factories can supposedly be built for as little as 20–30 percent of the cost of a U.S. plant equipped for flexible automation—which has, in many industries, proved very costly—and can achieve comparable reductions in lead times. In addition, while such disposable factories tend to be inflexible in terms of product mix or batch sizes, their advantages in terms of costs, lead times, and reduced exit barriers may in fact make them particularly advantageous wherever uncertainty is high—reminding us that there is more than one way of normalizing risk.

Having stressed the potentially wide-ranging benefits of adaptation, I must add that it can have negative as well as positive effects on multiple components of the ADDING Value scorecard. Issues related to economies of scale, particularly the link between volume and costs, loom particularly large in this context. The reason is that adaptation—and this is the fundamental limitation of this broad strategy—essentially involves sacrificing global scale economies. The sacrifice is apt to be particularly painful when adaptation involves incurring significant country-specific fixed costs in situations where either the size of the market or a company's share of it is quite limited.

For example, consider L'Oréal going up against AmorePacific in the Korean market for beauty care products. Chapter 2 discussed the array of disadvantages that L'Oréal, along with other multinationals, faces competing against this home-grown leader in Korea. But L'Oréal could address at least some of the cultural disadvantages that seem to be salient by developing products more tailored to Korean skin tones and conceptions of beauty. The trouble is that if it tried to match AmorePacific's R&D spending—reported to be 3.6 percent of AmorePacific's sales in 2006— that would, given a market share of less than one-sixth of AmorePacific's, escalate R&D to more than 20 percent of L'Oréal's revenues. And, because of its limited local scale, L'Oréal faces an even bigger hurdle in trying to imitate AmorePacific's door-to-door distribution system—even though that channel is AmorePacific's single most profitable. Instead, L'Oréal has focused on tapping global economies of scale—particularly through the cachet of being from France—or at least regional ones (e.g., its emphasis on skin whiteners throughout Asia as part of its "Geocosmetics" strategy).

The L'Oréal example is relatively simple in the sense that trying to adapt more to the Korean market would probably hurt the profitability of L'Oréal Korea as well as the company as a whole. The more tricky cases arise when the profitability of a country operation and of the overall corporation point in different directions regarding specific adaptation decisions—as we will see next.

Managing Adaptation

Examples in which countries champion more adaptation than makes sense from a corporate perspective are legion. To focus in on one, consider the case of Royal Philips Electronics, which has crossed borders for more than a century now.[42] Poor transport and communications links, protectionism, and the need to create local joint ventures to gain market acceptance led Philips, like many other early European multinationals, to establish a "federal" system of largely autonomous national organizations (NOs). Federalism was reinforced by World War II, which made Philips place its assets outside Continental Europe in independent trusts. After the war, Philips's management decided to rebuild the company through the NOs, which therefore added design and manufacturing capabilities to their previous focus on adaptive marketing. A second organizational axis of Main Industry Groups (MIGs) was supposed to coordinate product policy, but remained relatively powerless in the face of a cadre of elite expatriate managers—the so-called Dutch Mafia—who championed the NOs' country-oriented point of view.

As a result, by 1970 Philips operated five hundred plants scattered across nearly fifty countries and was experiencing pressure from competitors such as Matsushita, which had begun to reduce costs by consolidating factories and moving jobs to lower-wage areas. But Philips's efforts, starting in the early 1970s, to invest more power in the MIGs (which were renamed Product Divisions, or PDs) failed to make much headway. Philips had, by then, developed a "thick" culture: mature, complex, bureaucratic, and resistant to new information and incentives. As a parade of CEOs attempted to rebalance the geography-PD matrix away from the NOs and toward the PDs, Philips continued to lose market share and to restructure by exiting business after business. Finally, in 1996–1997, a new CEO, Cor Boonstra, brought in from the outside, took the drastic step of abolishing the geographic leg of the matrix. More than a quarter-century had elapsed since the first attempts to place less emphasis on adaptation through NOs and more on global economies of scale through the PDs!

In addition to illustrating that it is possible to overadapt, the Philips case shows that the optimal degree of adaptation varies by industry and can change over time, and that there may be—especially in mature organizations—long lags in changing the actual degree of adaptation. The case also has implications for the debate about whether there is one best way of organizing, at least from an adaptive perspective. Specifically, it has been suggested—particularly in Europe—that the European model of companies as multinational federations is inherently superior to the typically more centralized U.S. model of multinationals because of the diversity the former offers.[43]

The Philips example reminds us that it's not that simple: if you set up constitutional principles that prevent the adjustment of structures or processes in the face of changing realities, you are setting yourself up for enormous problems. Sometimes power must be concentrated centrally, whereas at other times, it must be dispersed locally. The trick is to concentrate and disperse proactively rather than to treat decentralization—or centralization—as *the* optimal approach. If we did, we would be back in the straitjacket we saw Coke struggling with in chapter 1.

The broader point is that it is possible to imagine errors of two types: overadaptation and underadaptation. The levers and sublevers discussed in the previous sections help relax the underlying tension between complete localization and complete standardization, but that still leaves open the question of how much to adapt.

Optimally exploiting adaptation possibilities—in a way that avoids the dangers of both over- and underadaptation—requires what might be termed a global mind-set. But this is easier said than done—as managerial self-assessments indicate. Thus, a survey of fifteen hundred executives in twelve large, multinational companies in the mid-1990s asked them to rate their performance along various dimensions deemed vital to international competitiveness. "The respondents rated their ability to cultivate a global mind-set to their organization dead last—34th out of 34 dimensions."[44]

To make matters worse, what executives mean by a global mind-set often discounts adaptation as a strategy lever. Thus, in another survey aimed at deriving bases for measuring the globalization of mind-sets, the researchers had to add responsiveness-related dimensions themselves because the respondents were apt to overlook these dimensions.[45] This presumably reflected a tendency to conflate global mind-sets with standardization and centralization.

What is to be done in the way of remediation? Experts agree that rote learning about the beliefs, customs, and taboos of foreign cultures—for instance, that a thumbs-up is a gesture of contempt in India rather than an indication that everything is OK—will never prepare people for every situation that arises, although it is the approach that corporate training programs often take.[46] What are required, instead, are mechanisms for cultivating both openness and literacy about diverse cultures and markets (see the box "Fostering Openness, Knowledge, and Integration Across Countries"), mechanisms that also help with the other strategies for dealing with differences described in this book—aggregation and arbitrage.

Fostering Openness, Knowledge, and Integration Across Countries

Beyond the mere rote learning of discrete facts about foreign cultures, successful adaptation requires a company to employ as many open-ended opportunities to develop literacy about diverse cultures as it can.

1. **Hiring for adaptability:** People vary in their ability to act appropriately and effectively in new contexts or among people with unfamiliar backgrounds. While training and experience can help in this regard, it is best to start by hiring people attitudinally disposed to mastering such situations.

2. **Formal education:** Formal education occurs not only in classrooms, but also through interactions with colleagues from other locations around the world. Of course, the appropriate content of such formal education is highly contingent: it would be dysfunctional to emphasize the importance of more localization to Philips's managers, for instance, and of standardization to Wal-Mart's, instead of the other way around. When I work out a training program on global strategy for a corporation, I tend to spend more time on design than on delivery.

3. **Participation in cross-border business teams and projects:** Team and project work can be key in developing interpersonal ties that cross borders—a very important complement to formal authority in getting things done. The coordination of globally distributed teams has been eased in recent years by information technology, which might itself be cited as a key enabler of the creation of high-bandwidth international links.

4. **Utilization of diverse locations for team and project meetings:** I recently attended a meeting for IBM stock analysts held in Bangalore. As CEO Sam Palmisano explained it to me, this was primarily about signaling commitment to and helping integrate an operation that had grown from less than ten thousand people to close to fifty thousand in three years, and not because IBM's strategy could be explained only in Bangalore.

5. **Immersion experiences in foreign cultures:** The Overseas Area Specialist course that Samsung initiated in 1991 is still a role model in

this regard. Every year, more than two hundred carefully screened trainees select a country of interest, go through three months of language and cross-cultural training, and then spend a year there—without a specific job assignment or contact with the local Samsung office—followed by a two-month debrief in Seoul.

6. **Expatriate assignments:** An even more intense form of immersion, expatriate assignments are also very expensive economically and in terms of personal wear and tear. As a result, they need to be targeted at high-potential managers rather than as a way of exiling people whom one would rather not see.

7. **Cultivating geographic and cultural diversity at the top:** It is still easy to find large companies with significant operations outside their home markets whose top management—and board of directors—is still (almost) entirely domestic. China provides a particularly dramatic example: the number of large Western companies with any Chinese representation at the top is still tiny.

8. **Dispersion of business unit headquarters or centers of excellence:** P&G's CEO, A. G. Lafley, regards the company's geographically dispersed business unit headquarters as a key point of difference from many of its competitors. Of course, the locations must be selected carefully: P&G's attempt to locate the headquarters of one of its global business units in Caracas quickly ran into problems and had to be revised.

9. **Defining and cultivating a set of core values throughout the corporation:** A strong one-firm culture can help override parochialism despite the diversity of locations and market conditions. A number of professional service firms provide good examples.

10. **Opening up across organizational boundaries:** To frame the problem as one of creating openness within the organization is to frame it too narrowly: interest in open innovation, for instance, is a reminder of the gains that can be tapped by opening up the organization to the outside world. Of course, such opening up to the outside also entails risks.

Source: Adapted (and extended) with permission from Vijay Govindarajan and Anil K. Gupta, *The Quest for Global Dominance* (San Francisco: Jossey-Bass, 2001), 129–136.

Even with all these mechanisms in hand, overcoming all the barriers to strategy change may require a major organizational push. The Samsung Corporation offers a particularly dramatic example.[47] Despite a number of initiatives over the years, including the immersion program described in the box, Chairman Lee Kun Hee was dissatisfied with the pace of globalization efforts and, in 1993, launched his New Management Initiative by summoning 150 senior executives to a luxury hotel in Frankfurt. He began his presentation to them at 8 p.m. and lectured them nonstop for seven hours about the need to "transform Samsung into a true world-class company"—without once going to the bathroom, according to one participant—culminating in a call to "change everything but your family." After he finished, he ordered the participants to stay on in Frankfurt for a week as a way of exposing them to the outside world. He took the entire senior management on other trips as well, including to Los Angeles to "show them our actual position was much lower than what we had thought." The symbolism of these efforts was backed up by a substantive emphasis on quality—and innovation—instead of quantity, which would make it more like Sony. Samsung restructured its portfolio to exit sunset businesses and tripled the percentage of production overseas to 60 percent of the total by 2000, through a program that involved regionalization as well as major acquisitions and strategic investments.

More than a decade later, this Frankfurt meeting is still recalled as having sparked a cultural transformation. Samsung, alone among the major Korean *chaebol*, not only survived the Asian financial crisis intact, but also achieved more than twice the market capitalization of Sony and overtook the Japanese company—and Philips and Matsushita's Panasonic—as the world's most valuable consumer electronics brand.[48] The example also reminds us that cultivating openness and literacy about diverse markets and cultures is about the heart as well as the head.

Conclusions

The box "Global Generalizations" summarizes the specific conclusions from this chapter. More broadly, adaptation clearly subsumes a range of different approaches, all of which must be thought through, instead of being a mechanical, paint-by-the-numbers process. The good news is that a comprehensive perspective on adaptation tremendously expands the headroom available to adjust to differences. The bad news is that even with full exploitation of adaptation-related possibilities, adaptation as a strategy for dealing with semiglobalization suffers from two distinct sets of limitations. First, assuming that centralized decisions are made at the global level and decentralized decisions at the local level fails to account for cross-border aggregation mechanisms that operate at levels intermediate to the country and the world. Second, adaptation strategies almost, by definition, treat differences across countries as constraints to be coped with and thereby ignore the possibilities of capitalizing on them. The two types of generic strategies for dealing with semiglobalization that are discussed next, aggregation and arbitrage, explicitly target these two limitations of adaptation strategies.

Global Generalizations

1. Very few businesses can operate on either a totally localized or a totally standardized basis across borders.

2. There are numerous levers (and sublevers) for adaptation intermediate to the extremes of localization and standardization: variation, focus, externalization, design, and innovation.

3. It is possible to adapt too much or too little—although the latter may be more common.

4. Industry characteristics have a great deal of influence on the optimal degree of adaptation, which may increase or decrease over time.

5. Changing the actual degree of adaptation can be subject to very long lags.

6. Change is aided by a flexible, realistic, and open mind-set—and may require a major organizational push.

7. Most companies have much headroom to improve how they adapt.

8. Adaptation decisions cannot be made independently of decisions about aggregation and arbitrage.

5

Aggregation

Overcoming Differences

We intend to continue moving forward with globalization . . .
by further enhancing the localization and independence
of our operations in each region.

—Fujio Cho, Toyota, 2003

CHAPTER 4 DEALT WITH the first of our AAA strategies for dealing with distances and crossing borders successfully: adaptation to adjust to differences. This chapter deals with the second of the three As, *aggregation* to overcome differences. Aggregation is all about using various grouping devices to create greater economies of scale than country-by-country adaptation can provide.

Aggregation means inventing and implementing cross-border mechanisms that operate at levels somewhere between an individual country and the whole world. And it generally engages intermediate levels within a company, rather than only the moguls at corporate and the locals. Think of aggregation as calling heavily on the upper-middle ranks of the organization. The objective is to exploit the similarities among countries more aggressively than traditional adaptation strategies do, but less aggressively than complete standardization would. The key underpinning is the idea, stressed in chapter 2, of differences in differences: there is much to be gained by grouping things so that within-group differences are minimal compared with between-group differences.

Although this chapter will discuss the many different kinds of aggregation strategies, its principal approach—in contrast to that of chapter 4, which emphasized variety—is to dig in deep into *one* type of aggregation strategy, by geographic region (the G dimension of the CAGE framework). The chapter first explains why regionalization is particularly salient in a cross-border context and then reviews a range of different regional strategies—with Toyota serving as the lead example—before turning to a broader discussion of different bases of aggregation and the challenges that arise in managing them.

The Reality of Regions

The most common pitch for regionalization has been that since globalization has stalled, strategy at the regional level is more important than ever.[1] But this marginalizes regionalization by treating it as a second-best alternative to globalization. In fact, geographic regions *haven't* been submerged by the rising tide of globalization: they are arguably *of increasing importance*. Consider some data, starting with trade.

Figure 5-1 shows how trade within regions has evolved since 1958 as a percentage of total international trade. For example, in 1958, some 35 percent of trade in Asia and Oceania took place between countries in that geographic region. In 2003, the proportion was over 54 percent—coincidentally, also the proportion of intraregional trade averaged across all regions. The only significant decline has been in Eastern Europe, but that is explained by the collapse of Communism. In other words, the data in figure 5-1 indicate that in the postwar period, generally considered a period of galloping globalization, intraregional trade has had more influence than interregional trade on the large increases in international trade. Figure 5-1 also casts doubt on the hypothesis that intraregional trade is somehow inferior to or is less indicative of truly valuable involvement in the international economy than interregional trade: low levels of intraregional trade—that is, high or sharply increasing levels of interregional trade—are generally associated with poor economic performance in a region (compare Africa, the Middle East, and the East European transition economies).

Regionalization is evident not only in trade, but also in other markers of cross-border economic activity. Thus foreign direct investment (FDI)—while obviously less regionalized than trade because it relaxes some of the geographic barriers to which trade is subject—*does* exhibit significant regionalization, as well. Country-level data from the United Nations Conference on Trade and Development show that for the two dozen countries

FIGURE 5-1

Intra-regional trade, 1958-2003

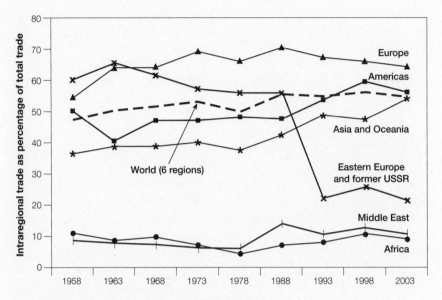

Source: United Nations, International Trade Statistics Yearbooks.

that account for nearly 90 percent of the world's outward FDI stock, the median share of intraregional FDI in total FDI was 52 percent in 2002.[2]

Company-level data point in the same direction. Among U.S. companies operating in only one foreign country, there is a 60 percent chance of that country's being Canada.[3] Mexico also turns out to exert a disproportionate pull on U.S. companies. And while those data cover all U.S. companies with foreign operations, even the largest multinationals exhibit a significant regional bias. Analysis by Alan Rugman and Alain Verbeke shows that of the 366 companies in the *Fortune* Global 500 for which such data were available, 88 percent derived at least 50 percent of their sales in 2001 from their home regions—with the share of sales in the home region averaging 80 percent for this subgroup.[4] In contrast, just 2 percent of their sample—or nine companies—had sales of 20 percent or more in each of the "triad" regions of North America, Europe, and Asia, although this proportion does seem sensitive to the cutoff points used.[5]

And even when companies do have a significant presence in more than one region, competitive interactions are often regionally focused. Reconsider the home appliance industry. The two largest players, Whirlpool and

Electrolux, were both biregional in the sense that North America and
Europe each accounted for 20 percent or more of their sales (until Whirlpool's acquisition of Maytag reduced the European share of its total below
this threshold level). But competition between them took place and was
managed largely at the regional level. And the significance of regionalization in that industry is further underscored by the ability of Indesit and
Arçelik, two of the three most profitable competitors among the top ten
and the fastest growing, to achieve that performance despite—one might
say because of—their focus on a single region. In other words, power-
house positions are often built up at the regional level.

I could go on to cite other markers of regionalization. While hard data
are hard to come by, experts generally agree that Internet traffic has become increasingly regionalized in recent years with the declining importance of the United States as an interregional switching hub.

The extent, persistence, and, in at least some instances, increasing regionalization of cross-border activity reflect the continuing importance of
both geographic proximity and proximity along the other CAGE dimensions: cultural, administrative, and, to some extent, economic. These factors
are related: countries that are relatively close to each other geographically are
likely to share commonalities along the other dimensions. What's more,
those commonalities have intensified in some respects over the past few
decades because of free-trade agreements, tax treaties, other regional preferences, and even currency unification, with NAFTA and the European
Union supplying the two most obvious examples. And ironically, some of
the differences between countries within a region can combine with their
similarities to expand the regional share of total economic activity. Thus,
Whirlpool exemplifies a pattern that applies to U.S. firms in many industries: "nearshoring" production facilities to Mexico, thereby arbitraging
across economic differences between the two countries while retaining
the advantages of geographic proximity and administrative and political
similarities, which more distant countries, such as China, do not enjoy.
Similarly, many Western European firms prefer to "nearshore" production
to East Europe. Later chapters will discuss such aggregation-plus-arbitrage
plays in greater detail.

Regionalization at Toyota

While the data and examples in the previous section reinforced the idea
that regionalization is one of the clearest manifestations of semiglobalization, they may still have left you with the sense that regionalization is
merely a watered-down version of globalization. The best way to dispel

that notion is to consider the example of Toyota, a global heavyweight that has embraced regionalization as one of the cornerstones to its strategy for competing across borders.

Toyota passed General Motors as the world's largest automaker in 2007 and has a revenue distribution that is highly globalized (biregional), even by the standards of the *Fortune* Global 500. The company has, nevertheless, pursued a very elaborate array of strategic initiatives at the regional level. The discussion will be organized according to Toyota's own summary of its evolution (figure 5-2).

- Phase 1 lasted for Toyota's first fifty years in the automobile industry and featured one production base (in Japan). As recently as 1985, overseas production accounted for less than 5 percent of the total. This figure reached nearly 15 percent by 1990, almost 30 percent by 1995, and 46 percent by 2006—a fundamental change that led to major shifts in regional emphasis.

- Phase 2, in the 1980s, witnessed Toyota's first significant FDI, particularly in the United States, where sales of Japanese cars had mushroomed, as had protectionist policies and sentiments. Building more cars where they were sold both reduced the likelihood of further import restrictions and minimized potential losses if those restrictions materialized.

- Phase 3 began in the 1990s and involved the creation of bases or hubs for individual regions to improve poor performance while lessening dependence on Japan. Initial production of a limited number of locally exclusive models—traditionally taboo at Toyota—signaled the company's seriousness about building more complete, capable organizations in each of its regions.

- Phase 4 overlaps with phase 3 and has seen (further) promotion of global cars—the Corolla, Camry, Yaris, and Hilux—with significant commonalities across regions to share the fixed costs of development and engineering. Concurrently, Toyota is reducing its number of major production platforms from eleven to six.

- Phase 5 involves consolidation and specialization by region, with some plants or regions receiving near-global mandates. Thus, Toyota's global pickup truck project funnels common engines and manual transmissions from Asian plants to four assembly bases there and in Latin America and Africa, and on to almost all the major markets around the world. (The exception is the United States, where pickups tend to be larger.)

FIGURE 5-2

Toyota's past and future production structure (as of 2004)

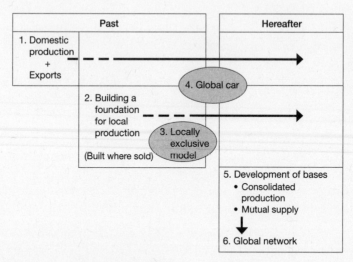

Source: Toyota investor presentation, September 2004.

Note: Numbers have been added to differentiate between phases, but otherwise, the text and layout are unmodified from the slide in a Toyota company presentation.

- Phase 6, the creation of a global network, will involve even more extensive attempts to optimize global production and supply. According to Chairman Fujio Cho, the network will be organized around regions because Toyota expects expanded free-trade agreements *within* the Americas, Europe, and East Asia, but not *across* them.[6]

The case of Toyota is a particularly useful reference point because its evolution, especially since the 1980s, illustrates the entire set of regional strategies that are introduced in the next section.

Regional Strategy Archetypes

Figure 5-3 summarizes the six regional strategy archetypes suggested by the six phases in Toyota's evolution, along with the basic strategic imperatives typically associated with each. Note that the focus of boxes 1 through 3 is intraregional, in a sense, while that of boxes 4 through 6 is interregional. The boxes represent progressively more complex—and less common—approaches to dealing with regional boundaries. So Toyota is truly unusual in terms of its progression from box 1 toward box 6. But applause for what it has accomplished—becoming the world's largest car-

FIGURE 5-3

Regional strategies

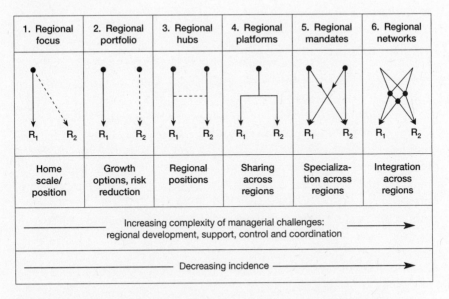

1. Regional focus	2. Regional portfolio	3. Regional hubs	4. Regional platforms	5. Regional mandates	6. Regional networks
Home scale/ position	Growth options, risk reduction	Regional positions	Sharing across regions	Specialization across regions	Integration across regions

Increasing complexity of managerial challenges: ————➤
regional development, support, control and coordination

———————— Decreasing incidence ————————➤

Note: The solid circle (●) can be interpreted as distinct product types; R_1 and R_2 represent two regions.

maker while making money in the process!—should not obscure the point that there is no natural order of progression through these regional strategy archetypes. Different regional strategies make sense for different businesses if value, not complexity, is being maximized. The rest of this section discusses the objectives and limitations of each strategy, using examples to highlight the range of choices that they entail.

1. Regional or Home Focus

While we have already discussed focus, focus along geographic or regional dimensions is worth reemphasizing because virtually all companies start off in this box, except for the very few that are "born global," often in high-technology areas (e.g., Logitech and Checkpoint). This is also the box in which nearly 90 percent of the *Fortune* Global 500 still reside, in terms of the revenue-based definition introduced above. Many of the companies that *have* moved on from this box, such as Toyota, stayed regionally or domestically focused for long periods. And some companies eventually return to a regional focus, often as part of deglobalization: for example, Whirlpool in home appliances or Bayer in pharmaceuticals.

For other companies, regional focus is a matter of neither default nor devolution, but, instead, the desired long-run strategy. Thus, in the highly globalized memory chip (DRAM) business, Samsung sells worldwide—in fact, it has one of the most balanced worldwide distribution of sales of *any* major business—but considers the co-location of most R&D and production around one main site in South Korea a key competitive advantage. Given how low transport costs are relative to product value, global concentration—which permits rapid interactions and iteration across R&D and production—dominates geographic dispersion.

In a somewhat different vein, Zara, the low-priced fashion apparel chain, designs and makes fashion-sensitive items near its manufacturing and logistics hub in northwestern Spain and trucks those goods to West European markets within two to four weeks of design origination. The enhanced customer appeal or rapid response and the reduced incidence of markdowns have so far been more than enough to offset the extra costs of producing in Europe instead of Asia—at least when it comes to West European markets. But "fast fashion" does not travel well from the Spanish hub to other regions, because the costs of the air shipments required for rapid response compromise the low-price positioning pursued in Europe.

The Samsung and Zara examples illustrate different conditions under which regional or home focus can prove attractive: when global scale economies are strong enough to permit centralization of at least some activities in one region or location, or when the key economies of scale operate at the regional, rather than local or global, level. A regional-to-regional focus like Zara's is also favored over a regional-to-global focus like Samsung's in a number of specific circumstances, including the following:

- A particularly profitable regional or home market (e.g., home appliances in the United States for Whirlpool), although this is likely to attract entrants from other regions (e.g., Haier)

- A need for deep local knowledge that reduces efficient breadth (e.g., Li & Fung's Asian focus in setting up and managing international supply chains for retailers)

- A high sensitivity to regional free-trade arrangements and regional preferences (e.g., in automobiles, given the amount of two-way trade in parts and vehicles)

- Other factors that effectively collapse the distance *within* regions, relative to the distances *between* them (e.g., regional energy grids)

Many of the risks associated with regional or home focus relate to the erosion of these conditions that underpin its viability relative to more globally standardized strategies. Conceptually, there is also the risk of being outperformed by more locally focused strategies. This is usually not an issue at home; rather, it tends to surface in nonhome countries, usually in the form of debates about how much the home country should dominate strategizing for the region.

Finally, regional focusers can also run out of room to grow or fail to hedge risk adequately. Growth within Europe is becoming more of an issue for Zara. And the lack of risk hedging has already emerged as a major concern because—as of 2006—the decline of the dollar against the euro has inflated Zara's costs of production in Europe, relative to competitors that rely more on dollar-denominated imports from Asia.

2. Regional Portfolio

Box 2—the regional portfolio—comprises strategies that involve more extensive operation outside a single region. When companies look to move from box 1 to box 2, they often cite growth options and risk reduction (in other words, avoiding the challenges that Zara faces). Particular stimulants to move in this direction include faster growth in nonhome regions, significant home positions that generate substantial free cash flow, local investment requirements to access foreign markets (the story of Toyota's early FDI, in a sense), and the opportunity to "average out" shocks, cycles, and so forth, across regions.

While such geographic broadening can take many forms, including total dispersion, moves that are more coherent usually target the buildup of a presence in particular regions or subregions. Even if the necessary resources are available, this can easily take a decade or longer, as illustrated by Toyota's North American buildup, which started with the New United Motor Manufacturing, Inc. (NUMMI) joint venture with General Motors in the early 1980s. Remember, too, that Toyota possessed a crucial competitive advantage: its Toyota Production System, which it "simply" had to transplant to non-Japanese locations. For an automaker lacking this kind of advantage, the organic buildup of a significant presence in a new region could take far longer.

Comparably long lags are seen even in the purest cases of portfolio management, which involve the assembly of a regional presence through acquisitions rather than organic growth. GE's buildup in Europe is an example. When CEO Jack Welch began GE's globalization initiative in the late 1980s, he targeted expansion in Europe in particular and accelerated the process by giving a trusted confidant, Nani Beccalli, wide latitude for deal making. Largely as a result of these acquisitions, GE had built up European revenues to one-half of its total non-U.S. revenues by the early 2000s.

But enhanced revenues are far from the whole story. Welch's successor, Jeffrey Immelt, provided a blunt assessment. "Europe is a big focus of mine," Immelt admitted a few years ago, "basically because I think we stink in Europe today." What explains the poor performance? GE chose to run its European businesses as stand-alone operations that reported up through their business structures to the U.S.-based global headquarters, purportedly run by "global leaders"—many of whom were Americans who had never lived or worked outside the United States. Meanwhile, most of GE's toughest competitors in its nonfinancial businesses were European. They knew their home turf and were prepared to compete effectively on it.

After the European Union blocked its attempted merger with Honeywell, GE felt the need to develop more of a European face and to set up a significant presence in Brussels. The company also decided to dedicate more corporate infrastructure and resources to Europe, partly as a way to attract, develop, and retain the best European employees. As a result, GE finally moved beyond a regional portfolio strategy by establishing a regional headquarters structure in Europe in 2001—organized around a new post of CEO of GE Europe—and following up in 2003 with a parallel organization in Asia. Jeff Immelt describes the regional teams as the key change agents in the company's various globalization initiatives.

GE's new regional headquarters mark a transition from the regional portfolio approach to a minimalist version of the regional hub strategy elaborated on in the next section. The lesson here, though, is that GE's regional portfolio strategy persisted for quite a long time—despite GE Europe's poor performance and despite GE's being a very well-managed company overall.

More generally, regional portfolio strategies tend to migrate some resource allocation and monitoring roles from corporate headquarters to regional entities. Apart from that migration, however, they offer little opportunity for regional considerations to influence what happens on the ground at the local level.

3. Regional Hubs

A more active alternative for adding value at the regional level was originally articulated by Kenichi Ohmae in his notion of "triad" strategy. This involves building regional bases or hubs that provide a variety of shared resources or services to the local (country) operations. The logic is that these hubs may—because of lumpiness, or increasing returns to scale, or externalities—be hard for any one country to justify, but may still be worth investing in from a cross-border perspective. Although a single or a few locations often provide such shared resources and services, in some cases, the hub may be a virtual one.

Regional hub strategies in their purest form—that is, those focused solely on regional position—represent a structured multiregional version of the regionally focused strategies discussed in box 1 of figure 5-3. For example, if Zara were to add a second hub in Asia, it would shift from being a regional focuser to a multiregional hubber. Therefore, some of the same conditions that favor a regional focus also favor regional hubs: (1) economies of scale at the regional level, (2) factors that effectively collapse the distance within regions relative to the distances between them, and (3) other conditions that lead to battles to build position at the regional level. The difference is that with more than one region, considerations of interregional heterogeneity also come into play. The more that regions differ in their requirements, the weaker the rationale for the multiple, regionally focused entities within such a company to share resources and services.

A regional headquarters (RHQ) can be seen as a minimalist version of a regional hub. The impact of an RHQ is typically limited, however, by a focus on support functions, with limited links to operating activities. Thus, while there is a president for Asia within Wal-Mart International, he performs a communication and monitoring role, but otherwise seems to exert only limited influence on strategy or resource allocation.

For an example of a powerful regional hub strategy that *does* tie into operations and supporting functions, consider Dell.[7] The company sells relatively standardized personal computers around the world (with some adaptation for variations in communications protocols, power supplies, etc.) using a business model that relies on unique operating capabilities for building-to-order and bypasses local distribution barriers. As Dell ascended to leadership in the PC business in North America, it shifted its strategy to also achieving leadership in its other regions—the Americas, Asia-Pacific and Japan, and Europe—in part by keying off its mainstay global accounts/corporate business, which varies less than its consumer business around the world.

Dell's regional operations are still at different levels of development: North America is farthest along, with Europe (particularly the English-speaking areas that were targeted early) being the next best developed, followed by Asia and then South America. That said, each of the regions has developed along similar lines, with its own RHQ, manufacturing, marketing, and IT infrastructure. Manufacturing, in particular, featured hubs organized around assembly facilities that were added in Ireland (1990), Malaysia (1996), China (1998), and Brazil (1998). Hub locations emphasize serving regional markets with quick response times: thus, the Brazil

The Uses and Limits of Regional Headquarters

Researchers and practitioners alike have paid a great deal of attention to the comings and goings of regional headquarters (RHQs).[8] RHQs do deserve some attention because they can serve important purposes if well thought out and well located. Thus, Philippe Lasserre of INSEAD has developed a list of key RHQ functions, including scouting (business development), strategic stimulation (helping organizational subunits understand and deal with the regional environment), signaling commitment to a region (to internal and external audiences), coordination (ensuring the exploitation of synergies and the pursuit of consistent policies across the region), and pooling resources (to take advantage of regional scale economies).[9]

Lasserre has also proposed a typology of RHQs based on their roles in multinationals' strategies. These include *initiators,* which emphasize strategic stimulation and coordination to support local operations; *facilitators,* which combine integration, strategic stimulation, and signaling; *coordinators,* which concentrate on strategic and operational synergies; and *administrators,* which focus on supporting functions, such as clerical, taxation, and treasury.[10] Michael Enright's work on RHQs in Asia-Pacific supplies some empirical support for this typology.[11]

But to focus on the role of RHQs in regional strategy is a little like focusing on the briefcase rather than on its *contents.* Without a clear sense of how a regional overlay is supposed to add value, it is impossible to specify the coordination requirements at the regional level, let alone whether an RHQ can help meet them. In the worst case, the RHQ becomes a substitute for thinking through your company's regional strategy. Phrased more positively, a company with few or no RHQs may still use regions as important building blocks in its overall strategy.

For an illustration, reconsider the case of Toyota. With an RHQ perspective, one might pick up on the establishment of Toyota Motor North America in 1996, of Toyota Motor Europe in 2002, and perhaps of its Southeast Asian subregional hub, but probably not much more. In that sense, RHQs are an inadequate basis for characterizing regional strategies.

---

site is located far from established Brazilian IT clusters, but sits halfway between South America's two largest cities, São Paulo and Buenos Aires.

Proximity to both suppliers and customers has been key in implementing this strategy because, with the unbundling of supply chains in the PC industry, the costs of logistics often exceed the cost added through particular manufacturing operations. As a result, the hubs also feature a concentration of local suppliers, as well as supply logistic centers where global suppliers maintain parts (at their own expense) until Dell's build-to-order assembly system calls for them (figure 5-4). These links let the production system source an estimated 70 percent of its components from Asian suppliers, despite their being geographically dispersed. This approach to managing global supply-chain relationships and logistics has even attracted Toyota's attention, not to mention that of Dell's direct, PC-making competitors (which have imitated elements, narrowing Dell's advantage).

Regional hubs, like most regional strategies, have to be assessed relative to approaches that are both more localized *and* more standardized. (In other words, both local and global predators could, conceivably, attack such a structure.) Since Dell's strategy doesn't target the very-low-cost PC market, in the teeth of local competitors focused on that segment, it has given up its leadership goals in the Chinese market, where customers are also thought to demand more of a relationship with suppliers. The threat from even more standardized approaches, in contrast, is limited: rather, the company's recent, widely reported problems stem more from front-end difficulties ranging from declining overall demand growth to service problems.

Regional hub strategies that *are* more responsive to interregional variation run the risk of adding too much cost or sacrificing too many opportunities to share costs across regions.[12] Taking advantage of such sharing opportunities is the central concern of the regional platform strategies examined next.

4. Regional Platforms

Regional hubs, as we've seen, spread fixed costs across the countries within a region. Regional platforms, by contrast, spread fixed costs across regions—and could, therefore, also be described as "interregional platforms." Platforming is typically emphasized for back-end activities that deliver scale and scope economies if coordinated across regions. Thus, most major automakers are, like Toyota, attempting to reduce the number of basic platforms they offer worldwide to achieve greater economies of scale in terms of design costs, engineering, administration, procurement, and operations. The goal is not to reduce the *amount of product variety* on offer, but instead *to deliver variety more cost effectively* by building local customization atop common platforms explicitly engineered for adaptability along these lines. Also note that platforming has worked better in this industry than in home appliances because of the much greater capital intensity and

FIGURE 5-4

Dell's regional manufacturing hubs, 2001

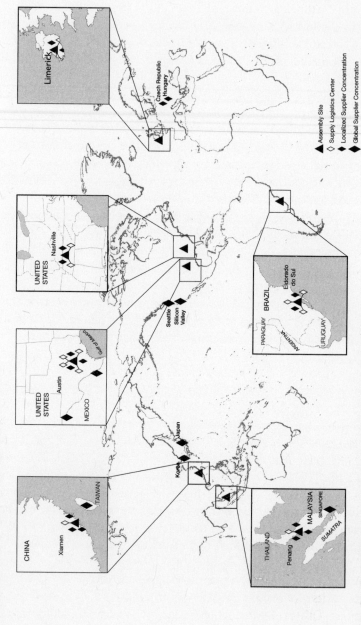

Source: Gary Fields, *Territories of Profit* (Palo Alto, CA: Stanford University Press, 2004), 212.

R&D intensity and associated economies of scale in automaking. (Auto companies accounted for four of the six top corporate spenders world-wide on R&D in 2005–2006, for example.)[13]

It is worth adding that despite aggressive platforming, initiatives such as Toyota's still have to stop well short of global standardization in the auto industry. As Sir Nick Scheele, former chief operating officer of Ford, points out: "The single biggest barrier to globalization [in autos] . . . is the rela-tively cheap cost of motor fuel in the United States. There is a tremendous disparity between the United States and basically the rest of the world, and it creates an accompanying disparity in some of the most fundamen-tal of vehicle characteristics: size and power."[14]

The subtext here is that Ford made a major misstep in the mid-1990s—the Ford 2000 program—that illustrates the principal risk inherent in platforming strategies: they can take standardization too far, at the ex-pense of the variation required in the local marketplace.[15] Ford 2000 was a highly ambitious integration initiative developed to combine Ford's re-gions—principally North America and Europe—into one global opera-tion. (One analyst described it as the biggest business merger in history, up to that point.) Ford's attempt to reduce duplication across North America and Europe created enormous internal turmoil and largely destroyed Ford's European organization. The program sacrificed regional product de-velopment capabilities and pushed unappealingly compromised products into an unreceptive marketplace. The result? Nearly $3 billion in losses in Europe through 2000, as well as a drop in European market share from 12 to 9 percent.

Such risks are of broader relevance, given the centralizing impulses of many corporate headquarters. (Some managers, especially those in the field, may say that this understates the problem.) A tendency toward cen-tralization reinforces the risks of excessive standardization of platforms across regions.

5. Regional Mandates

Regional mandates could also be described as interregional mandates, be-cause they involve awarding of broader mandates to certain regions to supply particular products or to perform particular organizational roles in order to tap economies of *specialization* as well as scale. The mandates that Toyota gave various Asian plants to supply engines and manual transmis-sions for its global (non-U.S.) pickup truck project were cited earlier as an example. Others abound. Thus, Whirlpool worldwide will source most of its small kitchen appliances from India—easier to do than for major home appliances, given small appliances' higher value-to-weight/bulk ratios. And a host of global companies are in the process of broadening the mandates of their production operations in China. Again, the scope for such mandates generally increases with product "standardizability" around the world, even though they involve focused resource deployments at the regional, national, or local levels.

(Inter)regional mandates also show up in areas that go beyond product development and production. Thus, global firms in consulting, engineering, financial services, and other service businesses often feature centers of excellence—repositories of particular knowledge and skills that are charged with making that knowledge available to the rest of the firm. Such centers are often concentrated in a single location, around an individual or a small group of people, rather than being geographically dispersed. As a result, their geographic mandates are much broader than their geographic footprints.[16]

Again, there are several risks associated with assigning broad geographic mandates to particular locations. First, they can supply cover for local, national, or regional interests to unduly influence, or even hijack, a firm's global strategy. Second, broad mandates are not well suited to picking up on variations in local, national, or regional conditions, although overlaying other approaches such as platforming can be of some help here. And finally, carrying the degree of specialization to extremes can create inflexibility and a lack of redundancy. In a volatile world, these are not trivial concerns.

6. Regional Networks

To achieve complementarities across different regions while avoiding excessive specialization and inflexibility, regional networks involve *integration* as well as the division of labor among resources located in different regions. Although academics have discussed networking extensively, most companies still merely *aspire* to such integration. So, our discussion of networks will be relatively brief and will focus on Toyota, one of the few companies that seem to have taken serious steps toward regional and global networking.

Perhaps the most relevant insight from the Toyota story is that, for practical purposes, it is better to think of networking not as a specific way to manage regions, but as *a state of mind that involves looking broadly at cross-border configuration and coordination*. (Indeed, from this perspective, every organization stands to gain something by thinking of itself as a network.) Thus, as Toyota has progressed through the various regional strategy archetypes (boxes 1 through 6 in figure 5-3), new modes of cross-border value creation have supplemented old ones instead of substituting for them—as Toyota's own figure 5-2 indicates.

Consider the numbered components of figure 5-2 in sequence. While Toyota has moved beyond a Japanese manufacturing base (regional focus), exports from Japanese manufacturing facilities to the rest of the world continue to account for more than one-quarter of its volume and a significantly larger share of its profits. Similarly, although Toyota has moved beyond a regional portfolio approach, concerns about protectionism and home bias of the sort that motivated the first investments in the United States still abound and are reflected in ads that highlight its record of job creation and environmental friendliness.

In terms of regional hubs, the ones in North America and Asia are relatively mature (if still growing), but the loss-making European operations are still being built up. In addition, the promotion of Katsuaki Watanabe, a production and procurement specialist, to succeed Fujio Cho as president signals an increased concern about, and commitment to, deep transplantation of the Toyota Production System from Japan to the newer production hubs at a time when overseas production is being ramped up rapidly. Toyota also continues to work to reduce its major production platforms and to pursue additional specialization through interregional mandates. So it is not so much that Toyota has progressed through the six regional strategy archetypes in figure 5-3 as it is that Toyota is now trying to cover all six boxes.

Second, Toyota's ability to pull all this off—to employ a range of regional strategies to create value—is inseparable from the basic competitive advantage mentioned earlier: the Toyota Production System's ability to produce high-quality, reliable cars at low costs. Without a fundamental advantage of this sort, some of the more complex modes of coordination that Toyota is attempting might well drown in a sea of red ink.

And finally, as noted above, Toyota's starting point is not a grand, longer-term vision of some distant globality when autos and auto parts can flow freely from anywhere to anywhere. Rather, the company anticipates expanded free-trade agreements within the Americas, Europe, and East Asia, but not across them. Again, *regions* turn out to be the best unit for expressing and implementing this more modest—but realistic—vision of a semiglobalized world in which neither the bridges nor the barriers between countries can be ignored.

Before finishing this section, take a couple of minutes to assess the potential for regional strategies for your company by working through the diagnostic in the box "Regionalization Potential Diagnostic."

Regionalization Potential Diagnostic

Circle one response to each of the eight questions that follow. If you are very uncertain about a particular response, just skip that question. Note that the scaling of the quantitative responses is approximate, even though it generally has some (rough) basis in the data.

Company Footprint

1. Number of countries with significant operations:
       (a) 1–5   (b) 6–15   (c) >15
2. Percentage of sales from home region:
       (a) > 80   (b) 50–80   (c) <50

Company Strategy

3. Objective for interregional dispersion:
       (a) decrease   (b) maintain   (c) increase
4. Number of bases of aggregation to be pursued:
       (a) 1   (b) 2   (c) >2

Country Linkages

5. Percentage of trade that is intraregional:
       (a) < 50   (b) 50–70   (c) >70
6. Percentage of FDI that is intraregional:
       (a) <40   (b) 40–60   (c) >60

Competitive Considerations

7. Differences in profitability across regions:
       (a) small   (b) short run   (c) long run
8. Key competitors' strategies:
       (a) deregionalizing   (b) unchanged   (c) regionalizing

The scoring is similarly rough-and-ready. Give yourself –1 for each (a) answer, 0 for each (b) answer, and +1 for each (c) answer, and then add them up. A positive score indicates a significant potential for strategy at the regional level. The higher the score, the greater the potential.

From Regionalization to Aggregation

Thinking through a range of regional strategies—both their attractions and their limitations—is a useful way of analyzing aggregation possibilities. But aggregation actually offers a broader canvas for companies thinking about how to tap greater economies of scale across national borders.

Rescaling Regions

While most of my examples up to this point have implied definitions at the continental level, I have avoided providing any clear definition of the term *region*. The goal was not to be elusive, but to avoid unduly specializing the argument by restricting the term to a particular geographic scale. Given large enough national units, the logic of the different archetypes can carry over from international to intranational regions. For example, the oil companies divide the market for gasoline in the United States into five intranational regions. Similarly, one can look at regional opportunities in contexts as diverse as cement in Brazil or beer in China, where transport costs are relatively high in relation to product value, and markets geographically extensive. And we can step up from the continental level rather than down. If a transatlantic free-trade agreement ever came to fruition—and there are many reasons it might not—this would create a superregion accounting for over 55 percent of the world's GDP. Such a region would, in some industries at least, become *the* focus of strategy development efforts.

This is also the appropriate place to mention the multilevel geographic aggregation schemes that a number of companies practice. Thus, drinks company Diageo is organized in terms of four regions: North America, Europe, Asia Pacific, and International, which consists of Africa, Latin America and the Caribbean, and Global Travel and Middle East "hubs." Note that the inclusion of Global Travel (duty-free) is a reminder that irregular or asymmetric structures may be more practical than the aesthetically pleasing (and, in some respects, simpler) symmetry that our discussion thus far has implied.

The broader point is that there are different geographic levels at which one can interpret the essentially geographic archetypes discussed in the previous section. Assessing the level—global, continental, subcontinental, national, intranational, or local—at which scale is most tightly tied to profitability is often a helpful guide to appropriate geographic scaling. Put differently, the world economy is made up of many overlapping layers—from local to global—and the point is not to focus on one layer, but to think in terms of the multiple layers. Geographic rescaling fosters flexibility by helping adapt ideas about regionalization to different geographic levels of analysis.

Aggregating Along Other CAGE Dimensions

In addition to rescaling geographic distance, one can be even more creative and focus on distance—and regions—along nongeographic dimensions: cultural, administrative or political, and economic. Aggregation along these other dimensions of the CAGE framework will sometimes still imply a focus on geographically contiguous regions. (Toyota's grouping of countries by existing or expected free-trade areas is a case in point.) At other times, though, such redefinition will yield pseudo-regions that aren't geographically compact.

An example of *cultural* aggregation is provided by Tata Consultancy Services (TCS), the largest Indian software services firm, which operates in more than thirty-five countries around the world. While later chapters will discuss TCS more fully, here we will consider the regional delivery centers—meant to supplement its global delivery centers in India and China—that it has pioneered. In 2002, TCS established a regional delivery center in Montevideo, Uruguay, and later set up one in Brazil, to serve not just Latin America, but also Spain and Portugal. TCS followed this up with a regional delivery center in Hungary—where many people speak German as a second language—that focuses on markets in Central Europe. And the company is currently exploring the possibility of establishing a center in Morocco, where there are many French speakers, with an eye to serving France and other Francophone countries. Aggregation on the basis of language is particularly attractive to TCS since linguistic distance matters a great deal in its business.

In the *administrative* realm, we can look to the example of Raytheon's "Commonwealth marketing group." Several years back, this Massachusetts-based defense contractor decided that the British Commonwealth was a logical organizational basis on which to organize its marketing to clients in those countries. Part of the rationale was that many of these countries shared similar procurement procedures and practices.

As for *economic* aggregation, the most obvious examples are companies that distinguish between developed and emerging markets and, at the extreme, focus on one or the other. Thus, after its first foreign direct investment in Spain, Mexico's Cemex grew through the rest of the 1990s by aggregating along the *economic* dimension. That is, the company expanded into other emerging markets that shared similarities with its home base, such as a significant volume of cement sold in bags, with the intent of creating a "ring of grey gold" circling the globe close to the equator. (In the last few years, though, Cemex has started to pay more attention to aggregation on a geographic basis, which seems to make sense, given the salience of geographic distance in its industry.) And many financial institutions that operate in both developed and emerging markets house the latter in a separate part of the organization.

It is worth adding that a number of companies with significant international and interregional operations are investing significantly in modern mapping technology to visualize new definitions of regions and pseudo-regions. This technology is backed up by enhanced clustering techniques; better measures for analyzing networks; expanded data on bilateral, multilateral, and unilateral country attributes, and so on. At the very least, this sort of mapping sparks creativity and therefore deserves to be taken seriously.

Aggregating on Noncountry Bases

The CAGE framework naturally focuses attention on countries (or other geographic units, broadly defined) as the basis for grouping. But there are many other, noncountry bases of cross-border aggregation that companies have implemented: channels (e.g., Cisco, which also aggregates by type of partners); client industries (e.g., Accenture and many other IT service companies); global accounts (e.g., Citicorp in its corporate banking business); and, most obviously and most intensively studied, businesses (e.g., global business units at Procter & Gamble, among many other companies).

Each of these aggregation schemes makes particular sense under certain conditions—and carries its own risks. Thus, global account management has attracted considerable attention in a business-to-business context as a way of providing customers with a single point of contact, coordination, and standardization.[17] But it raises a host of concerns: potential increases in the bargaining power of customers designated as global accounts, difficulties in managing local accounts alongside global ones, and the risk of creating consumer silos. And aggregation by business is particularly attractive for diversified companies for which the differences across businesses often loom even larger than the differences across countries, suggesting that businesses should constitute the primary basis of pursuing cross-border economies of scale. But once again there are risks that must, at a minimum, be managed. In this case, the risk is that business silos might compromise economies of scope that cut across businesses.

To summarize, aggregation represents a potentially powerful way of going beyond country-by-country adaptation strategies. And each basis of aggregation offers multiple possibilities for crafting strategies intermediate to the local and global levels by grouping things (although regions were the only basis for grouping that was looked at in detail in this chapter). That said, aggregation is no panacea, for several reasons. First, aggregation always carries the risk of creating silos that disrupt organizational functioning. Second, aggregation also tends to increase organizational complexity, given all the linking mechanisms that it necessitates—especially when aggregation is attempted along multiple dimensions rather than just one. Third, since it is usually impossible to implement all imaginable forms of aggregation, it is important to select among them—a task aided by the analytical frameworks developed in chapters 2 and 3. And fourth, frequent shuffling of bases of aggregation is almost invariably a recipe for disaster since it tends to take years to make a basis of aggregation work. The last two points will be addressed in the next two sections.

Analyzing Aggregation

Since aggregation is essentially an organizational response to the challenges of dealing with differences, it needs to flow from a clear sense of the company's strategy—and that strategy has to be anchored in the realities of the industry (or industries) that a company operates in and the value creation opportunities that it affords. So, both the CAGE distance framework and the ADDING Value scorecard are often useful in guiding cross-border choices about how to aggregate. The role of the CAGE framework in helping select among possible bases of aggregation has already been discussed, so this section will focus on applying the ADDING Value scorecard to two examples discussed in the previous section: TCS's decision to open up a second region, and P&G's reconsideration, in the late 1990s, of the role of regions in its global strategy.

I had a chance to observe TCS firsthand as it decided whether to open up regional delivery centers in Latin America. The major drawback TCS faced was the recognition that cost levels would be higher than in India because of higher local salaries, (initially) subscale operations, and various liabilities of foreignness. But that consideration was not decisive: TCS had to weigh it against a stack of benefits from adding a Latin American leg to the organization, as opposed to just continuing to expand in India (table 5-1). I will elaborate on the benefits shaded in gray, which TCS's management team considered particularly important.

First, TCS's strategy called for an increasing focus on larger, more sophisticated deals. However, in at least some cases, the large global clients signing such outsourcing deals had begun to prefer one vendor (or a few) with delivery centers in the multiple locations where they wanted work done—or with capabilities that spanned multiple languages and time zones. An early validation of this intent came when ABN-Amro selected TCS for a €200-million worldwide outsourcing contract—the largest IT services deal won up to that point by an Indian competitor—at least partly on the basis of its delivery centers in Latin America, an important region for the client.

Second, the Latin American delivery centers helped TCS try to position itself as the provider of "one global service standard" around the world. While large Western competitors such as Accenture had much more ex-

TABLE 5-1

TCS's decision to open regional delivery centers in Latin America

Value Components	Comments
Adding volume	+ Latin American business
	++ Large global deals requiring Latin American component
Decreasing costs	− Higher absolute costs in Latin America
	+ Indian costs rising
Differentiating, or increasing willingness-to-pay	+ Language advantages
	+ Time zone advantages
	++ Targeting provision of "one global service standard"
Improving industry attractiveness	+ Ability to counter multinational companies' claims that TCS is not global
	+ Prospect of seizing sustainable lead over Indian competitors
Normalizing risk	+ Reduction in "India risk"
Generating and upgrading resources, including knowledge	+ Buzz
	++ Multiculturalism
	++ Attempt to propagate delivery capabilities internationally

tensive global delivery networks, the service quality of those networks was considered inconsistent, given their reliance on local partners.

Third, and related to the first two points, the Latin American delivery centers helped generate substantial buzz around TCS's trademarked Global Network Delivery Model. In a 2006 *New York Times* column devoted to TCS's Latin American operations, Thomas Friedman wrote:

TCS Iberoamerica can't hire workers fast enough. When I visited its head office, people were working on computers in hallways and stairwells . . . It turns out that many multinationals like the idea of spreading out their risks and not having all their outsourcing done from India . . . The firm runs on strict Tata principles, as if it were in Mumbai, so to see Uruguayans pretending to be Indians serving Americans is quite a scene . . . [I]n today's world having an Indian company led by a Hungarian-Uruguayan [Gabriel Rozman, head of TCS's Latin American operations] servicing American banks with Montevidean engineers managed by Indian technologists who have learned to eat Uruguayan veggie is just the new normal.[18]

Fourth, as the last part of that quote suggests, the move fit with the intent of injecting additional multiculturalism into a company that did more than 90 percent of its business outside India but whose staff was more than 90 percent Indian.

Finally, and perhaps most important, was the idea of trying to propagate the company's delivery capabilities internationally. Given the increasingly tight market for software developers in India—discussed in more detail in chapter 6—developing an ability to achieve the same high delivery standards out of other locations was potentially a game-changing move.

These benefits and the others listed in table 5-1 were enough to overcome the concerns about higher costs. So this example should serve as a reminder of the usefulness of the comprehensive coverage—including qualitative as well as quantitative elements—encouraged by the ADDING Value scorecard.

A second illustration concerns P&G's reconsideration, under CEOs Durk Jager and A. G. Lafley, of the role of regions in its global strategy. P&G spent much of the 1980s and 1990s replacing country-centered organizations with more of a regional apparatus, particularly in Europe. But at the end of the 1990s, an increased emphasis on innovation and quicker global rollouts led to a shift to global business units as the primary basis of aggregation. Chapter 7 discusses the organization structure that resulted, but it is important to mention that P&G didn't entirely lose sight of regions; instead, it refocused its attention on the elements where regional economies of scale were strongest, along the lines suggested by table 5-2, which characterizes the economics of a representative fast-moving consumer good (FMCG) business.

Note from the table that the big regional economies of scale are in manufacturing and, to a lesser extent, general overhead; marketing support, often the focus of discussions about whether or not to standardize, comes in third. These simplified numbers focus attention on just the first two components of the ADDING Value scorecard, but they suffice to explain why P&G's aggregation efforts in Europe have involved supplying multicountry subregions through megafactories and clustering countries (e.g., Belgium and the Netherlands, the Iberian Peninsula, the Nordic countries, and the United Kingdom and Ireland) so as to reduce overhead.

Of course, the changes at P&G (and those described earlier at Toyota) also suggest the need for sequencing instead of either myopia or a "one aggregation choice for the ages" approach. Shifts to new structures or coordinating devices may be required to deal with problems created by old ones—but the pace of change is slow! For this reason, it is important to think things through ahead of time instead of treating aggregation as a

TABLE 5-2

Regional economies of scale: an illustration

	Brand A (regional brand) (millions of euros)	Brand B (sum of local brands) (millions of euros)
Total turnover	100	100
Manufacturing cost	40	48
Transport		(3)
Marketing support	10	12
Trade support	10	10
R&D	4	5
General and administrative	10	13
Profit	26	15

Source: Leading fast-moving consumer good (FMCG) company.

choice that is freely variable, as the example discussed in the next section will highlight.

Managing Aggregation

The range of possible bases of aggregation may suggest a fairly freewheeling approach to selecting among them. But making a basis of aggregation work usually requires a commitment to it over a number of years—often, in large companies, for the better part of a decade.

For a cautionary example along these lines, consider the case of ABB, a multinational corporation formed in 1988 by the merger of electrical equipment and machinery manufacturers Asea of Sweden and Brown Boveri of Switzerland. ABB's organization design, according to one authority, "probably received more attention in the 1990s than was given to all other MNEs [multinational enterprises] combined, both from the business press and from academics."[19] Given the reams written about ABB in what are now many different contexts, I will simply provide the briefest characterization of the shifting bases of aggregation at ABB since the late 1980s—shifts that are summarized in table 5-3 (which is *not* drawn to temporal scale) and are described in a bit more detail below.

After the merger of Asea and Brown Boveri, ABB's new CEO, Percy Barnevik, decided to break up the bureaucracy and geographic fiefdoms he had inherited. He flattened the organization and fragmented the company's

TABLE 5-3

Shifting bases of aggregation at ABB

	CEO OR ERA					
Premerger (up to 1988)	Barnevik (1988–1993)	Barnevik (1993–1998)	Lindahl (1998–2001)	Centerman (2001–2002)	Dormann (2002–2004)	Kindle (2004–?)
Countries	• Business areas	• Business areas	• Business areas	• Technol- ogies	• Core divisions	• Business areas*
	• Countries	• Countries	• Countries	• Customer industries		• Countries
		• Regions	• Global accounts			• Regions

*Effective January 1, 2006.

businesses into small, local operating companies that would report both to a country manager and to a business area manager ("the matrix"). And in 1993, Barnevik added a regional overlay to the geographic dimension of the matrix by clustering countries into three regions.

Critical to making this structure was the establishment of a common management information system that reported data on seven parameters personally reviewed by Barnevik for each of what eventually became two thousand profit centers. The modularized interfaces also facilitated the digestion of additional acquisitions and the reconfiguration of business areas over time. But the number of profit centers combined with modest profitability and further acquisitions to sow the seeds for a fundamental crisis later on in the decade.

After ten years of relative stability at the macro-organizational level, the pace of organizational change heated up at ABB as the Asian crisis, in particular, started to expose problems with the company's structure and strategy. Barnevik's successor as CEO, Goran Lindahl, removed the regional overlay as being too costly and tried to move ABB toward a three-dimensional structure in which a global account management structure was overlaid on top of Barnevik's original business area and country matrix.

External pressures on ABB continued to mount, however. In addition to the demand slowdown after the Asian crisis, there were challenges associated with marketing systems that integrated products from different business areas or for which the key customers were global or regional, not local. And there were other problems associated with what continued to be very autonomous local companies. In 2001, new CEO Jorgen Center-

man responded by replacing the matrix with a front-end/back-end organization that was intended to make ABB a "knowledge-based company."
Specifically, four main customer or front-facing units, defined by customer industry rather than geography, were supposed to enhance ABB's
capabilities for creating value for global and regional customers in particular. And they were to be linked to two back-end technological units,
Power Technologies and Automation Technologies, that were supposed to
integrate technology development across the businesses in ABB's two main
areas of technological competency.

Centerman was forced out in 2002, as ABB teetered at the edge of bankruptcy because of a continuing demand slowdown, pressures associated
with billions of dollars' worth of asbestos-related liabilities inadvertently
picked up in the United States with the acquisition (under Barnevik) of Com-
bustion Engineering, and the sluggishness of the new organization. Chairman Jurgen Dormann, who took over as CEO, dismantled the front-end/
back-end organization, sold off portions of the front end, and aggregated
the remaining business areas into two core divisions, Power Systems and
Automation.

The last few years at ABB have, under Dormann and his successor as
CEO, Fred Kindle, seen a focus on business and financial restructuring to
clean up the problems that resulted from the prior period of overly rapid
growth and shifts in the bases of aggregation. Aided by improvements in
the external environment as well as internally, the company finally does
seem to have recovered from the pressures that came to a head in the
early 2000s: sales are finally close to levels posted in the late 1990s, with
only one-half the head count. And recently the company has disaggregated the two core divisions into the five business areas that composed
them as well as regrouped the countries into regions, which have their
own profit-and-loss statements. The matrix is back!

The ABB saga is extremely rich in implications for organization design in
general and managing aggregation in particular. Consider just half a dozen:

1. There is no perfect aggregation scheme for abolishing the integration-
   responsiveness trade-off, despite the claims that were made about
   Barnevik's original implementation of the matrix. This conclusion
   is only amplified by the recognition that none of the schemes described above really addressed the challenges of arbitrage—which
   GE, to cite a company that ABB once considered its arch-rival, pursued much more effectively (see chapter 7) and which is discussed
   at length in the next chapter. More generally, bursts of optimism
   about new approaches to the problems of complex organizations
   should be tempered with the realization that the hunt for an

all-purpose organizational structure represents a triumph of hope over experience.

2. Despite the drawbacks of any aggregation scheme, the challenge of aggregating across multiple dimensions clearly remains an important and interesting one. The strategic challenge is magnified by the number of possible bases of aggregation, many of which ABB tried out over a short time span. The focus on a particular subset of the possible bases of aggregation should, ideally, be chosen for well-thought-out reasons rather than on the basis of unjustified assumptions.

3. Even more important than the number of dimensions of aggregation one selects is how effectively one manages them. It is easy to think of three or even four successful dimensional matrixes, (particularly in the information technology or IT sector), as well as cases where companies have been challenged to manage even a single dimension of aggregation effectively. Appropriate linking mechanisms that go well beyond the formal structure are very important in this regard. In addition, despite ABB's recent reversion to a matrix structure, there is an emerging sense, rooted in the experience of many large companies (e.g., Philips prior to CEO Boonstra, as described in chapter 4), that when a company *does* pursue multiple bases of aggregation, putting more than one of them on the same plane can be a recipe for gridlock. In other words, a pecking order often seems necessary.

4. Shallow analogies sometimes play a more important role in the choice of aggregation approaches than they should. Consider the shortest-lived aggregation scheme at ABB, Centerman's institution of a front-end/back-end structure in apparent emulation of IT companies. ABB's shift to this organizational structure does not seem to have properly accounted for the differences between it and them. Many of the IT companies served a broader range of industry verticals, arguably enhancing their need to explicitly span and aggregate across this dimension. And most of them moved to the front-end/back-end structure from a functional structure—an easier transition than the one at ABB, for reasons described next.

5. Appropriate choice among aggregation approaches requires analysis—analysis that attends to industry dynamics, company history, and company performance. Thus, the matrix came under pressure at ABB because of industry dynamics—the slowdown in demand, pricing pressures, and the increasing emphasis induced for global

integration as opposed to local responsiveness. ABB's history militated against the shift to the front-end/back-end structure in the sense that ABB was starting out with a business organization that would have to be chopped up into functions. In contrast, the barebones divisional structure into which Dormann aggregated distinct business areas arguably *did* make sense, given the urgency of restructuring.

6. In the long term, the single most powerful criterion for selecting bases of aggregation is the enhancement of the competitive advantage that is being targeted through cross-border operations (see chapter 7 for additional discussion). Embedding the primary bases of aggregation in the formal organizational structure is a necessary, but insufficient, condition for such enhancement. And pushing boxes around on the organizational chart should be done only from an urgent sense of necessity: the costs, in terms of time lags in changing organization behavior, disruption, and the like, are very high. We can learn from the contrast between ABB's hyperactivity and, for instance, Toyota's constancy or P&G's focus on making aggregation on a regional basis work for the better part of two decades before it shifted to a primary emphasis on global business units.

Conclusions

The box "Global Generalizations" summarizes the specific conclusions from this chapter. More broadly, aggregation further expands our strategy toolkit for dealing with the differences across countries. However, aggregation has its limits. Like adaptation, it still focuses on exploiting the similarities across countries as sources of value creation—that is, aggregation treats differences across countries as constraints. Yet, examples such as TCS remind us that differences, at least along selected dimensions, can also be powerful sources of value creation potential, rather than just a problem. The next chapter digs deeper into this point: it focuses on arbitrage as the third of our three As for broadening thinking about global strategy.

Global Generalization

1. Not only does the world remain regionalized in many respects—a manifestation of semiglobalization—but, along at least some dimensions, the levels of regionalization have been increasing rather than decreasing.

2. An overwhelming majority of companies, including the largest ones, still derive the bulk of their sales from their home region. And even very successful companies with significant operations in multiple regions (e.g., Toyota) often rely on regions as their primary bases of aggregation.

3. There are a number of distinct regional strategies rather than just one: regional focus, regional portfolios, regional hubs, regional platforms, regional mandates, and regional networks.

4. Regions or pseudo-regions can be defined in terms of CAGE dimensions other than the geographic one.

5. Regions themselves represent just one basis of cross-border aggregation; others include channels, client industries, global customers, and—particularly important for diversified companies—global business units or product divisions.

6. Aggregation schemes attempt to reduce within-group differences and, for that very reason, risk missing out on cross-group interactions.

7. The pursuit of multiple bases of aggregation greatly increases complexity—and often requires some kind of pecking order to work.

8. The CAGE framework and the ADDING Value scorecard can be very helpful in selecting bases of aggregation, although it is also important to recognize the importance of sequencing.

9. Rapid reshuffling of the bases of aggregation is usually a recipe for poor performance; putting a basis of aggregation into practice usually takes years in large, complex organizations.

6

Arbitrage

Exploiting Differences

*Globalization is about producing where it is most cost
effective, sourcing capital from where it's cheapest
and selling it where it is most profitable.*

—N. R. Narayana Murthy, Infosys, August 2003

THE THIRD OF OUR AAA STRATEGIES for dealing with distances
and crossing borders successfully is *arbitrage*. Arbitrage is a way of *exploiting*
differences. It implies seeking *absolute* economies, rather than the scale
economies gained through standardization. It treats differences across borders as opportunities, not as constraints.

This chapter begins by underscoring the absolute importance of arbitrage. It then uses the CAGE framework to unpack the cultural, administrative, geographic, and economic bases of arbitrage. To illustrate the
variety of arbitrage strategies, I use a complex case drawn from the pharmaceutical industry, where both the administrative and economic bases
of arbitrage are important. The chapter concludes with further discussion of
how to use the ADDING Value scorecard to analyze arbitrage, and of some
of the managerial challenges that arise in exploiting arbitrage opportunities.

The Absolute Importance of Arbitrage

Arbitrage, of course, is the original cross-border strategy. Many of the great traders throughout history got their start by trading luxuries that were subject to extreme differences in absolute costs and availability. Thus, Europe's spice trade with India developed because spices could (initially) be sold in Europe for several hundred times what they cost in India. Furs and fish that were abundantly available only in North America helped create a transatlantic trade and, incidentally, led to the colonization of that continent. Similar, essentially geographic differences drove the global whaling fleets of the late eighteenth century (which, with their floating factory ships, can be said to have originated offshore manufacturing), as well as the vertically integrated agricultural and mining companies that emerged early in the nineteenth century.

The freestanding enterprises that dominated British foreign direct investment at the end of the nineteenth century attempted to arbitrage across differences in administrative structure (and power) by pursuing foreign investment opportunities under British law. Additionally, exports of light manufactures (e.g., garments) became important in the nineteenth century. These, too, involved arbitrage, but it was an arbitrage across *economic* differences, rather than geographic or administrative ones.

Despite this long history, arbitrage is often glossed over in contemporary discussions of globalization and strategy. Take Wal-Mart, for example: most of the general discussion about its internationalization revolves around its international store network. Wal-Mart has more than 2,200 international stores, which together generated $63 billion in sales (one-fifth of the company total) and $3.3 billion in operating income (closer to one-sixth of the total) in 2006. What attracts significantly less attention is Wal-Mart's global sourcing effort, particularly from China. In 2004, the company claimed to buy about $18 billion worth of goods directly from China, not counting merchandise in its stores obtained indirectly from there via suppliers. Even if one takes just the $18 billion figure and applies the usual estimates of how much that reduces Wal-Mart's costs, the implied savings approach $3 billion—that is, they are comparable to the operating income generated by the international stores, but on a much smaller investment base.[1] And going by the results of a store check I conducted in a small sample of Wal-Mart stores in 2004, Wal-Mart's *total* procurement, direct and indirect, of Chinese-made goods may be two to three times as much as this official figure, implying that savings from sourcing from China are substantially greater than the operating income from the international stores! In that sense, buying Chinese goods cheaply and reselling them at a profit in the United States is a far more important part of Wal-Mart's cross-border strategy than its international store network.

As a second example—one concerning a company that should have paid more attention to arbitrage sooner than it did—consider the sad case of Lego, the Denmark-based manufacturer of children's building blocks and associated paraphernalia. Lego's performance began to suffer in the late 1990s due to excessive diversification and aggressive competition in its core business, particularly from Canada-based Mega Brands, Inc., which started to sell much cheaper blocks (MEGA Bloks) sourced from China. But Lego continued injection-molding its own blocks in Denmark and Switzerland, which resulted in products that were up to 75 percent more expensive and inferior in financial performance (figure 6-1).[2] Lego's performance has since rebounded as it has refocused on its core business and outsourced most of its production to contract manufacturer Flextronics, which is moving production offshore. However, Lego faces a much more serious, established competitor in MEGA Brands—in a category that Lego created and of which it was the namesake.

These examples suggest an asymmetry between the attention devoted—by commentators and sometimes even managers—to arbitrage opportunities versus other reasons for extending operations across borders. There

FIGURE 6-1

MEGA Brands versus Lego

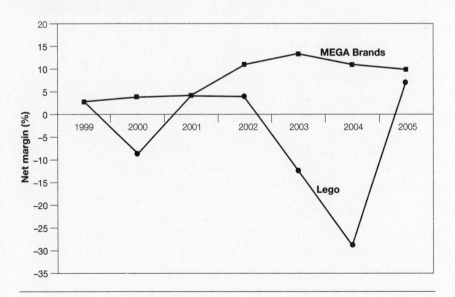

are multiple reasons why arbitrage often doesn't get the attention that it deserves—and they need to be identified before they can be corrected.

First, there seems to be a general sense that the activities underlying the traditional forms of arbitrage—hunting, fishing, farming, digging, weaving, and so on—are, well, *backward*. When it comes to the glamorous task of making money across borders, haven't we progressed beyond hunting and gathering? If you are inclined to agree, think harder about what it actually *means* to purchase tens of billions of dollars of goods a year from China—in a world in which distance still matters—and to use them to feed a lean-mean sales machine in the United States. This challenge and opportunity has led Wal-Mart's Global Procurement Center in Shenzhen, China, to develop some very sophisticated capabilities.

Second, there is a belief that arbitraging fundamental factors, such as capital or labor, offers only limited opportunities for competitive advantage.[3] After all, can't these factors be sourced globally at the click of a mouse, rendering them a weak competitive reed to lean upon? My response is to point to the reality of semiglobalization discussed earlier in this book, particularly in chapter 1, as well as the implication that even apparently unspecialized factors such as labor and capital *are* specialized at the level of location (even if in no other way). Sourcing from China by many companies, including Wal-Mart, hasn't yet lifted Chinese labor costs to U.S. levels and is unlikely to do so for decades—although it *has* played a role in raising them. I will return to this issue of sustainability in the last section of this chapter.

A third stereotype, related to the second one, involves the notion that the profit potential from arbitrage is quite limited. My response? Look at the above calculations concerning Wal-Mart or at other sectors, such as Indian software services, which I discuss at greater length later on. For now, note that TCS, the Indian leader, has averaged a return on capital employed of more than 100 percent over the last five years while growing revenues at a 30 percent-plus rate. Although TCS is beginning to aggregate at a regional level, its core strategy has historically been one of labor arbitrage.

Fourth—and this gets to the issue of why companies don't do more to talk up arbitrage opportunities even when they recognize them—there is a great deal of political sensitivity about arbitrage, particularly labor arbitrage, even though it is happening all around us. One does not have to be a conspiracy theorist to guess that this has something to do with the claim by Wal-Mart—a company with a supply chain and information systems unmatched in its industry—not to know the total volume of goods from China flowing through its store network. Again, the management of this challenge, among others, will be discussed at more length later in this chapter.

Finally, much of the discussion about arbitrage focuses—as did the Wal-Mart example—on obtaining labor-intensive goods (or services) from emerging markets and selling them in developed ones. This is a very important form of arbitrage, but it is far from the only one. If we are to give arbitrage its due, then we have to broaden our view of it.

One way to stretch our thinking about arbitrage possibilities is to cite exotic examples. Let's consider some, mostly from recent headlines. Zhang Yin, the world's richest self-made woman, with a net worth of over $3 billion, got her start importing waste paper from the United States and recycling it.[4] Bumrungrad Hospital in Thailand, a pioneer in medical tourism, annually treats close to half a million foreign patients in its five-star facilities.[5] A number of East European countries also attract many patients across borders in distinct specialties: the Czech Republic in cosmetic surgery, Latvia in knee surgery, Hungary in dentistry, and Slovenia in fertility treatments.[6] Portuguese investors are contemplating building enormous retirement complexes for wealthier North Europeans.[7] About 3,500 very wealthy individuals from all over the world have become Swiss citizens to benefit from local laws that set tax payments as a multiple of housing costs, without accounting for foreign wealth and income.[8] LanChile has outperformed the averages for the airline industry with a strategy that capitalizes on Chilean exports of perishables such as salmon, fruit, and flowers: cargo accounts for 40 percent of its revenues, compared with 5 percent or less for large U.S. carriers.[9] Some of Africa's better boarding schools in countries such as Ghana, Kenya, and South Africa draw students, mostly of African extraction, from overseas.[10] Remittances from emigrants account for more than 20 percent of GNP in a number of small countries, such as Moldova and Nicaragua.[11] And importing used cars is a bigger business, in terms of number of vehicles, than the new-car business in countries as diverse as Bulgaria, Jamaica, New Zealand, and Nigeria.[12]

CAGE and Arbitrage

The preceding examples all represent departures from—or at least variations on—the usual notion of low-cost manufactures from emerging markets being sold in developed ones. In particular, a number of examples illustrate the increasing incidence of cross-border arbitrage in services. But they do have a motley character. For a more comprehensive perspective on arbitrage, look at it through the lens of the CAGE framework since each type of difference between countries highlights a potential basis for arbitrage.[13]

Cultural Arbitrage

Favorable effects related to country or place of origin have long supplied a basis for cultural arbitrage. For example, French culture or, more specifically, its image overseas has long underpinned the international success of French haute couture, perfumes, wines, and foods.

But cultural arbitrage can also be applied to newer, more plebeian products and services. Consider, for example, the extraordinary international dominance of U.S.-based fast-food chains, which, at the end of the 1990s, accounted for twenty-seven of the top thirty fast-food chains worldwide and for over 60 percent of global fast-food sales.[14] In their international operations, these chains exploit—to varying degrees—the global spread of American popular culture by serving up slices of Americana (at least as it's perceived locally) along with their food. An even more extreme example is supplied by Benihana of Tokyo, the "Japanese steakhouse." Although there was a predecessor outlet in Tokyo, the company's Web site lists its first restaurant as opening on Broadway in New York. Benihana serves up a theatrical version of teppan-yaki cooking that the company describes as "eatertainment" and others as ersatz Japanese—and still has only one outlet in Japan, out of more than one hundred worldwide (heavily focused on the United States).

Nor are such "country-of-origin" advantages reserved for rich nations. Poor countries, too, can be important platforms for cultural arbitrage. Examples include Haitian compas music, Jamaican reggae, and dance music from the Congo, all of which enjoy image advantages in their respective regions.

We often hear claims that the scope for cultural arbitrage is decreasing over time, as the world becomes more consistently "vanilla." But this clearly does not apply to all countries and product categories, as attested to by the launch of a number of successful place-branding consultancies in recent years. Or to be more specific, the persistent association of Brazil with football, carnival, beaches, and sex—all of which scream youth—is a case of cultural-arbitrage potential that companies have just begun to recognize. Thus, Inbev of Belgium, the world's largest brewer in terms of volume, is now taking Brazil's Brahma beer global—although the export version has a different formulation from the Brazilian one, a fancier bottle, and a premium positioning. According to Devin Kelley, Inbev's vice president for global brands, Inbev saw the beer as a product that captured the essence of Brazil—even before considering what it tasted like. "The emotional context of Brahma, at the heart and soul of this incredible country called Brazil, was the single most important factor."[15]

In fact, new opportunities for cultural arbitrage are appearing all the time. Thus, the push by the European Union to tighten rules for geographical designations on food products such as "Parma ham" and "Cognac brandy" would reinforce the natural advantages of particular countries or places of origin. What's more, as Finland's recently developed reputation for excellence in information technology indicates, in certain product categories, such advantages can now be created much faster than before: in years rather than decades or centuries. Meanwhile, reductions in other dimensions of the CAGE differences—tariffs or transport costs, for example—can also increase the viability of cultural arbitrage. For example, selling products or services to diaspora based on "back-home" appeal has become easier than ever before.

Administrative Arbitrage

Legal, institutional, and political differences from country to country open up another set of strategic arbitrage opportunities. Tax differentials are, perhaps, the most obvious example. Through the 1990s, to cite just one case, Rupert Murdoch's News Corporation paid income taxes at an average rate of less than 10 percent, rather than the statutory 30 to 36 percent of the three main countries in which it operated: Britain, the United States, and Australia. By comparison, major competitors such as Disney were paying close to the official rates.

These tax savings were critical to News Corporation's expansion into the United States, given the profit pressures on the company: net margins consistently less than 10 percent of sales in the second half of the 1990s and an asset-to-sales ratio that had ballooned to three to one. By placing its U.S. acquisitions into holding companies in the Cayman Islands, News Corporation could deduct interest payments on the debt used to finance the deals against the profits generated by its newspaper operations in Britain. Overall, the company has incorporated approximately one hundred subsidiaries in havens with no or low corporate taxes and limited financial disclosure laws. The intangibility of its informational assets has helped in this regard. As one accounting authority put it, "There's absolutely no reason why a piece of paper, which is the right to show something, couldn't sit anywhere, so it could be sitting in the Cayman Islands."[16]

Most companies that cross borders do pay attention to international tax differentials and other administrative bases of arbitrage because of the large implications for value. However, they tend to be wary of discussing such considerations because the administrative gray areas that underpin them might substantially be curtailed or even eliminated. Thus, in a phenomenon known as round-tripping, many mainland Chinese businesspeople channel investment funds through foreign parties and then back into China, often through Hong Kong, in order to secure better legal protection, tax concessions, or otherwise favorable treatment. In fact, one-third or more of the FDI ostensibly flowing into China is estimated to have *originated* in China! And the tiny island nation of Mauritius (population 1.2 million) is, in most years, the top "source" of FDI flowing into India (population 1 billion) because of a tax treaty as well as, to a lesser extent, cultural links (two-thirds of Mauritians are of Indian extraction). More broadly, enclaves, tax havens, free-trade areas, export-processing zones, cross-border cities, and the like tend to be hot spots for administrative arbitrage. And some do very well out of it. The richest country in the world in 2006 was Bermuda, with an average GDP per person of almost $70,000, or 60 percent more than the average for the United States.

Much of what goes on under the rubric of administrative arbitrage is legal or at least semilegal—even when it has an odor to it, as in the relocation of economic activity, ranging from manufacturing activities to waste dumps, to exploit lax environmental rules. But cross-border criminal activity—drug production and distribution, human trafficking, illegal arms dealing, other forms of smuggling, counterfeiting, money laundering, to cite the major categories—also tends to involve some component of arbitrage, especially administrative arbitrage.[17] The size of such arbitrage opportunities helps explain why the cross-border component of total criminal activity probably exceeds the 10 percent presumption—although it is obviously impossible to be certain.

The kinds of companies discussed in this book tend to work within or around the rules instead of breaking them. They can and do, however, try to use their political leverage to change rules that they do not like. Thus, in late 2006, the Confederation of British Industry warned that the burden of taxation in the United Kingdom could cause an exodus of corporations—clearly a pitch for limiting taxes and compliance burdens.[18] A somewhat different kind of example is provided by companies using powerful home governments to pressure foreign governments into granting favorable treatment. Enron, for example, enlisted the help of the U.S. State Department, which obligingly threatened to cut off development assistance to Mozambique—one of the poorest countries in the world—if it granted a gas deal to a South African competitor instead of to an Enron-led consortium.

Sordid? Yes, especially since the story involves Enron. But such stories remind us that companies help shape the administrative rules of the game: that they can be rule makers instead of simply rule takers, and that power differentials—at the governmental level as well as the company level—matter.

Geographic Arbitrage

Considering all that has been said and written about the alleged "death of distance," it's not surprising that few strategy gurus take geographic arbitrage very seriously. Yes, it's true that transportation and communication costs have dropped sharply in the last few decades. But that drop does not necessarily translate into a decrease in the scope of geographic arbitrage strategies.

Consider the case of air transportation, the cost of which has declined more than 90 percent in real terms since 1930—a steeper drop than experienced by other, older modes of transportation over the same period. In fact, thanks to air transport, *new* opportunities for geographic arbitrage have been created. For example, in the international flower market in Aalsmeer, Netherlands, more than 20 million flowers and 2 million plants are auctioned off *every day,* with customers in the United States or Europe buying blooms flown in from, say, Colombia on the day they arrive. While this is a special example, the trade-related boom that transport companies—all of which can be thought of as geographic arbitrageurs—experienced between 2003 and 2006 reminds us that geographic distance still matters: if it didn't, they would be facing bleak futures. The example of LanChile emphasizing cargo has already been cited. Note that the boom also extends to purely domestic transporters—for example, U.S. railways carrying Chinese goods from West Coast ports to other parts of the country—since geographic distance continues to matter within as well as between countries.[19]

Although communication costs have dropped even more sharply than transportation costs, they haven't eliminated opportunities for geographically based arbitrage either. Thus, Cable & Wireless (C&W), the U.K.-based telecommunications company, generated 37 percent of its revenues but 74 percent of its earnings from its international operation in 2005–2006.[20] High international profits involve taking advantage of residual distance by serving thirty-three relatively small markets around the world—many of them islands, whose communications links with the outside world are still dominated by C&W.

In fact, the overall evolution of international telephony has been greatly influenced by administrative arbitrage over residual administrative distance, even as some of the effects of geographic distance have weakened. Basically, regulatory regimes that prop up prices have consistently lagged advances in technology. In the days of telecom monopolies, a customer living outside the United States might call a personal computer in the United States, which would then call back the customer and the destination number (in a third country) and connect them, taking advantage of typically lower U.S. outbound rates. And currently, services such as Skype arbitrage the difference between distance-sensitive, administered pricing of long-distance calls, and the distance-invariant costs of Internet protocol (IP) telephony.

The geographic arbitrageurs that *have* lost some ground in recent decades are the great general trading companies of the past, which traditionally took advantage of large international variations in prices for a broad array of products by getting them from country A to country B. Lower transportation costs and greater connectivity have made it much easier for manufacturers and retailers to exploit these opportunities themselves.

Nevertheless, the savviest trading companies have found ways of staying in business. Thus, instead of simply trading on its own account, Hong Kong–based Li & Fung derives most of its revenue from more sophisticated geographic (and economic) arbitrage. It uses its offices in forty countries to set up and manage multinational supply chains for clients—or what might better be described as supply nets. For example, a down jacket's filling might come from China, the outer shell fabric from Korea, the zippers from Japan, the inner lining from Taiwan, and the elastics, label, and other trim from Hong Kong. Dyeing might take place in South Asia, stitching in China, and quality assurance and packaging in Hong Kong. The product might then be shipped to the United States for delivery to a retailer such as The Limited or Abercrombie & Fitch, to which credit risk matching, market research, and even design services might also be provided.[21]

What's all this activity about? It's about creating multiple possibilities for arbitrage by slicing up the value chain ever more finely across geographies—or engaging in what economists have recently labeled "trade in tasks."[22] Thus, the major impact of decreasing transport and communications costs has not been on geographic arbitrage per se, but on the *scope* for economic arbitrage, which they have greatly increased and to which we turn next.

Economic Arbitrage

In a sense, all arbitrage strategies that add value are "economic." But I use the term here to refer to *the exploitation of economic differences that don't derive directly from cultural, administrative, or geographic differences.* These factors include differences in the costs of labor and capital, as well as variations in more industry-specific inputs (such as knowledge) or in the availability of complementary products.

The best-known type of economic arbitrage is the exploitation of cheap labor, which is common in labor-intensive, capital-light manufacturing (e.g., garments). What is worth emphasizing here is that high-tech companies can use that strategy just as effectively.

Consider the case of Embraer, the Brazilian firm that is one of the world's two major suppliers of regional jets. While many factors, including managerial and technical excellence, contribute to Embraer's success, labor arbitrage has also played a key role. To be specific, Embraer's employment costs came to $26,000 per employee in 2002, versus an estimated $63,000 for the regional jet business of its archrival, Montreal-based Bombardier. If Embraer had had Bombardier's employment cost structure, its operating margin would have fallen from 21 percent of revenues to 7 percent, and its net income would have turned negative. Not surprisingly, Embraer has focused its operations on final assembly, the most labor-intensive part of the production process, and has outsourced other operating activities to its supplier partners in richer countries with higher labor costs.[23] And labor arbitrage is also one of the bases of the challenge to Bombardier and Embraer being mounted by China Aviation Industry Corp I, a state-run manufacturing group, that is, with the help of a network of international suppliers, developing large regional jets to be offered at 10–20 percent lower list prices.[24]

Capital cost differentials might seem, at first blush, to offer slimmer pickings than labor cost differentials—after all, the former are measured in single percentage points rather than in multiples of up to ten or twenty like the latter. But most companies (at least in the United States) earn returns within two or three percentage points of their cost of capital, so such differences *are* consequential, especially in capital-intensive industries. The Cemex case supplies a potent example of arbitrage in financing (chapter 3).

While we generally focus on economic arbitrage in the context of operations and financing, it can also be exploited in other functional activities. Consider Starent Networks, a company founded in August 2000 in Tewksbury, Massachusetts, with the mission of switching wireless networks to all-IP (Internet protocol) telephony. Soon after its founding, the company ran into what founder Ashraf Dahod describes as the "nuclear winter" of the meltdown in the telecommunications sector.[25] The company survived—and thrived—by migrating its product development function to India. And Starent is far from an unusual example: more U.S. companies seem to have offshored product development than call centers or help desks, even though the offshoring of call centers and help desks has attracted much more attention.[26]

The preceding discussion rounds out our understanding of each of the four broad dimensions of distance embedded in the CAGE framework as a potential basis for arbitrage. Even more numerous than the bases for arbitrage are the variety of arbitrage strategies. To further broaden our thinking about arbitrage, let's consider a detailed example that illustrates this variety.

Varieties of Arbitrage: The Example of Indian Pharmaceuticals

When people think of the pharmaceutical industry, they typically think of "Big Pharma": a dozen-odd multinational firms headquartered in the United States and Europe that account for about one-half of the world-wide market in terms of value.[27] Big Pharma firms historically generated high returns by developing and marketing drugs protected by patents—particularly *blockbuster* drugs, defined as ones that generate more than $1 billion in annual revenues.

In recent years, however, Big Pharma has come under a great deal of pressure: Accenture calculates that the overall market value of the pharmaceutical sector—mostly accounted for by Big Pharma—dropped from more than $2 trillion in 2000 to less than $1.5 trillion by 2005.[28] Big Pharma's problems are various and include declining R&D productivity and general bloat. As my retired Harvard colleague Mike Scherer puts it, "[High] prices drive costs."[29] But the challenge I concentrate on here is that from copycat generic drugs. Although generics have long threatened drugs coming off patent, soaring drug costs and buyer consolidation, among other structural changes, have recently intensified their impact on branded pharmaceuticals. Thus, according to Medco Health Solutions, three big drugs that came off patent in 2005 had 87 percent of their prescriptions switched over to generics within *one* month.[30]

Generic drugs must meet the same quality standards as branded drugs, but are typically sold—after a six-month period of exclusivity for the first generic in the United States—at prices that are 20 to 80 percent lower than their branded counterparts. Generic drugs account for between 10 and 15 percent of the pharmaceutical market by value and significantly more by volume.[31] Moreover, they are thought likely to attack another 30 percent of the current market in the United States alone over the next five years, as key drugs go off patent.[32]

There are many generic-drug manufacturers worldwide—about 150 significant ones by one count. The largest, Teva of Israel, had $5.3 billion in sales in 2005. Teva's success is rooted in administrative arbitrage: according to Eli Hurvitz, who ran it for twenty-six years, it owes its existence to the Arab boycott of companies doing business with Israel.[33] In response, Israel let local companies copy drugs patented overseas if their owners didn't market them locally—which is how Teva built up its process expertise.

A similar administrative loophole underlies the success of a more recent wave of Indian challengers in generic drugs. Pharmaceutical manufacturing in India long reflected a policy that recognized process patents but not product patents, and thereby rewarded the reverse engineering of imported drugs. Since 2005, Indian patent laws have adjusted toward international norms as a result of the country's accession to the World Trade Organization (WTO). But because of this history, low labor costs and buyer willingness to pay, and cutthroat domestic competition, the larger Indian manufacturers have developed low-cost manufacturing capabilities that have let them build up a significant position in generic drugs. One indication is that Indian companies account for 25 percent of the Abbreviated New Drug Applications (ANDAs) filed with the U.S. Food and Drug Administration (FDA) to launch generic drugs. Very diverse strategies underlie this level of market penetration—even if one focuses just on the top ten Indian firms out of several thousand.

Some Indian firms have continued to focus on *imitating* drugs coming off patent or drugs that are still under patent in some places but can be marketed in other, unregulated markets. The first approach is the one traditionally followed by generic drugs competitors. The second approach is illustrated by the second-largest Indian pharmaceutical firm, Cipla. In 2000, Cipla announced generic anti-HIV antiretrovirals that reduced the annual price of treatment from $11,000 per patient to $400 per patient. Cipla's products are thought to account for one-third of the anti-HIV/AIDS medications taken in Africa, and the company stands to gain additional markets if other governments invoke WTO provisions that let them declare a national emergency and license the production or sale of drugs without the permission of the patent holders—as happened in Thailand at the end of January 2007.[34]

Other Indian firms have started *collaborating* with Western firms by either in-licensing the latter's products—usually with a view to manufacturing and marketing them in India—or manufacturing active pharmaceutical ingredients and intermediates that are then marketed by Western firms outside India. One example of a company that has pursued both approaches is Nicholas Piramal, India's eighth-largest pharmaceutical firm, which has essentially avoided generic exports—and associated frictions with Big Pharma—in order to focus on such partnerships. It has licensed in drugs from several Western firms and has emphasized custom manufacturing for and R&D partnerships with them (see below).

Yet other Indian pharmaceutical firms, such as its largest, Ranbaxy, have come to focus on *innovating* or, more broadly, pioneering.[35] Like most other

Indian firms, Ranbaxy built up overseas sales—now 80 percent of its total—with generic exports, but in recent years, it has pushed the envelope in a number of ways. To benefit from a statutory six-month period of exclusivity in the United States, Ranbaxy has been particularly aggressive in its attempts to be the first to manufacture generic versions of drugs going off patent. This approach has entailed extensive litigation, sometimes unsuccessful (e.g., its challenge to Pfizer's patent on the world's top-selling drug, the anticholesterol drug Lipitor), but other times offering rich rewards (e.g., the anticholesterol drug simavastatin). Another set of innovation initiatives has aimed to improve off-patent drugs (e.g., through novel delivery systems) to develop so-called branded supergenerics. Thus, in 1999, Ranbaxy licensed its once-a-day formulation of ciprofloxacin, an antibiotic, on a worldwide basis to Bayer. More recently, the company has emphasized patented inhalation devices and transdermal patches. While subject to a more complex approval process, supergenerics benefit from three years of marketing exclusivity in the United States.

Another, even more important innovative approach employed by Ranbaxy—and other larger Indian firms—has been to invest in developing entirely new drugs. In total, Indian firms are estimated to have as many as three dozen "new chemical entities" at relatively advanced stages of development. But the cost (including failures) of discovering and developing a new drug is estimated, in the West, to exceed $1 billion—more than the annual turnover of all Indian pharmaceutical companies but Ranbaxy. Thus, most Indian firms that *are* attempting to develop new drugs—for example, Dr. Reddy's, the third-largest—have been explicit about their intent to out-license promising drug candidates as a way of defraying the costs and risks of clinical trials and launch.

Out-licensing also suggests a variety of related strategies involving focus on value-chain activities other than drugs manufacturing:

- *Contract R&D:* Instead of simply engaging in contract manufacturing, a number of Indian firms are also undertaking contract R&D for Western manufacturers. Such an approach focuses on the largest arbitrage differentials in the sector: Pfizer estimates that Indian chemists make about $5 an hour, versus more than $50 an hour for U.S. scientists. Thus, in early 2007, Nicholas Piramal and Eli Lilly signed an agreement under which the former will be responsible for the global design and execution of pre-clinical and early-stage clinical work for some of the latter's new drugs.

- *Clinical trials:* A new medicine must go through clinical trials—the final and most expensive stage of trials—on a carefully selected sample of patients. These trials have also attracted great attention from drug-industry arbitrageurs. More than 40 percent of all clinical trials are now conducted in poor countries.[36] India attracts particular attention because of a large supply of patients, many of whom are "treatment-naive" (i.e., don't consume lots of pharmaceuticals), and of English-speaking doctors.[37]

- *IT-enabled services:* India has been successful as a destination for IT-enabled services, accounting for nearly half of total offshoring activity in 2005.[38] As a result, the pharmaceutical sector has shown great interest in exploiting its potential to contain the surging costs of data management and informatics support during the drug development process in areas such as data entry, database management, and trial study design, customer support services, and data analytics.

This characterization is far from complete—one could distinguish further among strategies by mode of growth (internally or by acquisition, with the latter mode attracting many Indian firms recently), areas of specialization, geographic focus, and so on. One could also look at cultural or geographic bases of arbitrage by considering India's traditional medicine systems—Ayurveda, Siddha, and Unani—and its biodiversity. But the variety of possible arbitrage strategies should already be clear.

The responses from Big Pharma have also been varied. Novartis, the fifth-largest pharmaceutical company in the world, is one example. Novartis bought out Hexal of Germany for $8.3 billion in 2005 to cement its position as one of the two largest generic-drug manufacturers in the world, and has tried to bundle generic and branded medicines to offer health-care providers "one-stop shopping."[39] As far as India is concerned, Novartis participates in the market there, as the fifth-largest foreign player. It also undertakes clinical trials and software development in India and, in early 2006, opened a global R&D center for over-the-counter medicines near Mumbai. But Novartis's big resource commitment has been to China, which a number of Big Pharma companies view as having even more potential than India. In late 2006, it announced an investment of $100 million in an R&D facility in Shanghai that would initially focus on cancers caused by infections—a significant proportion of Chinese cancer cases. And Novartis has also been active on the legal front: in January 2007, it filed a challenge in an Indian court to a decision not to grant it a patent on a modified form of its leukemia drug, Glivec—prompting an official of Médecins Sans Frontières to comment, "Novartis is trying to shut down the pharmacy of the developing world."[40] Arbitrage clearly poses a number of choices for Big Pharma, not just for second-tier players.

Analyzing Arbitrage

Given the variety of arbitrage strategies, there is no one way to analyze them. But, again, the ADDING Value scorecard can be used to structure the analysis and helps suggest some specific dos and don'ts. The key point to remember is that arbitrage can affect all the components of the ADDING Value scorecard, not just the first D of decreasing costs.

Adding Volume

Arbitrage can affect volume in a number of ways. Sometimes, arbitrage opportunities can open up entirely new businesses—for example, the cut-flower business in the Northern hemisphere in the winter. At other times, the volume increments come from the fact that, in the absence of arbitrage, one might have to turn business away—a particularly sore point for many executives in the high-tech sector, who complain about the difficulty of finding the right kind of technical talent in many developed countries.

A somewhat different source of volume growth involves securing market access. Reconsider Novartis's decision to establish a major R&D lab in Shanghai. While cost arbitrage is presumably one motive for the move, analysts have stressed another: improving relationships with governmental authorities who will decide what kind of medicines to buy for their citizens.[41] So, in assessing such a move, it is important to factor in the positive effects on future volumes instead of simply adopting a perspective focused purely on costs. Otherwise, one would reject some moves that made sense.

All these mechanisms presumably combine to account for the finding, in a recent survey, that growth is the second most frequently cited reason for offshoring, after cost reduction.[42] It is not necessary to assess their relative importance to conclude that the idea of arbitrage adding volume has to be taken seriously.

Of course, along with the possible volume-expanding effects of arbitrage, it is important to verify the expansibility of the basis of arbitrage that underpins it. GEN3 Partners, based in Cambridge, Massachusetts, provides a good example of such constraints. The core business of GEN3 Partners is innovation consulting for major U.S. companies using Russian specialists trained in TRIZ, a rigorous Soviet-era methodology for inventive problem solving.[43] At the end of 2005, GEN3 had about one hundred personnel in Russia, of whom about half were PhDs or Doctors of Science who also met the company's requirements of at least five years of practical experience. It was possible to imagine expanding this pool to several hundred, perhaps, but not beyond that number. Given those volume constraints, GEN3 had to pursue a much-higher-end business model than did, say, Indian software services firms with access to hundreds of thousands of new technical personnel every year. GEN3 was already operating at a revenue-per-employee level of $100,000 and was targeting $200,000-plus, versus $50,000 to $70,000 for Indian software services firms, even though Russian salaries per employee were still somewhat lower.

Decreasing Costs

While cost reductions are the most frequently cited reasons for arbitrage-related moves, analyses of them are often flawed in conceptually simple but practically dangerous ways. One frequent problem is a focus on snapshots of relative costs. As the GEN3 example suggests, this can be very misleading: in that case, the cost of personnel with the requisite training in TRIZ was bound to escalate sharply if GEN3—and other consulting firms tapping into the same resource base—proved successful at monetizing the resource. Other frequent, related problems include a failure to adjust for likely shifts in exchange rates (the Chinese yuan, for instance, is probably significantly undervalued relative to Western currencies, suggesting that forward-looking assessments based on today's exchange rates will overstate the likely Chinese cost advantage) and for differentials in productivity (in many Chinese and Indian cases, still a fraction of Western levels). Even apparently authoritative estimates can be subject to such problems. For example, the Organisation for Economic Co-operation and Development (OECD) recently came out with a report that had China's R&D level surpassing Japan's. This "finding" was based on the idea that because China's scientists and engineers cost one-quarter of Japan's at official exchange rates, why not just multiply China's R&D expenditures times four![44]

Nevertheless, while acknowledging some reasons why labor arbitrage may be less advantageous than it appears at first blush, it is also important to recognize some positive factors that often get overlooked. Consider the kind of calculation that I tend to frown on when I encounter it in the classroom: "The costs of Indian software personnel are (say) one-third those of U.S. software personnel but are escalating at 15 percent per year, so the Indian cost advantage will get wiped out within eight years." As an argument against arbitrage, this misses out on several key points:

- The opportunity costs of turning business away (see "Adding Volume")
- The likelihood of even greater pressures on cost and availability in developed countries—which leads to predictions that the total surplus generated by India and other countries that are currently

low-cost suppliers of IT workers will increase rather than decrease over the next few years (figure 6-2)

- The possibility of faster productivity improvements and cost containment in India—as achieved in the 1990s through a shift from on-site to offshore development

FIGURE 6-2

Evolution of global IT workforce (hourly labor cost versus thousands of FTEs*)

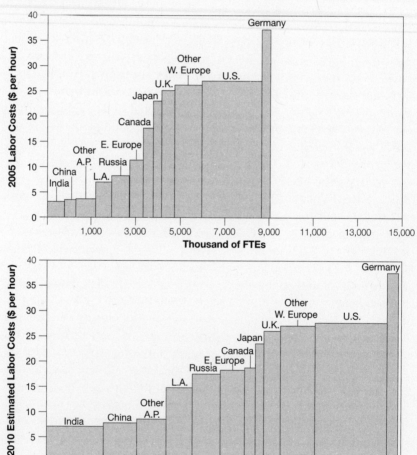

Source: Compiled from industry sources and consultants' reports.

*Full-time equivalents.

- Quality differentials that, in this case, may actually favor Indian competitors, as discussed in the next subsection

The broader point to be made here is that it is important to go beyond naive labor cost comparisons to look a bit more deeply at the kinds of negatives and positives outlined above. Not considering them amounts to an assumption that they will exactly cancel out, which will happen only by accident.

Yet another problem has to do with the common focus on labor costs (and productivity). But as chapter 3 emphasized, we need to look at costs comprehensively. Thus, work by the Boston Consulting Group (BCG) has highlighted the capital that can be saved by building plants in rapidly developing economies such as China.[45] BCG estimates that for discrete manufacturing processes, it is possible to reduce typical capital investments by 10 to 30 percent below Western levels by using local equipment suppliers; by 20 to 40 percent by also targeting process improvements such as replacing capital with labor and rethinking make-or-buy decisions; and by 30 to 60 percent by totally overhauling the operating model by revamping entire production chains, redesigning products for local manufacturability, and moving to continuous utilization from a five-days-per-week model. The benefits include not just higher returns on investment, but lower fixed costs and breakeven points and reduced exit barriers in case operations have to be discontinued—that is, lower risks as well as costs.

The ultimate objective of the analysis should be, of course, to build up a comprehensive picture of costs rather than to focus on a single cost element, whether labor, capital, or something else. This, along with the differentiation-related factors discussed next, is the key determinant of whether a product or service is likely to be offshored. Cost-related flags of "offshoreability" include not only the factors already discussed, but also high value-to-bulk ratios, short supply chains, and broad availability of required inputs and skills. But to understand the *degree* of incentive to move products or services offshore rather than treating offshoreability as "on" or "off"—it is usually better to look comprehensively at costs instead of relying on flags of this sort.

To take a concrete example, why have Indian software services companies been able to grow much more quickly and profitably than Indian pharmaceutical companies? Part of the answer lies in the greater labor-intensity in software, with employee-related costs accounting for one-half or more of revenues. A more comprehensive answer is that Indian software firms' total costs (per employee) are still one-third or less of the costs of the Western competitors that the Indian firms are trying to take business away from, whereas Indian pharmaceutical firms' costs are probably two-thirds or more of the costs of Western generic companies. An even more comprehensive answer would also take into account the administrative barriers to economic arbitrage in pharmaceuticals.[46]

Differentiating

The impact of arbitrage on differentiation or willingness-to-pay has attracted much less attention than its impact on costs, but can be at least as important. Cultural arbitrage, for instance, often involves raising willingness-to-pay based on country-of-origin effects. Of course, as the discussion in chapter 3 should have warned us, such effects can, depending on the situation, have negative rather than positive effects.

Examples of economic arbitrage reinforce the importance of actually analyzing the implications of arbitrage for differentiation. While economic arbitrage often reduces willingness-to-pay as well as costs, there are important exceptions to this rule. Software services seem to be one such exception. The Indian software firms are lower priced as well as lower cost than their Western competitors, but this seems to reflect reputational stickiness rather than quality differences. In fact, there is evidence that some of the larger Indian firms—such as TCS, the largest firm, which has also taken the lead at compiling such data—actually offer both higher quality and lower costs for software maintenance, in particular, than some of their better-known Western counterparts.[47] Corroboration comes from the fact that India still accounts for one-half of the software development centers certified to operate at the highest levels of process compliance even though it accounts for only about one-tenth of the total global IT workforce. This example and TCS's inauguration, in the first quarter of 2007, of a marketing campaign focused on communicating its dual competitive advantage, underlines the importance of:

- Not treating price as a proxy for quality or willingness-to-pay in the long run.

- Really digging deep into buyer economics. Thus, TCS's campaign stresses the implications of poor software quality for buyers' total costs of quality, including rework—which is estimated to be one-half or more of the total IT spending at a typical large organization.

- Actively communicating such benefits instead of simply assuming that buyers will figure them out for themselves.

As in the case of costs, it is possible to flag differentiation-related correlates of offshoreability: a product or service is less likely to move offshore when considerable customization is required, demand is very changeable, local presence or service requirements are high, and purchasing decision makers are public rather than private. But, once again, it is usually better to try to build up a comprehensive, ideally quantitative picture of relative viability—of the comparative width of the wedge between willingness-to-pay and costs—instead of simply relying on such flags.

Improving Industry Attractiveness or Bargaining Power

In addition to possibly lowering costs or raising willingness-to-pay, arbitrage may improve industry attractiveness or one's own bargaining power within it. Thus, IBM has increased its head count in India from nine thousand to fifty thousand in less than three years not only to improve its own economics, but also to put pressure on its Indian rivals by attacking what is still probably their single most important source of advantage.

Again, it would be rash to assume that arbitrage always has a particular type of effect in this regard. Thus, while global companies have implanted many R&D centers in China and India—with a focus on electronics and telecoms in China, and software and engineering in India—the protection of intellectual property rights remains a major concern. One study of global companies with R&D centers in China indicates that they have found several ways to address this issue. One particularly important method is to split R&D efforts across a company's global network in such a way that the value of the projects undertaken in China is highly contingent on projects being pursued elsewhere in the global network or, more broadly, on firm-specific expertise.[48] Also note that this strategy is unavailable to local firms, probably contributing to their lower expenditures on, and returns from, R&D.

Such splits are not a perfect solution: think of Cisco's allegations, since settled, that Huawei Technologies Co., Ltd., of China poached its switching technology across multiple geographies. But the concept does suggest two important lessons about strategy. First, in the study cited above, the firms that did particularly well with their Chinese R&D centers appear to have been ones with stronger internal linkages, reminding us that competitive advantage can be developed in dealing with institutional failures as well as on more traditional bases. Second, it should be clear that the external environment need not be taken as given: elements of it can and, ideally, *should* be influenced through firm strategy.

Normalizing Risk

Arbitrage is subject to an extensive array of risks, both market and non-market. With regard to the former, think of all the (greater) hazards to which supply chains that cross borders are subject: exposure to unknown and potentially less reliable suppliers and to exchange-rate fluctuations; the possibility of infrastructural and other bottlenecks at borders; the compounding of risks associated with supply chains that are very thinly sliced across multiple countries, as in the earlier example of the down jacket from Li & Fung, and so on.

Li & Fung's network also affords numerous insights, however, in how to cope with such risks. After the 9/11 terrorist attacks on the United States, it reportedly took Li & Fung less than three weeks to relocate time-sensitive activities from partners in Pakistan to partners in other countries deemed more politically secure. Li & Fung obviously practices such dynamic arbitrage over longer time frames as well, in response to changes such as major shifts in exchange rates. Such moves occur within the context of a broader strategy in which capacity and materials subject to long lead times or stable demand are locked in well ahead of time, but decisions concerning attributes that are highly sensitive to market fluctuations are deferred for as long as possible.

A particular type of risk associated with arbitrage has to do with its political sensitivity—particularly evident around but not confined to labor arbitrage. Note that such risk isn't confined to external constituencies: as IBM, for example, moves offshore, its top managers must be careful not only in their public communications, but also in internal ones. Successful arbitrageurs offer several lessons in this regard. First, be discreet: emphasize viability and growth as objectives rather than (just) cost reductions, and be cautious about capitalizing on health, safety, and environmental standards that are looser than at home. Second, think through a range of mechanisms—lobbying, working with natural allies, including companies who are otherwise competitors, investing in job creation, and so forth—for expanding your freedom of action. A final suggestion is to favor strategies that exhibit some degree of robustness to changes in the political climate.

The political risk associated with arbitrage strategies should be balanced with recognition of the possible political risks of counterstrategies. Think of the example mentioned in the last section: the lawsuit in an Indian court by Novartis. Risks, like the other components of the ADDING Value scorecard, should be looked at in comparative perspective, across alternatives.

Generating Knowledge—and Other Resources and Capabilities

The final component of the ADDING Value scorecard, which I'll mention briefly, is generating knowledge—and other resources and capabilities. Again, arbitrage strategies can have either positive or negative implications. On the positive side, IBM and Accenture's efforts to expand in India probably will help bolster their long-run capabilities, even if the short-run impact on operating economics is negative because of lower price realizations, setup costs, and the internal disarray associated with very rapid expansion. On the negative side, a major investment bank that has outsourced many analytical functions to India is just starting to realize that the move will significantly deplete its pool of senior analysts in a few years—unless it significantly changes its hiring and promotion policies.

This discussion of the importance of analyzing arbitrage and, especially, applying the ADDING Value scorecard, should have clarified why arbitrage is often thought about far too narrowly. Individual CAGE bases of arbitrage can be used to target different components of the ADDING Value scorecard; in addition, complex cases involving multiple bases of arbitrage further expand the possibilities, as illustrated by the discussion in the previous section of pharmaceuticals.

Managing Arbitrage

This chapter, like chapters 4 and 5, was meant to stretch one's thinking about how to deal with differences—in this instance, by expanding on the potential for exploiting them through arbitrage strategies. A number of challenges arise in managing arbitrage strategies, though. Some, such as the risks that arbitrage engenders, particularly political risks, have already been discussed. But what deserve additional attention are the sustainability of arbitrage strategies and how they are influenced by firm-level resources, particularly management capabilities, as opposed to market-level differences in prices, costs, et cetera.

Note, first of all, that while sustaining competitive advantage from arbitrage can be a worthwhile objective, it is not necessary for arbitrage to make sense. Reconsider the example of Wal-Mart. Even if arbitrage didn't offer Wal-Mart a sustainable advantage, it would probably be worth undertaking, if only to avoid ending up at a cost disadvantage relative to other competitors—a serious obstacle to Wal-Mart's pursuit of its low-cost strategy.

The Lego versus MEGA Brands example is even clearer. Lego chose to deal with arbitrage opportunities by essentially outsourcing them to a contract manufacturer, Flextronics. That is, Lego moved to neutralize arbitrage as a source of competitive advantage or disadvantage and to focus on advantage from its intangible assets: its brand name, its relationships, and its innovation capabilities. In contrast, Wal-Mart, in keeping with its traditional emphasis on back-end efficiencies, has opted to try to build a competitive advantage around arbitrage by developing distinctive capabilities to manage what is probably the world's biggest cross-border sourcing operation. This contrast highlights a second theme that is worth underscoring: building a sustainable competitive advantage through arbitrage

generally requires a commitment to building firm-specific capabilities—
a commitment that takes years if not decades to implement. Zero firm-
specific capabilities, in contrast, may allow you to achieve parity, but not
much more.

The same theme stands out from some of the other examples considered in this chapter. Embraer certainly benefits from cheap Brazilian
labor, but its ability to turn that labor—theoretically available to all—into
a source of competitive advantage depends on capabilities that it has developed to run a world-class aerospace operation amid the turbulence of
contemporary Brazil. And Ranbaxy's innovation-driven vision of success
in pharmaceuticals was already in place a decade ago, when I first wrote a
case on the company and invited its president to come talk to my Harvard MBA class.

For a somewhat more detailed example of what is involved in converting
such visions into reality, let's look once again at Tata Consultancy Services
(TCS), the largest Indian software services firm. TCS arbitrages in the reverse
direction from Wal-Mart: it buys cheap at home (in the form of software
developers) and sells dear overseas. But this model, which TCS pioneered,
is no longer unique: it is also used by virtually everyone else involved in
software exports from India, ranging from Infosys, the second-largest firm
(whose founder was quoted in the epigraph to this chapter), to the smallest
body-shopping operation. The result of all this has been a large run-up in
the cost of Indian software developers. How has TCS managed to sustain
superior performance despite the sharp escalation of labor costs?

Figure 6-3 tracks TCS's revenues per employee, costs per employee, and
net profit per employee since the end of the 1980s. TCS's costs per employee have more than tripled since then. To sustain its performance, TCS
has had to increase the revenue per employee even faster: revenue has
quadrupled rather than tripled over this period, and as a result, profit per
employee has jumped severalfold! The revenue-per-employee performance is even more impressive when one accounts for a significant shift in
business from on-site development over this period to more efficient offshore development out of India today: this reduces revenue per employee
by 30 to 40 percent, although it does boost absolute profit per employee.

What lies behind these numbers? In addition to moving work offshore,
TCS has, over time, migrated to working on projects that are larger and
more complex and that offer higher realizations per employee—a shift in
which it seems to lead the Indian software sector. And with revenues per
employee that are still significantly less than those of Accenture and IBM
Global Services—as well as quality advantages along some dimensions, as
discussed—there is clearly headroom to do even better. The target for the

FIGURE 6-3

Upgrading by Tata Consulting Services

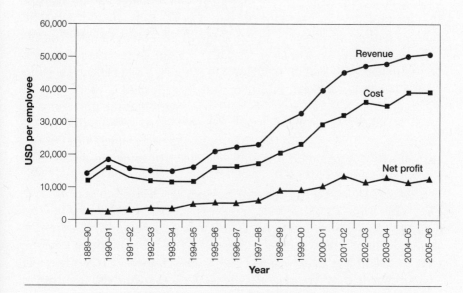

medium run is to boost revenue per employee by another 25 to 30 percent. But, of course, the achievement of these targets, not to mention past accomplishments, has required a level of firm capability that goes well beyond the insight that Indian software developers are relatively inexpensive.

Similar capability requirements are discernible on the demand as well as the supply side of this business. To successfully offshore some or all of its software service requirements, a client company must have some ability to specify those requirements—greater than if the work were simply being done in-house, at corporate headquarters—and to track outcomes. In recognition of this fact, as some of the larger software outsourcing deals negotiated in the mid-1990s come up for renewal, sophisticated companies seem to be increasingly chunking them up and splitting them across multiple vendors instead of single-sourcing them from them a megavendor. But, as in any group, it is still possible to find companies well behind the curve. My most cautionary example is the large European bank that has hired Indian software companies to complete more than one thousand of its projects, but still does not track performance across projects or vendors.

If this last example sounds too extreme to be true or widely relevant, note that only 1 percent of the respondents to a recent survey by Duke

University's Arie Lewin say that their companies have corporatewide strategies for offshoring.[49] Yet, in the absence of such a strategy, one might see offshoring efforts run amok or, probably more likely, an insufficient amount of offshoring due to internal barriers. The solution to this state of affairs is partly strategic and partly organizational, involving mechanisms such as the creation of internal champions for arbitrage, incentives for project managers as well as top managers, and pull-through commitments by top managers.

To summarize this section, a sustained commitment is required to develop and deploy capabilities to arbitrage effectively—and not all commitments are possible at any one organization at any given point in time. Put differently, firms may have to make trade-offs between arbitrage and the other elements of their strategy. Some mixing and matching may be possible across the AAAs of adaptation, aggregation, and arbitrage—recall that TCS has managed to overlay a degree of regional aggregation on its core strategy of arbitrage. However, pursuing all three strategies, or even two of them, full-tilt may lead to inconsistencies.

For a cautionary example of a company that failed, for a while, to grasp such trade-offs, consider Acer of Taiwan, one of the world's largest computer manufacturers. Acer entered into the contract manufacturing of personal computers early and made good money with that arbitrage play. But in the early 1990s, the company began to push Acer as a global brand (and a basis for aggregation) across countries, particularly developed ones. This two-track approach turned out to be problematic. While the branded own-product business did grow to significant volumes, it continued to generate losses. Meanwhile, customers for its contract manufacturing arm worried about the spillover of business secrets to, and cross-subsidization of, Acer's offerings under its own brand. Matters came to a head in 2000, when IBM cancelled a major order, reducing its share of Acer's total contract manufacturing revenues from 53 percent in the first quarter of 2000 to only 26 percent in the second quarter of 2001. Eventually, Acer made some hard choices. Its contract manufacturing continued to focus on customers in advanced countries and was gradually spun off into a separate company called Wistron. Meanwhile, Acer refocused its own-brand sales on the East Asian region, particularly Greater China. While the revised strategy faces its own challenges, it certainly seems to have worked better than the old one.

In my MBA classroom presentations, this is usually about the time that I show a PowerPoint slide of a celebrated and controversial beast: the *jackalope* (figure 6-4). I won't go into the debates surrounding this animal, which may or may not inhabit the American West, lure cowboys to their

FIGURE 6-4

The jackalope

doom with uncanny imitations of human song, or produce a milk that is a powerful aphrodisiac.[50] I invoke the jackalope here simply to make the point that asking an animal—or an organization—to be more than one thing at one point in time can lead to some very awkward results. *Some degree of internal consistency* is a basic requirement for a good strategy—or organization. A jackrabbit with a full rack of horns probably can't hold its head up, let alone run down the road.

For now, I'll let my jackalope metaphor serve as a placeholder for a more serious discussion of one of the most challenging questions in contemporary global strategy: *To what extent is it possible to mix and match across the AAA strategies of adaptation, aggregation and arbitrage?* Chapter 7 deals with that question at length.

Conclusions

The box "Global Generalizations" summarizes the specific conclusions from this chapter. More broadly, arbitrage further expands our strategy toolkit for dealing with the differences across countries. As the Acer example emphasizes, however, decisions about arbitrage cannot be made independently of decisions about the other elements of a firm's strategy. The next chapter digs deeper into this point.

Global Generalizations

1. Arbitrage involves exploiting differences across countries instead of treating them as constraints to be adjusted to or overcome.

2. Very few companies can afford to ignore arbitrage opportunities.

3. There are multiple possible bases of arbitrage—cultural, administrative, geographic, and economic—and even if a company focuses on just one or two of them, it faces many variants on arbitrage strategies.

4. Arbitrage has the potential to improve all elements of the ADDING Value scorecard—but is also subject to numerous risks that must be managed.

5. Arbitrage may be worth undertaking even if it doesn't yield a sustainable competitive advantage, but an emphasis on arbitrage opportunities usually does require a long-term commitment to the development of firm-specific capabilities.

6. Even companies that do engage in arbitrage often have a great deal of headroom to improve how they do so.

7. Arbitrage decisions cannot be made independently of decisions about other elements of a company's strategy.

7

Playing the Differences

The AAA Triangle

*The MNC [multinational corporation] of the late twentieth century
had little in common with the international firms of a hundred years
earlier, and those companies were very different from the great trading
enterprises of the 1700s. The type of business organization that is now
emerging—the globally integrated enterprise—marks just as big a leap.*

—Sam Palmisano, Chairman and CEO, IBM,
"The Globally Integrated Enterprise" (2006)

COMPARE THE WORDS of Sam Palmisano with those of Ted Levitt at
the beginning of chapter 1. Levitt was clearly excited about the globalization of markets. What Palmisano is excited about, in contrast—I've had a
chance to check this with him—is the globalization of production and of
services delivery. In the *Foreign Affairs* article from which the quote was
excerpted, Palmisano notes that an estimated sixty thousand manufacturing plants were built by foreign firms in China alone between 2000 and
2003, and discusses how IBM has sought to capitalize on its expanded
sense of the possibilities.

I think that Palmisano is onto something fundamental—something that
extends beyond the justification of a particular corporation's strategy or

even a heightened appreciation of the possibilities afforded by arbitrage. Attention to the globalization of production as well as the globalization of markets heralds something new in global strategy—something that changes our understanding of the variety of global strategies as well as the challenge of selecting among them. This chapter begins by explaining why. It then discusses progressively more ambitious responses that are characterized in terms of the AAA strategies, i.e., in terms of strategies for playing the differences. The chapter concludes with some broader lessons for global strategy and organization.

The Need to Redefine Global Strategy

Figures 7-1a and 7-1b compare the strategic issues raised by the globalization of markets with those raised by also considering the globalization of production. Figure 7-1a focuses on the globalization of markets. With limited globalization of markets, adaptation is in order; with extensive globalization of this sort, aggregation merits more emphasis; and in between, the two have to be traded off against each other—*the* strategic choice on which the literature on global strategy has traditionally focused.[1]

FIGURE 7-1

The globalization of markets and production

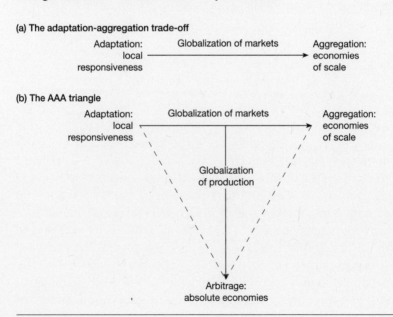

(a) The adaptation-aggregation trade-off

Adaptation: local responsiveness ——— Globalization of markets ———→ Aggregation: economies of scale

(b) The AAA triangle

Adaptation: local responsiveness / Globalization of markets / Aggregation: economies of scale

Globalization of production

Arbitrage: absolute economies

Figure 7-1b summarizes the implications of also accounting for the globalization of production. This obviously transforms the adaptation-aggregation trade-off into the adaptation-aggregation-arbitrage (AAA) triangle.[2] And just as obviously, it adds significantly to the range of ways in which companies can think of playing cross-border differences.

But attention to the globalization of production does more than simply expand the range of possible strategies: it also suggests a new, expanded set of trade-offs. As the literature in economics on multinational companies (MNCs) reminds us, vertical MNCs that exploit the differences across countries have very different operating and organizational characteristics from horizontal MNCs that perform many of the same activities in each major market (and that mush together the categories of adaptation and aggregation).[3] Table 7-1 highlights the strategic differences across the AAA strategies.

TABLE 7-1

Differences across the AAA strategies

Characteristics	Adaptation	Aggregation	Arbitrage
Competitive advantage: why globalize at all?	To achieve local relevance through national focus (while exploiting some scale)	To achieve scale and scope economies through international standardization	To achieve absolute economies through international specialization
Coordination: how to organize across borders?	By country; emphasis on adjustments to achieve a local face within borders	By business, region, or customer; emphasis on horizontal relationships for cross-border economies of scale	By function; emphasis on vertical relationships, including across organizational boundaries
Configuration: where to locate overseas?	To limit the effects of cultural, administrative, geographic, or economic distance by concentrating on foreign countries that are similar to the home base		To exploit some elements of distance by operating in a more diverse set of countries
Controls: what to watch out for?	Excessive variety or complexity	Excessive standardization or emphasis on scale	Narrowing spreads
Change blockers: whom to watch out for internally?	Entrenched country chiefs	All-powerful headquarters, business, regional, or account heads	Key functions or vertical interfaces
Corporate diplomacy: which external issues might arise?	Relatively discreet and robust, given emphasis on cultivation of a local face	Appearance of, and backlash against, homogenization or hegemony (especially for U.S. companies)	The exploitation or displacement of suppliers, channels, or intermediaries; potentially most prone to political disruption

Most fundamentally, the three As involve the pursuit of different sources of advantage from operating across borders and, relatedly, are associated with different organizational types. If a company is emphasizing adaptation, a country-centered organization is often indicated. If aggregation is the primary objective, cross-border groupings of various sorts—global business units or product divisions, regional structures, global accounts, and so on—make sense. And an emphasis on arbitrage is often best pursued by a vertical, or functional, organization that tracks the flow of products or work orders through the organization. Clearly, not all three modes of organizing can take precedence in one organization at the same time. And although some approaches to corporate organization (such as the matrix) can combine elements of more than one pure mode, they carry costs in terms of managerial complexity.

Given these—and other—differences across the three As, strategy often requires choices about which of the As to emphasize or, equivalently, about how to play the differences. Figure 7-2 summarizes the variety of global strategies implied by the AAA triangle, arrayed in four levels of increasing ambitiousness, that are meant to summarize the possibilities rather than to suggest a sequence through which all border-crossing companies must pass. The sections that follow discuss these four levels of global strategy one by one.

Level 0: AAA Awareness

For the three As to be minimally useful, a company must be aware of them. This might seem like a requirement too trivial to be worth stressing, but

FIGURE 7-2

Levels of global strategy

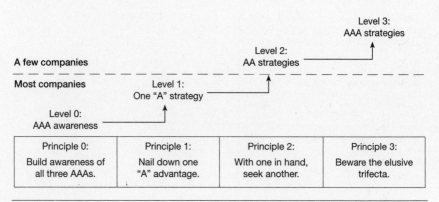

Principle 0:	Principle 1:	Principle 2:	Principle 3:
Build awareness of all three AAAs.	Nail down one "A" advantage.	With one in hand, seek another.	Beware the elusive trifecta.

many companies, judging by the examples in this book, fail to meet it. The patterns of failure themselves seem quite diverse. Global neophytes often tend to implant themselves overseas in the same form as they did domestically, expecting instant aggregation, and often endure significant losses as they learn that some adaptation is typically needed as well. Unless they go global to exploit arbitrage opportunities, they are likely to be oblivious to these opportunities in the early stages as well. In experienced companies, history can also be a key conditioner: a company that has grown through acquisitions or has a long tradition of federalism is likely to fail to achieve the requisite focus on real aggregation. Country of origin matters as well. U.S. companies often pursue aggregation and arbitrage more aggressively than their European counterparts, but are often less attuned to adaptation. And the best Chinese and Indian companies tend to be better at arbitrage than they are adaptation and aggregation.

One way to counteract undue biases in this regard is to use the AAA triangle to build your company's awareness of the full range of strategic objectives that it might pursue, and different levers and sublevers for doing so. In this context, granularity and specificity are helpful. That is, it makes sense to stress the (often overlooked) levers discussed in chapters 4 through 6 (see table 7-2) and, even better, to take the discussion down to the level of individual sublevers, backed up by interesting examples.

A second approach to broadening awareness of the three As is to use the AAA triangle to develop a globalization scorecard. While there are both advantages and disadvantages to the use of scorecards, they offer room for significant improvement on the state of current practice: most companies seem to lack any systematic global performance measurement system beyond tracking the percentage of revenues derived from foreign operations and ensuring that the profitability of the foreign operations is acceptable, or at least not unsustainably bad.

TABLE 7-2

Global strategy levers

Adaptation: adjusting to differences	Aggregation: overcoming differences	Arbitrage: exploiting differences
• Variation	• Regions	• Cultural
• Focus	• Other country groupings	• Administrative
• Externalization	• Noncountry groupings	• Geographic
• Design	○ Business or product	• Economic
• Innovation	○ Global accounts	
	○ Client industries	
	○ Channels	

Figure 7-3 is a simplified example of a globalization scorecard. It was developed for a financial services company focused on the capital markets side of the business, rather than on retail financial services that had grown through acquisition. The quantitative targets attached to the scorecard elements in figure 7-3 were supplemented with qualitative ones, initiatives were defined to help achieve both types of objectives, and progress was tracked in terms of value creation (along the lines of the ADDING Value scorecard) as well as these operating measures.

Note that while the globalization scorecard in the figure covers all three As, the treatment is deliberately imbalanced. This reflected a clear sense that, given the company's industry, history of growth through acquisition, and strategy, additional aggregation was the highest strategic priority globally—and that there were trade-offs between pursuing that strategy and the others, particularly adaptation.

That last point can and should be generalized. Building awareness of all three As is essential, and many companies—particularly those that lag behind—have the headroom to improve along each of them. Nevertheless, most companies will need to prioritize across the AAA strategies, as discussed next.

Level 1: One "A" Strategy

The need for strategic prioritization—as opposed to simply pushing as hard as possible along all three As—stems from the differences across the

FIGURE 7-3

A sample globalization scorecard

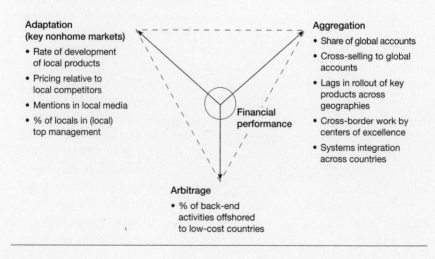

Adaptation
(key nonhome markets)
- Rate of development of local products
- Pricing relative to local competitors
- Mentions in local media
- % of locals in (local) top management

Financial performance

Aggregation
- Share of global accounts
- Cross-selling to global accounts
- Lags in rollout of key products across geographies
- Cross-border work by centers of excellence
- Systems integration across countries

Arbitrage
- % of back-end activities offshored to low-cost countries

AAA strategies that were laid out in table 7-1. The literature on competitive strategy has long emphasized that such heterogeneity usually forces companies to choose how they are going to beat their competitors, instead of simply planning to beat them on all dimensions—and that companies that fail to face up to this reality have to reckon with significant conflict and coordination costs.[4] As discussed in chapter 6, Acer exemplifies such conflict: its private-label business, built around arbitrage, lost customers when it also began to aggregate by building up its own brands. And the best way of making the point about coordination costs is to note that if everything is meant to be a priority, nothing, in effect, will be.[5]

The emphasis on clarity about which one of the three strategies will be the basis of cross-border advantage is *not* meant to imply obliviousness to the remaining strategies. As emphasized above, most border-crossing companies need to at least think through all three. But the point is that having done so, *every top manager of a company with aspirations to create value through border-crossing activities should be able to specify clearly, in his or her own head, which of the three As will be the basis for cross-border competitive advantage.*

Most companies that have built up profitable operations outside their home base have done so by stressing one of the three As. While such strategies are referred to here as "pure," that should not be equated with "simple." Wal-Mart's international stores have performed poorly—particularly in markets dissimilar to the United States—largely because of intrinsic as well as self-imposed difficulties in *adapting* a business model that worked well for Wal-Mart at home. Unilever has underperformed P&G in areas of overlap such as beauty care largely because Unilever still has trouble, for all its recent efforts, at *aggregating* to achieve cross-border economies of scale and scope. Or to consider a case of success rather than failure, Embraer's ability to outperform Bombardier in the regional jet business can be entirely imputed to labor *arbitrage*—but the easy arithmetic of cheap labor notwithstanding, it is far from simple to actually run a world-class aerospace operation out of Brazil.

While firms that have achieved global success are likely to have already developed resources and capabilities around a particular strategy, less experienced or less successful firms sometimes need to figure out which of the AAA strategies to target. Again, the AAA triangle can be helpful in this context. One approach is to calibrate how intensive an industry or a business is in various categories of expenditure that serve as rough proxies for the headroom afforded by the three As. The percentage of sales spent on advertising indicates how important adaptation is likely to be; the percentage spent on R&D is a proxy for the importance of aggregation; and the percentage spent on labor helps gauge the importance of (labor) arbitrage.[6]

More specifically, I recommend plotting industries or companies on a calibrated version of the AAA triangle, as in figure 7-4 (which is based on data for U.S. manufacturing industries). If an industry or a company scores above the median along a particular dimension of intensity—delineated by the solid line in the figure—the corresponding strategy merits some attention. If it scores close to or past the dashed line, which delineates the 90th percentile, the corresponding strategy may be perilous to ignore.

Another, related approach involves using the AAA triangle to map a company's position relative to its competitors—in terms of either the expenditure intensities just described or a broader set of considerations (see figure 7-7 below). This provides some additional insight into which strategy or strategies to stress—particularly important when a company is up against formidable competitors.

Level 2: Compound (AA) Strategies

Although pure A strategies are the most obvious types of global strategies, at least a number of leading-edge global companies I have had a chance to discuss the AAA triangle with seem to emphasize two As rather than just one. Such compound AA strategies might actually involve a company's

FIGURE 7-4

Industry expenditure intensities

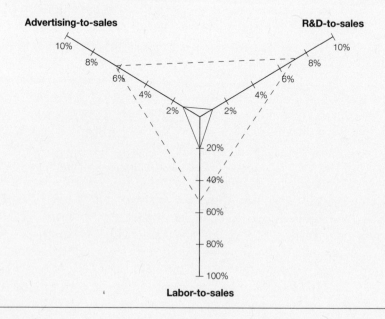

beating its competitors on two dimensions or, more probably, striking a better balance between two As than competitors are able to achieve. Under the latter interpretation, AA strategies can be thought of as generalizing the one key trade-off, between adaptation and aggregation, identified by the traditional focus on the globalization of markets to the three key trade-offs highlighted by the AAA triangle once account is also taken of the globalization of production (compare figures 7-1a and 7-1b). These AA strategies, corresponding to the sides of the AAA triangle, emphasize the common focus underlying each trade-off: similarities in the case of the adaptation-aggregation trade-off, differences or variation in the case of the adaptation-arbitrage trade-off, and cross-border integration in the case of the arbitrage-aggregation trade-off.

Also note that allowing for AA strategies further expands the variety of global strategies from three to six—or to nine if one allows AA strategies with primary and secondary emphases (Aa strategies, in effect). For lessons about how to achieve the ambitious objectives implicit in AA strategies, it is best to look at leading-edge companies. The rest of this section will focus on four such company examples that are informed by discussions with the respective CEOs and other executives (figure 7-5).

IBM. For most of its history, IBM pursued an adaptation strategy, serving overseas markets by setting up a mini-IBM in each target country. Every one of these companies performed a largely complete set of activities (apart from R&D and resource allocation) and adapted to local differences as necessary. In the 1980s and 1990s, dissatisfaction with the extent to which

FIGURE 7-5

Evolution of leading-edge companies

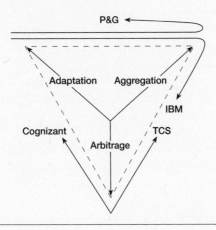

country-by-country adaptation curtailed international scale economies led to the overlay of a regional structure on the mini-IBMs. IBM aggregated the countries into regions in order to improve coordination and thus generate more scale economies at the regional and global levels.

More recently, however, IBM has also begun to exploit differences across countries. The most visible signs of this new emphasis on arbitrage (not a term the company's leadership uses) are IBM's efforts to exploit wage differentials by more than tripling its employees in emerging markets in three years—particularly in India, where head counts went from less than ten thousand to fifty thousand over that period—and by planning for additional, massive growth there. Most of the new employees are in IBM Global Services, the part of the company that is growing fastest but has the lowest margins—which they are supposed to help improve, presumably by reducing costs rather than raising prices. So IBM is pursuing an aggregation-arbitrage strategy. Adaptation remains important, particularly in market-facing activities, but is *not* being emphasized more than in the past.

One particularly interesting part of IBM's attempts to arbitrage by better matching the supply of talent globally to demand is a sophisticated matching algorithm that dynamically optimizes people's assignments across all of IBM's locations. Krishan Nathan, the director of IBM's Zurich Research Lab, describes some of the reasons that such a people-delivery model involves much more rocket science than, for example, a parts-delivery model. First, people's services usually can't be stored. Second, people's functionality can't be summarized in the same, standardized way—by serial number and associated description of technical characteristics—that parts are summarized. Third, in allocating people to teams, a company must pay attention to issues of chemistry that might, as a worst-case scenario, make the team less than the sum of its (human) parts. Fourth, for this reason and others (e.g., employee development), assignment durations and sequencing must satisfy some auxiliary criteria. Nathan also describes the resultant assignment patterns as "75 percent global and 25 percent local." While this may be more aspirational than actual, it is clear that, to the extent that better matching is being used to arbitrage more effectively, it embodies a massive power shift, the effective orchestration of which is a much broader organizational challenge.

Procter & Gamble. Like IBM, Procter & Gamble started out with mini-P&Gs that tried to fit into local markets, but it has evolved differently. Its halting attempts at aggregation across Europe, in particular, led to a drawn-out, function-by-function installation of a matrix structure through the course of the 1980s. But the business-geography matrix proved unwieldy, and in 1999, new CEO Durk Jager announced a major reorganization around global business units (GBUs) with ultimate profit responsibility, complemented by geographic market development organizations (MDOs) that would actually run the salesforce (shared across GBUs) and go to market.

The result of this ambitious attempt to achieve more aggregation was that all hell broke loose along multiple dimensions, including at the key GBU-MDO interface. Jager departed after only seventeen months. P&G has experienced more success under his successor, A. G. Lafley, who says that he retained the house that Jager built, but added wiring to the structure. Thus, decision tables, devised after months of negotiation, lay out protocols for how the different decisions are to be made, and by whom—the GBUs versus the MDOs—while generally reserving responsibility for profits (and the right to make decisions not covered by the tables) for the GBUs. But there is some flexibility within the system: the pharmaceuticals business, with distinct distribution channels, has been left out of the MDO structure, and in emerging markets, where market development challenges loom large, profit responsibility continues to be vested with country managers. Common IT systems and career paths that cross over between the GBUs and MDOs help tie those subunits together. The capstone is provided by an elaborately layered system of reviews that starts with growth objectives, then cascades down through strategies, innovations, and brands before being translated into operating plans and budgets with rolling two-year horizons.

Lafley also explains that while P&G remains willing to adapt as necessary to important markets, it ultimately aims to beat competitors—country-centered multinationals as well as local companies—through aggregation at the GBU level. He also explains that arbitrage is important to P&G (mostly through outsourcing), but that it takes a backseat to both adaptation and aggregation: "If it touches the customer, we don't outsource it." As a result, arbitrage—through multiyear outsourcing, via the Global Business Shared Services unit, of IT services to HP, employee services to IBM, and facilities management to Jones Lang LaSalle—has affected about 2.5 percent of P&G's employee base, versus closer to 25 percent at IBM. One obvious reason is that the scope for labor arbitrage in the fast-moving consumer goods industry may be increasing but is still much less substantial overall than in, say, IBM Global Services.

TCS and Cognizant. TCS's attempts to aggregate and its core strategy of arbitrage have already been discussed. As CEO S. Ramadorai puts it, both are integral to its future. But while ostensibly pursuing the same AA strategy as IBM, TCS places comparatively more emphasis on arbitrage, in line with its initial strategy. The contrast helps makes the point that there is room for variation in the definition and implementation of what might seem to be the same AA strategy and suggests, as does the example of P&G (which was majoring in aggregation and minoring in adaptation), that distinguishing between the primary and secondary emphases of AA strategies can indeed be helpful.

But even without drawing such distinctions there may be more than one route to success in a particular industry. This point will be illustrated with another example from Indian IT services, Cognizant, which has grown rapidly to become the fourth-largest competitor with delivery basically out of India. Cognizant has emphasized arbitrage and adaptation, rather than arbitrage and aggregation, by investing heavily in a local presence and "face" in its key market, the United States, to the point where the firm can pass itself off as Indian or U.S.-based, depending on the occasion.

Cognizant began life in 1993 as a captive of Dun & Bradstreet, with a more even distribution of power than in purely Indian firms: founder Kumar Mahadeva dealt with customers in the United States, while Lakshmi Narayanan (then chief operating officer, now chairman) oversaw delivery out of India. The company soon moved to deepen such pairings by setting up a "two-in-a-box" structure in which there were always two global leads for each project—one in India, and one in the United States. The leads had joint accountability and were compensated on the same outcomes in the same way. Francisco D'Souza, Cognizant's new CEO, recalls that it took two years to implement this structure and even longer for it to change mind-sets—at a time when there were only six hundred employees (compared with twenty-five thousand now). And two-in-a-box is just one element, albeit an important one, of a much broader effort to rethink the trade-offs between arbitrage and adaptation and get past what Cognizant's management describes as the key integration challenge in global offshoring: poor coordination between delivery and marketing that leads to "tossing stuff over the wall" (figure 7-6).

Taken together, all these examples illustrate that the pursuit of compound strategies rather than one is still challenging. The organizational elements of this challenge will be discussed further in the last section of this chapter.

Level 3: Trifecta (AAA) Strategies

Finally, consider a company trying to beat its competitors on all three strategies: adaptation, aggregation, and arbitrage. Success in this regard, while not impossible, is very rare. It is more likely—or less unlikely—in

FIGURE 7-6

Cognizant's arbitrage-adaptation strategy

Staffing	Delivery	Marketing
• Relatively stringent recruiting process • More MBAs and consultants • More non-Indians • Training programs in India for acculturation	• Two-in-a-box structure • All proposals done jointly (India and overseas) • More proximity to customers • On-site kickoff teams • Intensive travel, use of technology	• Indian and U.S. positioning • Use of U.S. nationals in key marketing positions • Very senior relationship managers • Proactive selling to a small number of large customers

environments where the tensions outlined in table 7-1 are weak or can be overridden by large-scale economies or structural advantages, or where competitors are constrained.

For an example that illustrates these points as well as the pursuit of an AAA strategy, or close to it, consider the case of GE Healthcare, or GEH, in medical diagnostic imaging. This industry has been growing rapidly and has concentrated globally in the hands of a big three: GEH, Siemens Medical Solutions (SMS), and Philips Medical Systems (PMS), with estimated revenue shares of the worldwide "big box" business of, roughly, 30 percent, 25 percent, and 20 percent, respectively.[7] The high global concentration seems to be related to what is most striking about the industry in terms of the strategies depicted in figure 7-4: medical diagnostic imaging ranks well within the top decile of manufacturing in terms of R&D intensity. Specifically, R&D-to-sales ratios have risen to more than 10 percent for the big three competitors and range even higher for smaller rivals, many of which face profit squeezes. These figures suggest that the aggregation-related challenge of building global scale has proven particularly important in this industry in recent years.

GEH, the largest of the big three, has also consistently been the most profitable. This reflects, first of all, success at aggregation, as indicated by the following:

- *Economies of scale:* GEH has higher total R&D spending than SMS or PMS, greater total sales, and a larger service force (constituting half of GEH's total employee head count)—but its R&D-to-sales ratio is lower, its other expense ratios are comparable, and it has fewer major production sites.

- *Acquisition capabilities:* Through experience, GEH has become more efficient at acquiring. It made nearly one hundred acquisitions under Jeffrey Immelt (before he became GE's CEO); since then, it has continued to make a lot of acquisitions, including the $9.5 billion Amersham deal in 2004, which moved the company beyond metal boxes and into medicine, and its purchase of two of Abbott Laboratories' diagnostics businesses in early 2007 for $8.1 billion, further extending its medical capabilities.

- *Economies of scope:* The Amersham and Abbott acquisitions reflect a drive to meld GE's traditional base of physics and engineering skills with skills at biochemistry; in addition, GEH finances equipment purchases through GE Capital.

In addition to its success at aggregation, GEH has even more clearly outpaced its competitors in terms of arbitrage. Under Immelt, but especially more recently, it has moved to become a "Global Product Company" by migrating production rapidly to low-cost production bases. Moves have been facilitated by a "pitcher-catcher" concept originally developed elsewhere in GE, with a "pitching team" at the existing site working closely with a "catching team" at the new site until the latter's performance meets or exceeds the former's. By 2005, GEH was reportedly more than halfway to its targets of obtaining 50 percent of its direct material purchases from—and locating 60 percent of its own manufacturing in—low-cost countries.

Finally, in terms of adaptation, GEH has invested heavily in country-focused marketing organizations, relatively loosely coupled to the integrated development-and-manufacturing back end, with objectives that one executive characterized as being "more German than the Germans." It also boosts customer appeal with its emphasis on providing services as well as equipment; for example, training radiologists and consulting about postimage processing, although such customer intimacy obviously has to be tailored by country.

Having outlined GEH's well-thought-out global strategy, I must add that even it is subject to some internal tensions, particularly in terms of adapting to the exceptional requirements of potentially large but low-income markets such as China and India versus integrating globally. As Jeff Immelt recently described it,

At a meeting last year, reviewing the value products for health care with Joe Hogan, who runs the business, we added $20 million in funding and took the responsibility for the value products away from the product lines and put it in China. That was how we removed an internal barrier:

the mother business was squeezing it. In the year since, sales have grown from $60 million to $260 million. At a recent update for those same products, we talked about an external barrier: how we might design knockdown kits so that we could design the thing and make a kit in India but have it assembled in China and avoid the tariffs and duties.[8]

It is also worth adding that GEH *isn't* clearly ahead on all dimensions: SMS has focused more on core imaging and is regarded as having achieved technological leadership in more imaging modalities. That is, SMS has aggregated more effectively from at least one perspective. This example reminds us that even when more than one competitor pursues a particular strategy, they may succeed by taking very different approaches.

What's more, GEH has managed to pursue the three As to this extent partly by separating out the pursuit of one of them, adaptation. This is one example of a range of mechanisms for economizing on managerial bandwidth. Such mechanisms are particularly in demand when a company is emphasizing the pursuit of two or, especially, three As: separation may be a better overall approach than forcing very diverse activities together in, say, the bear hug of a matrix structure. As A. G. Lafley explained to me, the reason P&G is able to pursue arbitrage up to a point as well as adaptation and aggregation is that the company has deliberately separated these functions into three subunits (global business units; market development organizations; and global business shared services, or GBSS) and has imposed a structure that minimizes points of contact and, thereby, friction.

P&G's emphasis on outsourcing through GBSS effectively externalizes arbitrage, calling to mind yet another sublever discussed in the context of adaptation in chapter 4. Some of the other sublevers discussed in chapter 4 also apply to this problem of optimizing the allocation of limited managerial bandwidth. Making different parts of the organization perform different functions is, after all, a matter of increasing internal variation efficiently, despite trade-offs and various indivisibilities that favor doing particular things one way throughout the organization.

Finally, GEH's performance has also depended, to some extent, on constrained competitors. In addition to facing a variety of size-related and other structural disadvantages relative to GEH, SMS and particularly PMS have simply been slow in some respects, such as in shifting production to lower-cost countries. For all these reasons, the temptation to treat the GEH example as an open invitation to pursue a trifecta of adaptation, aggregation, and arbitrage should stubbornly be resisted. If you still find yourself tempted, please read the box "The AAA Trifecta: Better Odds at the Racetrack?" with particular care.

The AAA Trifecta:
Better Odds at the Racetrack?

Despite my advice against trying to beat capable competitors along all three AAA dimensions, experience shows that energetic managers will consider that objective and even pursue it far more frequently than in the few cases in which it actually seems attainable. Instead of betting your company's resources on an AAA strategy, it might be safer to take them to the racetrack and wager them on a *trifecta*.

A trifecta, as aficionados of racing will know, involves picking horses to finish first, second, and third in a race. The successful selection of all three is unlikely enough that winning money through a trifecta is viewed in some racing circles as indicative of inside information.

Pick threes, in which you pick the winners in three separate horse races, are even riskier than trifectas (other things being equal, particularly the distribution of equine talent). In a trifecta, if a horse places first, it can't also place second, and so on.

The challenge of pulling off an AAA strategy in business seems substantially harder than successfully picking the winners in three separate horse races, because of the conflicts or trade-offs across the three As that were highlighted in table 7-2. Or to use a different mammalian metaphor suggested by chapter 6, attempts to create jacks-of-all-trades are likely to result, instead, in jackalopes.

The AAA Triangle and Strategy Development:
A Competitive Mapping Example

The previous section used the AAA triangle to illustrate the variety of global strategies. The triangle can also be helpful in deciding which strategy to pursue in the first place, a point already registered in regard to A strategies during the discussion of industry expenditure intensities (figure 7-4), but worth making in a extended way, over an extended strategy space.

The example concerns PMS, the smallest of the big three in diagnostic imaging. As described in chapter 4, Philips long followed a strategy that concentrated significant power in the hands of country managers and emphasized adaptation—until 1996, when a new CEO abolished the geographic leg of the geography-product matrix to aggregate more effectively around global product divisions. At the business level, in regard to PMS, it is sometimes suggested that Philips's traditional focus on adaptation has persisted and remains a source of competitive advantage over GEH or SMS. But any adaptation advantage for PMS is limited by SMS's edge at technology and GEH's edge at service quality. While these can be seen as global attributes of those two competitors' offerings, they *do* create customer lock-in at the local level.

Any residual adaptation advantage for PMS seems to be more than offset by disadvantages at aggregation, at which it trails GEH and SMS even though the supremacy Philips assigned to global product divisions in the second half of the 1990s was meant to move it in this direction. PMS's absolute R&D expenditures are one-third less than those of GEH and one-quarter less than those of SMS, and it is a much larger part of a much smaller corporation—with, apparently, a smaller acquisition war chest. In addition, PMS was stitched together out of six separate companies in an acquisition spree between 1998 and 2001 to complement its original, aging X-ray imaging business. It is somewhat surprising that this attempt has worked as well as it has—in a corporation without much acquisition experience to fall back on—but there are clearly still aftereffects. Most dramatically, PMS wrote down or paid more than €700 million related to past acquisition attempts—one consummated, another considered—in 2004, nearly wiping out its reported earnings for that year.

PMS's preoccupation until recently with getting its disparate parts stitched together is also partly to blame for its trailing at arbitrage. It did not start a manufacturing (joint) venture in China until September 2004, with the first output for the Chinese market becoming available in 2005, and the first supplies for export in 2006—even though Philips, the parent, is one of the largest multinationals in China. Overall, PMS's sourcing levels from low-cost countries in 2005 were comparable to levels achieved by GEH in 2001 and lagged SMS's as well.

These insights on positioning relative to the three As can usefully be pulled together into a single competitive map (figure 7-7). Mapping along these lines, while always approximate, calls attention to how competitors are actually located in strategy space as well as improving visualization of the trade-offs across different strategies—both important to thinking through where and where not to focus your efforts.

How might PMS use this competitive map—and, more broadly, the AAA triangle, for strategy development? In view of where PMS lags, there are probably certain operational givens about trying to narrow those gaps: continuing to try to improve how the different parts of PMS work

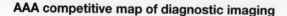

FIGURE 7-7

AAA competitive map of diagnostic imaging

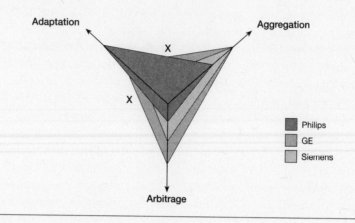

together (aggregation) and accelerating the shift of manufacturing to low-cost countries (arbitrage). But it seems unlikely that PMS can decisively beat its larger rivals at either strategy (unless it somehow successfully introduces a disruptive technology, but that is easier said than done). It also seems, however, that the increased emphasis industrywide on aggregation and arbitrage *has* undercut the viability of a strategy based just on adaptation.

The two most obvious strategy alternatives for PMS are the two AA strategies marked by Xs in figure 7-7: adaptation-aggregation or adaptation-arbitrage. Adaptation-aggregation comes closest to the strategy currently in place. Note, however, that it is unlikely to solve the aggregation-related challenges facing PMS as number three, so it had truly better offer some meaningful extras in terms of local responsiveness. Alternatively, PMS could give up on the idea of creating a competitive advantage and simply tap into average industry profitability, which is high: the big three are described as "gentlemanly" in setting prices. Either way, though, imitation of the larger rivals' large-scale moves into entirely new areas seems likely to *widen*, rather than narrow, this source of disadvantage.

The second of the AA alternatives for PMS, adaptation-arbitrage, would aim not just to produce in low-cost locations, but to radically reengineer and simplify the product so as to take large amounts of cost out for large emerging markets such as in China and India. However, this option does not fit with Philips's heritage, which is *not* one of competing through low costs. And GEH has clearly reduced the room for PMS to follow a strategy of this sort by an "in China for China" product that is supposed to have reduced costs by 50 percent. PMS, in contrast, talked of cost reductions of 20 percent with its first line of Chinese offerings.

Finally, if neither of these compound alternatives appeals—and frankly, neither seems likely to lead to a competitive advantage for PMS—the company *could* try to change the game that is playing. While PMS seems stuck with structural disadvantages in core diagnostic imaging relative to GEH and SMS, it could look for related fields in which it might have more advantages and fewer disadvantages. (In relation to the AAA triangle, this would best be thought of as a lateral shift, to a new area of business.) And in fact, PMS seems to be attempting something along these lines—albeit slowly—with its recent emphasis on medical devices for people to use at home, such as home defibrillators to treat sudden cardiac arrest. As former CFO Jan Hommen put it, PMS has an advantage here over both SMS and GE: "With our consumer electronics and domestic appliances businesses, we have gained a lot of experience and knowledge in how to facilitate consumers."[9] Since the resources emphasized in this go-to-home strategy—brand and distribution—operate at the local or national level, the new strategy can be seen as emphasizing adaptation (and some degree of aggregation) in a new market.

Three Organizational Principles

The preceding sections have highlighted the variety of global strategies and offered tools and several specific principles for choosing among them. It is useful to add three principles for organizing to achieve the selected strategic objectives.

Expanded coordination

While multinational companies have existed for several centuries, at least, they have greatly increased the amount of coordination that they attempt. Early multinationals such as the great trading companies operated in environments where information flows were slow and sparse, and the companies had correspondingly small headquarters: the Hudson's Bay Company, for instance, employed only twenty salaried managers centrally at the beginning of the eighteenth century.[10] By the late nineteenth century, some multinationals had worked out the functional and multidivisional forms of organization as responses to the challenges of coordination and control over long distances, but head offices continued to be small by today's standards: thus, the highly integrated oil behemoth, John D. Rockefeller's Standard Oil, had only a thousand people in general administration on the eve of its dissolution in 1911. Since then, leading-edge multinationals have looked beyond a single strategy (originally arbitrage) and have benefited—especially recently—from dramatic improvements in information technology. As a result, cross-border coordination in such companies extends well beyond the traditional emphasis on resource allocation across and monitoring of national operations by headquarters—and involves significant coordination across organizational boundaries. Yet many companies, not to mention the literature, still cling to minimalist conceptions of coordination.

New coordination mechanisms

Efficient expansion of the amount of coordination attempted has been greatly aided by the development of new coordination mechanisms. Consider examples from leading-edge companies discussed earlier in this chapter. In addition to IBM's human supply chain, the company has demonstrated creativity in devising "deal hubs" to aggregate across its diverse businesses and in reconsidering assumptions such as the collocation of global functional headquarters: it recently relocated its chief procurement officer from Somers, New York, to Shenzhen, China. Other examples already mentioned include P&G's cascading structure of reviews, TCS's global-regional-local delivery network, Cognizant's two-in-a-box structure, and GE's "pitcher-catcher" concept. Numerous others can be culled from current headlines. Thus, Cisco recently announced the appointment of a chief globalization officer, to be based in Bangalore, which has been designated Cisco Globalization Center East, as part of an initiative to set up a global, developing-technology hub in the Indian subcontinent to compete more effectively with the likes of Huawei of China.[11] (Actually, all of Cisco's primary business functions are supposed to be represented in India, and the company's target is to have 20 percent of senior managers working out of Bangalore by 2010.) The point of all these examples is that with new challenges, new responses are mandated, and leading-edge companies are good places to look for them.

The Evolving Agenda

Let's return to the example with which this chapter began, IBM. While IBM has gone a considerable distance in recent years in integrating arbitrage into how it runs its businesses, particularly IBM Global Services, it seems unlikely that the company will be able to beat Indian competitors at software services at their own low(er)-cost game, given employment costs that seem to be 50 to 75 percent higher than for local firms. Rather, what is distinctive about IBM is that despite recent divestitures, it still has the broadest product line in the industry, with hardware, software, and IT services. By analogy with PMS's seeking out unoccupied space—but arguably from a position of greater strength—one option for IBM is to realize the vision of "One IBM" by offering solutions that span all three sectors. The latest reports out of IBM headquarters indicate that an aggregation effort along exactly these lines seems to have been initiated as the company gets up to speed (or close to it) in terms of arbitrage. Sam Palmisano has formed integration and value teams out of the top several hundred managers at the company as a (relatively) bottoms-up way of trying to transform the organization more fundamentally than top-down dictates to the sector heads might achieve. Also note that such changes in relative emphasis are particularly likely, over the short-run, if compound strategies are being pursued.

The last principle and, in fact, all three organizational principles discussed in this section are meant to make a broader point. Nobody has yet figured out the optimal way to organize a complex global company, even conditional on the strategic target or targets that it is pursuing. But much can be learned from what leading-edge companies are trying to do, how they have chosen to pursue their agenda, and the challenges with which they continue to wrestle.

Conclusions

The box "Global Generalizations" summarizes the specific conclusions from this chapter. If the last few, in particular, seem open-ended, that is by design. This book was meant to broaden thinking about global strategy. This chapter has done its part by stressing the variety of global strategies: there are three pure strategies corresponding to the three As—with numerous variants on each—and at least as many compound (AA or AAA) strategies. In addition, one can imagine a number of organizational interpretations and implementations of the choice of a particular A or AA (or, sometimes, AAA) strategy. That is why, despite my insistence on choosing among the three As, taking semiglobalization seriously in setting strategy can be very liberating. There are many ways to play the differences.

Global Generalizations

1. The excitement around globalization has shifted since the 1980s from the globalization of markets to the globalization of production.

2. While the current enthusiasm for the globalization of production—or, more broadly, arbitrage—may pass, there is for the first time recognition of the full scope of the global strategy agenda.

3. This agenda can be summarized in terms of the AAA triangle, which, in addition to helping highlight the variety of global strategies, can be used to develop a globalization scorecard and force strategic prioritization.

4. Every top manager of a company with aspirations to create value by crossing borders should be able to specify in his or her own head which of the three As will be the basis for the company's cross-border competitive advantage.

5. My broad recommendations in this regard to the AAA strategies are these: nail down at least one of the As and, with one in hand, possibly seek another, but be careful about pursuing the elusive trifecta.

6. Applications or extensions of the AAA triangle that aid choices across the three As include careful consideration of the trade-offs across them and the mapping of expenditure intensities and competitive positions.

7. The effective pursuit of adaptation, aggregation, or arbitrage, or, especially, some combination of them typically requires expanded conceptions of coordination and arrays of coordination mechanisms.

8. Nobody has yet figured out *the* optimal way to organize a complex global company, but much can be learned from looking at leading-edge companies.

8

Toward a Better Future

Getting Started

Even if you're on the right track, you'll get run over if you just sit there.

—variously attributed to Arthur Godfrey and Will Rogers

IN THE 1980S, the rhetoric of globalization concentrated on markets. In the 2000s, it seems much more focused on production. In addition to the substantive content of this shift, it suggests some variability over time in how enthusiasts have thought about globalization up to now. There is similar variability in beliefs about the future of globalization.

Getting caught up in one of these debates is often no help in—and sometimes an obstruction to—deciding what to do about global strategy and getting started at doing it. This chapter begins by commenting briefly on forecasts about the future of globalization. It then offers several suggestions for improving paths to the future and concludes with a five-step framework for getting started by doing a global strategy audit for your business or businesses.

Forecasts About Globalization

Forecasts about globalization have a tendency to get too caught up in the times in which they are formulated. Thus, Karl Polanyi and coauthors

(1957) and Karl W. Deutsch and Alexander Eckstein (1961), writing before the full extent of the recovery of globalization after World War II became clear, emphasized that various measures of internationalization had declined significantly since the period before World War I, and asserted that this trend was unlikely to be reversed anytime soon.[1]

Contrary to the predictions by those eminent thinkers, cross-border economic activity surged in the postwar period and, as it breached prewar records, inspired forked responses, with optimists stressing that international economic integration had reached new heights, and pessimists insisting that it had barely returned to levels experienced nearly a century earlier. Optimism about globalization drew strength from the fall of the Berlin Wall in the late 1980s; rapid growth in Asia, particularly China (albeit qualified by the Asian currency crisis); and, more recently, the surging globalization of production. But, perhaps since optimism tends to provoke its own opposition, we are seeing, as I write this, serious suggestions that globalization—as in the rate of increase of cross-border integration—may be slowing down.

The level of seriousness with which I take such forecasts is limited, for reasons that aren't restricted to past performance, or nonperformance, but also include several other considerations:

- Skepticism about using blips in the business cycle and other high-frequency events as the basis for announcing changes in the direction or speed of a process with significant momentum that has unfolded over a long period

- Appreciation of the complexities of making precise predictions about organizations, let alone countries or the entire world economy, coupled with unease about how some of the forecasts that *are* made seem to be pulled out of thin air

- Belief that the semiglobalized state of the world, far removed from either complete localization or complete integration, is a better basis for company strategy than iffy forecasts about changes in that state or changes in the rate of change

To elaborate on that last point, think of somebody who is driving across the United States and who happens to be in the Midwest. The driver is going to be far from the coasts for quite some time, irrespective of whether he or she speeds up or slows down—or even changes direction. A similar argument applies to semiglobalization. Looking forward, levels of cross-border integration may increase, stagnate, or even suffer a sharp reversal if the experience between and during the two world wars is any indication of the possibilities. But given the parameters of the current situation, it seems unlikely that increases will anytime soon yield a state in which the differences among countries can be ignored. Or that de-creases could lead to a state in which cross-border linkages can be forgot-ten about. So one does not have to make a precise forecast to predict that semiglobalization as a condition is sufficiently broad to persist for some time to come. Achieving similar stability in attitudes toward global opera-tions would seem preferable to mood swings about the outlook—espe-cially since most global strategies cannot be changed on a dime.

So to summarize, the one forecast that I am comfortable with is that semiglobalization is likely to persist for the next decade, the next two decades, and (probably) beyond—although obviously, the confidence in-terval fans out as one moves farther into the future. If this diagnosis plays any role in preventing bipolar attitudes toward globalization, it will have been worthwhile. But readers are probably also looking for specific advice on what might be done to improve their companies' future global trajec-tories. In response, let me offer some tentative recommendations for mak-ing a path toward a better future.

Path Making

How might you improve the path that you follow from today to tomor-row and beyond if the future is shrouded in uncertainty? To be more spe-cific, how might your company improve, in the context of globalization, on the common expedients of sailing in one direction until hitting a sand-bar, or playing pinball to the headlines, or simply marking time?

1. Anticipate bumps and detours even if you do believe that the world will eventually become much more integrated. Even if you remain convinced that the apocalyptic vision of close-to-complete integration will be realized sooner or later, recognize that the road from here to there is unlikely to be either smooth or straight. There will be shocks and cycles, in all likelihood, and maybe even another period of stagnation or reversal that will endure for decades. (It's happened before!) Volatility of this sort is particularly worth allowing for in relation to the BRIC (Brazil, Russia, Indian, and China) economies that Thomas Friedman and other writers have recently emphasized as centers of value creation in the twenty-first century. But even companies that are supposed to be sophisti-cated about emerging markets trip up on this point. Goldman Sachs—the leader in investment banking in most major markets, the first major Wall Street bank to commit resources to post-Soviet Russia, and one of the in-stitutions responsible for popularizing BRIC countries as an opportunity set—ranked twenty-fourth among investment banks in Russian equity and debt underwriting in 2005.[2] Why so low? Because Goldman, like a number of other investment banks, exited after Russia's 1998 financial crisis and debt default, and let several years go by before trying to reestablish its foothold there. Note that strategies such as this often entail buying in at the top of the cycle and exiting at the bottom—usually not a recipe for financial success.

2. Pay attention to other "predictable surprises" as well. Bumps are just one manifestation of "predictable surprises," a term coined by Max Bazerman and Michael Watkins to describe situations where "leaders had all the data and insight they needed to recognize the potential, even the inevitability, of major problems, but failed to respond with effective preventative action."[3] A number of predictable or at least possible surprises are in the air as far as the general global environment is concerned: global warming; different kinds of meltdowns in the Middle East, China, and India, and the United States, among other possibilities; a global liquidity crisis; a general sociopolitical backlash against globalization; and so on.[4] Notions of a global governance gap reinforce the idea that a shock of this sort might have a persistent effect. How many such shocks is your company prepared for? At a minimum, I suggest articulating one or more deglobalization scenarios and analyzing their implications for your company's global strategy, as a prelude to thinking, possibly, of alternatives.

3. Add to predictive power by taking things down to the industry and company level. Shocks, cycles, and trends, even when they have crosscutting implications, vary greatly across industries and companies in their effects, in ways that greatly reduce the usefulness of trying to fit one world-historical conception to all of them. Focus on the risks and, more broadly, trends that are most likely to affect *your industry or company, and how they are actually to do so*. Thus, even the effects of something as potentially far-reaching as global warming depend on whether one looks at the issue from the perspective of a financial investor, a construction firm, an automaker (whose reaction would also depend on its focus on large versus small cars), or a potential supplier of cleaner energy, to cite some varied examples. And depending on the setting, other risks or trends may well be more salient and therefore worth prioritizing. For example, when I first started working with Indian software firm TCS on building useful scenarios about the future, we figured that it made the most sense to start with avian flu, given the nature of the company's business.

4. Recognize the importance of business in shaping broad outcomes—including those related to the future of globalization. The preceding discussion might have seemed to suggest that outcomes will unfold independently of what businesses decide to do. But for many key uncertainties, that is clearly not the case. Consider the broad process of globalization itself. Some of the concerns voiced by antiglobalizers include the following:

- A declining share of wages in total national income in developed countries at a time when the share of profits is at a multidecade high in many of them

- The lack of a globalization safety net in many of those countries (the United States, for instance, is estimated to gain $1 trillion per year from trade, but to spend about $1 billion on retraining)[5]

- The creation of a two-track world. As Muhammad Yunus, the microcredit pioneer put it in his speech accepting the 2006 Nobel Peace Prize, if globalization "is a free-for-all highway, its lanes will be taken over by the giant trucks from powerful economies . . . [at the expense of] Bangladeshi rickshaws."[6]

It is neither principled nor practical for companies to stick their heads in the sand in response to an issue as fundamental as the distribution of the globalization dividend. In terms of public discourse and action, in particular, I'd recommend the following steps for companies that favor greater integration (note that not all will do so):

- Be careful about your choice of words. Outsourcing often triggers negative vibes, as former Bush economic adviser Greg Mankiw discovered; so does globalization, which, according to U.S. pollster Frank Luntz, "frightens older workers."[7] (Luntz recommends talking about the free-market economy instead—although one suspects that this might work less well in continental Europe.)

- Try to be concrete rather than abstract about economywide benefits of globalization. Findings such as the McKinsey Global Institute's calculation that for every dollar the United States sends abroad through outsourcing, it gets about $1.12 back are more useful than appeals to the process of market equilibration described in economics textbooks.[8]

- Dispel globalization bogeymen that don't have a scientific basis, such as the myth, discussed and discredited in chapter 1 and my other work, that increased global integration necessarily leads to increased global concentration.

- Support job-retraining programs and, more broadly, social insurance. History shows that support for free trade tends to be fragile in the absence of such programs.

- Emphasize upgrading and productivity growth as the focus of public as well as business policy. These are what really matter in the long run for the wealth of nations as well as companies.

5. Don't let a focus on the future crowd out consideration of the here and now. The future, including whether the direction of globalization creates headwinds or tailwinds for global strategies, certainly has a bearing on the success or failure of those strategies. But it should not be allowed to crowd out consideration of other factors that also matter, including those in the here and now. A refrain throughout this book is that the current state of practice of global strategy leaves *significant* headroom for improvement. One way of exploiting that potential is to get started. Figure 8-1 depicts a five-step process for doing so, although the sequencing should not be taken too literally. The rest of this chapter focuses on these steps.[9]

FIGURE 8-1

Redefining global strategy: a five-step process for getting started

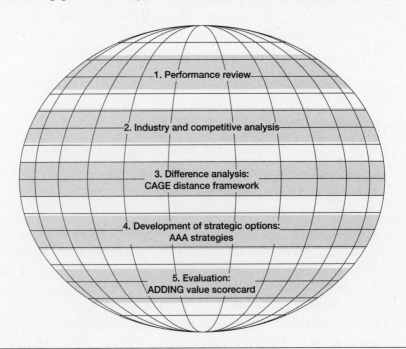

1. Performance review
2. Industry and competitive analysis
3. Difference analysis: CAGE distance framework
4. Development of strategic options: AAA strategies
5. Evaluation: ADDING value scorecard

Getting Started

Suggestions about how to use the ideas developed in this book to devise better global strategies have run through the previous chapters. But it seems useful to summarize the suggestions here, in a final chapter, to help the reader start putting them to some use. The five-step process described here starts with background analysis before turning to the articulation and evaluation of strategic options. Since the background analyses are the ones that haven't already had an entire chapter—or more—devoted to them, they are the ones that are discussed in a bit more detail below.

1. Performance review. As a backdrop to any attempt to set or reset global strategy, it is useful to review how global operations have been doing. At least one dimension on which it is useful to disaggregate performance is the geographic one (although the bases of disaggregation are as numerous as the bases of aggregation discussed in chapter 5). For a range of possible reasons—such as a belief in ultimate ubiquity, escalating commitment, and a focus on accounting profits rather than economic profits that also net out the opportunity costs of the capital employed—many companies get into but don't get out of unsuitable geographies. Some indications of the extent of the problem are provided by data that Marakon Associates analyzed at my request. Here are Marakon's findings:

> We found that half of the companies we have looked at (8 out of 16) have significant geographic units that earn negative economic returns . . . [We] know from our clients that their profitability by geography has stayed fairly stable over time unless they have specifically targeted action at specific countries/regions.

Figure 8-2 provides a fairly typical example of this type of problem. Note that in 2005, roughly one-fifth of this company's revenues generated negative economic returns. And if this seems bad, note that the same ratio for Toyota, a champion globalizer, was 25 percent rather than 20 percent.

The broader point is that instead of looking at international revenues, growth rates, and even accounting profits, it is critical to take a value-focused perspective. It is better still to take an even broader approach to global performance management and set up a globalization scorecard, as illustrated in figure 7-3. That is because a sense of how you have been doing generally improves discussions of what you should do next.

2. Industry and competitive analysis. Industry and competitive analysis is an essential part of the approach to global strategy development that

FIGURE 8-2

Economic returns by country: a fast-moving consumer goods company

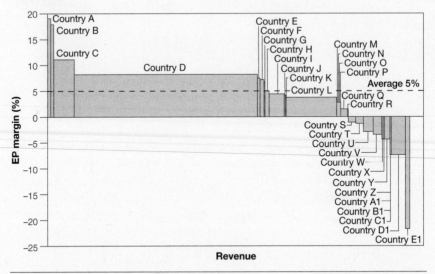

is described in this chapter. It actually cascades through the rest of the five-step process as well and will be cited when the respective steps are discussed. What should be emphasized here is that there are some very basic questions about one's own industry and interactions within it that it is foolhardy to start off without first answering. This is especially true since at least some generally held intuitions in this regard—about increasing global concentration or standardization, for example—turn out to be generally wrong.[10]

Nine basic questions of this sort—questions that you should be able to answer with data rather than intuition—are listed in the box "Basic Questions in Cross-Border Industry and Competitive Analysis." Many of these questions are or can be elaborated further in terms of levels at a point in time versus changes over time, and also in terms of global, regional, or local levels of analysis; and other kinds of segmentation schemes. Each must be looked at from the perspective of a particular industry. And changes over long time frames—often a decade or longer—are of interest, given the slowness with which many global measures move. In addition, compiling and comparing international data may entail much more effort than doing so at the national level. All of which is to say that "just" filling out this background picture of the industry and interactions within it can involve a great deal of work.

Basic Questions in Cross-Border Industry and Competitive Analysis

1. Concentration of sales among the top three to five players: Is it really increasing?

2. Leadership and changes in leadership or market shares: Is there a clear leader or core, and if so, how much turnover has been experienced in identities?

3. Cross-border trade as a percentage of world production, foreign direct investment relative to gross fixed capital formation, and international joint ventures or strategic alliances (perhaps relative to cross-border mergers and acquisitions): How do these normalized measures of cross-border integration stack up?

4. Cross-border standardization, most obviously of products: Again, is it really increasing?

5. Rate of real price declines: What do these imply about the minimal targets for productivity improvement?

6. Industry profitability, particularly economic profitability: How large, in particular, is cross-country variation in profitability?

7. Relationship between profitability and scale (if any): Does profitability depend on scale globally, regionally, nationally, or at the plant or customer level?

8. Distribution of economic profits across suppliers, competitors, complementors, and buyers: Where's the money?

9. Advertising/marketing, R&D, and labor (and capital and specialized inputs): Which of these categories of expenditure loom particularly large in your industry and, on that basis, what type of industry is it?

---

3. Difference analysis with the CAGE distance framework. Steps 1 and 2, while basic in terms of due diligence, were also generic in the sense that they didn't really key off the idea of semiglobalization developed in this book. Semiglobalization draws attention to differences across countries. Understanding the landscape of semiglobalization was the topic of chapter 2, which introduced a multidimensional framework (CAGE) for thinking about different degrees of difference between or among countries. The chapter emphasized distance-based measures of difference, with two objectives in mind:

- Moving the discussion beyond declarations of the existence and importance of cross-country differences by permitting some calibration

- Adding a bilateral or multilateral component to what still too often tends to be country analysis based on unilateral country characteristics uninformed by considerations of distance from home

If these points seem old hat by now, remind yourself of the state of practice, even sophisticated practice. I received a reminder recently when I found myself doing a panel on globalization with several well-known practitioners at an event in Vienna. The audience naturally craved local responsiveness, so one question we were asked was "How should Austrian firms be thinking about East Europe?" The panel generally agreed that East Europe *was* interesting, although of course, one had to be careful there. The CAGE distance framework goes considerably farther: it directs attention to East European countries where German is widely used, that were part of the Austro-Hungarian Empire, that are close to Austria as the crow flies, share a land border with it, are navigable along the Danube, et cetera. Moreover, the framework can also easily accommodate variation in per-capita income and other significant differences that exist across East Europe.

Chapter 2 also emphasized that much of the value of difference or distance analysis comes from taking it down to the industry level. The objective, in other words, is to look at your industry landscape from a semiglobalized perspective. It is therefore important to figure out the cross-country differences that matter the most *in your particular industry* and ideal to gain a more quantitative sense of distance-sensitivities. The strategy that is selected—the focus of the next two steps—should embody some coherence in how it deals with the critical dimensions of distance. Of course, this still leaves room for different approaches to dealing with distance, ranging from common proximity-first strategies to opposites such as the "difficult first, easy second" strategy espoused by Haier—although companies rarely do well by seeking out distance along *all* dimensions. What clearly *isn't* a good idea is ignoring distance altogether.

4. Development of strategic options around the AAA strategies. The development of strategic options was discussed in chapters 4–7, which introduced the AAA strategies and discussed how to play the differences off the implied menu of strategy options. In addition, these chapters embodied a number of procedural points, some of which are worth reemphasizing here. First, having two or more options to evaluate is a *lot* better than having one. Second, strategic options do not emerge spontaneously: they have to be developed and documented. And third, improving the set of strategic options considered should probably command at least as much attention as improving their evaluation.

Improving the set of strategic options has been a recurrent theme of this book. One way this book has tried to help is by stretching thinking about global strategy with reminders of multidimensionality and variation of several kinds:

- The multidimensional (CAGE) differences between countries, and differences in differences

- The multiple components of value that can be affected by cross-border moves

- The variety (and subvarieties) of strategies for dealing with cross-border differences

Additional insights about how to improve strategic options were provided by the discussion of creativity in developing options (chapter 3) and of creating an open, adaptive mind-set (chapter 4; see also my Web site, www.ghemawat.org). And the discussion supplied numerous specific examples of imaginative—as well as unimaginative—development of global strategies. The bottom line? It is always worth looking for a new and improved angle.

5. Evaluation of strategic options with the ADDING Value scorecard. In evaluating strategic options, it is useful to analyze the implications for value in terms of the six components of the ADDING Value scorecard that was introduced in chapter 3. Table 3-2 provided a long list of guidelines— twenty-eight in all—for analyzing these value components. But the length and structure of that list should not obscure the fundamental point that it is important to take a value-focused perspective on globalization.

Again, if this recommendation sounds innocuous, it is worth reviewing current practice. Many companies still see globalization primarily in revenue-related terms, and of the remainder, many focus on accounting profits rather than economic profits (net of capital costs). So a value-focused perspective still seems the exception rather than the rule. And even fewer companies seem to do a good job of connecting strategic decision making about globalization to their systems for corporate financial programming.

The juxtaposition of this focus on value and the need expressed earlier for creativity seems the appropriate note on which to conclude. It should be abundantly clear from this book that semiglobalization, as distinct from the polar abstractions of complete cross-border integration and complete segmentation, enriches the space of global strategies and makes them worth thinking about creatively. But it should also be clear that semi-globalization implies significant barriers to border-crossing activities, which is what makes the focus on value particularly necessary.

Notes

Introduction

1. An authoritative global history of football is provided by David Goldblatt, *The Ball Is Round* (London: Viking, 2006). The globalization of soccer is also discussed by Gerald Hödl, "The Second Globalisation of Soccer" (San Francisco: Funders Network on Trade and Globalization, 16 June 2006), available at www.fntg.org/news/index.php?op=view&articleid=1237&type=0; and Franklin Foer, *How Soccer Explains the World: An Unlikely Theory of Globalization* (New York: HarperCollins, 2004).

2. Kofi A. Annan, "At the UN, How We Envy the World Cup," *International Herald Tribune*, 10–11 June 2006, 5.

3. Geoffrey Wheatcroft, "Non-Native Sons," *Atlantic Monthly*, June 2006.

4. Ibid.

5. Alan Beattie, "Distortions of the World Cup, a Game of Two Hemispheres," *Financial Times*, 12 June 2006, 13.

6. The data on success on the playing field in this paragraph and the next one are based on Branko Milanovic, "Globalization and Goals: Does Soccer Show the Way?" *Review of International Political Economy* 12 (December 2005);: 829–850 and an e-mail from him dated 13 August 2006, regarding the goal differentials in the 2006 World Cup.

7. Deloitte, Sports Business Group, "Football Money League: The Reign in Spain," (Manchester, UK: Deloitte 2007), accessed at http://www.deloitte.com/dtt/cda/doc/content/Deloitte%20FML%202007.pdf.

8. Robert Hoffmann, Lee Chew Ging, and Bala Ramasamy, "The Socio-Economic Determinants of International Soccer Performance," *Journal of Applied Economics* 5, no. 2 (November 2002): 253–272.

9. Mike Kepp, "Scoring Profits?" *Latin Trade* (magazine), December, 2000.

10. Uwe Buse, "Balls and Chains," *Spiegel Online*, 26 May 2006.

11. "Blatter Launches Fresh Series of Blasts," ESPN SoccerNet, 13 October 2005, http://soccernet.espn.go.com/news/story?id=345694&cc=5739.

Chapter 1: Semiglobalization and Strategy

1. For the original article, see Theodore Levitt, "The Globalization of Markets," *Harvard Business Review*, May–June 1983, 92.

2. See, for instance, *Wikipedia*, s.v. "Global strategy," http://en.wikipedia.org/wiki/Global_strategy.

3. See, for instance, Richard Landes, "Millenarianism and the Dynamics of Apocalyptic Time," in *Expecting the End: Millennialism in Social and Historical Context,* ed. Kenneth G. C. Newport and Crawford Gribben (Wilco, TX: Baylor University Press, 2006).

4. This is due, of course, to the influence of Thomas Friedman's *The World Is Flat* (New York: Farrar, Straus and Giroux, 2005), which has spent more weeks on various best-seller lists than all its globalization-related predecessors combined. Friedman's book is hard to engage with directly, since its 450-plus pages contain no tables, charts, footnotes, or list of references. But see my article, "Why the World Isn't Flat," *Foreign Policy* (March–April 2007); as well as the exchange of letters with Friedman, among others, in the May–June 2007 issue of *Foreign Policy*.

5. Times TV, Mumbai, 10 August 2006.

6. Preliminary estimates for 2006 suggest that the merger wave for the year increased this ratio of FDI to gross fixed capital formation to about 12 percent.

7. Complete integration in the sense of borders not mattering will typically imply levels of internationalization somewhat less than 100 percent, to an extent that depends on the largest national shares of the activity in question. Thus, without any double-counting, the trade-to-GDP ratio for the world would, given the distribution of (nominal) GDPs, be about 90 percent at the borders-don't-matter benchmark (100 percent minus the Herfindahl concentration ratio of GDPs, for reasons that the interested reader can work out). Additional normalized comparisons related to trade will be provided in chapter 2.

8. One problem is the focus on *revenues* rather than *value added*—for example, shipments of car parts from the United States to Canada, with cars being shipped back.

9. U.N. Conference on Trade and Development, *World Investment Report, 2005* (New York and Geneva: United Nations, 2005).

10. Pankaj Ghemawat, "Semiglobalization and International Business Strategy," *Journal of International Business Studies* 34, no. 2 (2003): 138–152.

11. This is, for instance, the escape hatch employed by Thomas Friedman when confronted with figure 1-1. See our exchange on "Why the World Isn't Flat" in the May–June 2007 issue of *Foreign Policy*.

12. UNESCO, International Organization for Migration, *World Migration 2005: Costs and Benefits of International Migration* (Geneva: International Organization for Migration, June 2005).

13. Alan M. Taylor, "Globalization, Trade, and Development: Some Lessons from History," in *Bridges for Development: Policies and Institutions for Trade and Integration,* ed. R. Devlin and A. Estevadeordal (Washington, DC: Inter-American Development Bank, 2003).

14. It is worth noting that trade economists continue to try to explain why there is so little trade rather than why there is so much of it, as will be elaborated in chapter 2.

15. The driver emphasized by Levitt, the convergence of tastes, is no longer taken very seriously. See John A. Quelch and Rohit Deshpandé, eds., *The Global Market: Developing a Strategy to Manage Across Borders* (New York: Jossey-Bass, 2004), particularly my chapter, "Global Standardization vs. Localization: A Case Study and a Model," 115–145.

16. Technological improvements are also reported to have assumed that role in apocalyptic scenarios in general. See Kenneth G. C. Newport and Crawford Gribben, eds., *Expecting the End: Millennialism in Social and Historical Context* (Waco, TX: Baylor University Press, 2006).

17. Frances C. Cairncross, *The Death of Distance: How the Communications Revolution Will Change Our Lives* (Boston: Harvard Business School Press, 1997), 4.

18. The calculation is based on guesstimates of U.S. Internet traffic at the end of 2005 from Andrew Odlyzko of the University of Minnesota; of the U.S. share of worldwide traffic, from RHK/Ovum, market consultants; and of total cross-border traffic from TeleGeography's *Global Internet Geography*. For a discussion of Professor Odlyzko's methododology and its application to end-2002, see "Internet Traffic Growth: Sources and Implications," in *Optical Transmission Systems and Equipment for WDM Networking II*, ed. B. B. Dingel, Proc. SPIE, vol. 5247, 2003, 1–15. The figure for end-2005 was provided by him in a phone conversation on 22 March 2007.

19. National Association of Software and Service Companies, "The IT Industry in India: Strategic Review, 2006" (New Delhi: NASSCOM, December 2005). Thomas Friedman cites Nandan Nilekani, the CEO of the second-largest Indian IT services company, Infosys, as the inspiration for his image of a flat world. But Nandan has pointed out to me that although Indian software programmers can now serve the United States from India, access is assured, in part, by U.S. capital's being invested—quite literally—in that outcome. I read this as suggestive of barriers, and of the idea that country of origin matters—even for capital, which we often think of as stateless.

20. The characterization of Google's strategy in Russia in this paragraph is based on Eric Pfanner, "Google's Russia March Stalls," *International Herald Tribune,* 18 December 2006, 9, 11.

21. Jack Goldsmith and Tim Wu, *Who Controls the Internet? Illusions of a Borderless World* (New York: Oxford University Press, 2006), 149.

22. Jeffrey Sachs and Andrew Warner, "Economic Reform and the Process of Global Integration," *Brookings Papers on Economic Activity,* 25th Anniversary Issue (1995).

23. Francis Fukuyama, *The End of History and the Last Man* (New York: Free Press, 1992).

24. Samuel Huntington, *The Clash of Civilizations and the Remaking of World Order* (New York: Simon & Schuster, 1996).

25. Steve Dowrick and J. Bradford DeLong, "Globalization and Convergence," paper presented for National Bureau of Economic Research Conference on Globalization in Historical Perspective, Santa Barbara, CA, 4–5 May 2001.

26. "The Future of Globalization," *The Economist,* 29 July–4 August 2006, front cover.

27. Dani Rodrik, "Feasible Globalizations," in *Globalization: What's New?* ed. M. Weinstein (New York: Columbia University Press, 2005).

28. *The Cola Conquest,* video directed by Irene Angelico (Ronin Films, Canberra, Australia, 1998).

29. Ibid.

30. Roberto C. Goizueta, remarks made to World Bottler Meeting, Monte Carlo, 25 August 1997, available at http://www.goizuetafoundation.org/world.htm.

31. Roberto C. Goizueta, quoted in Chris Rouch, "Coke Executive John Hunter Calling It Quits," *Atlanta Journal and Constitution,* 12 January 1996.

32. Sharon Herbaugh, "Coke and Pepsi Discover New Terrain in Afghanistan," Associated Press, 26 November 1991.

33. The Coca-Cola Company, Annual Report, 1997.

34. "Coke's Man on the Spot," *BusinessWeek Online,* 3 May 1999, available at www.businessweek.com/1999/99_18b3627119.htm.

35. Douglas Daft, quoted in Betsy McKay, "Coke's Daft Offers Vision for More-Nimble Firm," *Wall Street Journal,* 31 January 2000.

36. Douglas Daft, "Back to Classic Coke," *Financial Times,* 27 March 2000.

37. Douglas Daft, "Realizing the Potential of a Great Industry," remarks at the *Beverage Digest* "Future Smarts" Conference in New York, 8 December 2003, posted in the "Press center/viewpoints" section of the Coke Web site, www2.coca-cola.com/presscenter/viewpoints_daft_bev_digest2003_include.html.

38. For additional discussion of hype around growth, see Pankaj Ghemawat, "The Growth Boosters," *Harvard Business Review,* July 2004.

39. Bruce Kogut, "A Note on Global Strategies," *Strategic Management Journal* 10, no. 389 (1989): 383–389.

40. Pankaj Ghemawat and Fariborz Ghadar, "Global Integration ≠ Global Concentration," *Industrial and Corporate Change,* August 2006, especially 597–603.

41. Reid W. Click and Paul Harrison, "Does Multinationality Matter? Evidence of Value Destruction in U.S. Multinational Corporations," working paper no. 2000-21, Board of Governors of the Federal Reserve System, Washington, DC, February 2000; and Susan M. Feinberg, "The Expansion and Location Patterns of U.S. Multinationals," working paper, Robert H. Smith School of Business, University of Maryland, College Park, 2003.

42. Orit Gadiesh, "Think Globally, Market Locally," *Financier Worldwide,* 1 August 2005.

Chapter 2: Differences Across Countries:
The CAGE Distance Framework

1. David Orgel, "Wal-Mart's Global Strategy: When Opportunity Knocks," *Women's Wear Daily,* 24 June 2002.

2. For purposes of the following discussion, I'll treat Puerto Rico as distinct from the United States—that is, as "international"—except as otherwise noted.

3. For further discussion of gravity models, see Edward E. Leamer and James Levinsohn, "International Trade Theory: The Evidence," *Handbook of International Economics,* vol. III, ed. G. Grossman and K. Rogoff (Amsterdam: Elsevier B.V., 1995).

4. Note that the median distance across all possible country-pairs falls in between these two distances.

5. The estimates reported here are based on my own work with Rajiv Mallick and, although still very large in absolute terms, are significantly lower than the ones reported in Pankaj Ghemawat, "Distance Still Matters: The Hard Reality of Global Expansion," *Harvard Business Review,* September 2001, whose estimates were based on early work by Jeffrey Frankel and Andrew Rose, "An Estimate of the Effects of Currency Unions on Growth" unpublished paper, University of California, Berkeley, 2000. Our lower estimates mostly reflect our greater care in dealing with numerous observations coded as zero and our stricter focus on separate countries as opposed to politically distinct entities.

6. I'm counting "Colony/Colonizer" because both countries shared the same colonizer: Great Britain.

7. John F. Helliwell, "Border Effects: Assessing Their Implications for Canadian Policy in a North American Context," in *Social and Labour Market Aspects of North American Linkages,* ed. Richard G. Harris and Thomas Lemieux (Calgary: University of Calgary Press, 2005), 41–76.

8. For examples of each, see, respectively, Prakash Loungani et al., "The Role of Information in Driving FDI: Theory and Evidence," paper presented at the North American Winter Meeting of the Econometric Society, Washington, DC, 3–5 January 2003; Richard Portes and Helen Rey, "The Determinants of Cross-Border Equity Flows," *Journal of International Economics* 65 (February 2005): 269–296; Juan Alcácer and Michelle Gittelman, "How Do I Know What You Know? Patent Examiners and the Generation of Patent Citations," *Review of Economics and Statistics,* forthcoming; and Ali Hortacsu, Asis Martinez-Jerez, and Jason Douglas, "The Geography of Trade on eBay and MercadoLibre," working paper, University of Chicago, 2006.

9. Gert-Jan M. Linders, "Distance Decay in International Trade Patterns: A Meta-analysis," paper no. ersap679, presented at 45th Congress of the European Regional Science Association, Vrije Universiteit, Amsterdam, 23–25 August 2005, available at http://www.ersa.org. For additional evidence on the regionalization of international trade, see chapter 5.

10. For a more detailed review of frameworks for country analysis, refer in particular to "Note on Country Analysis," on my Web site, www.ghemawat.org.

11. See Geoffrey G. Jones, "The Rise of Corporate Nationality," *Harvard Business Review,* October 2006, 20–22; and, for a more detailed discussion, Geoffrey G. Jones, "The End of Nationality? Global Firms and 'Borderless Worlds,'" *Zeitschrift für Unternehmensgeschichte* 51, no. 2 (2006): 149–166.

12. Jan Johanson and Jan-Erik Vahlne, "The Internationalization Process of the Firm: A Model of Knowledge Development and Increasing Foreign Market Commitments," *Journal of International Business Studies* 8, no. 1 (1977): 22–32.

13. See, for instance, "Marketing Mishaps," *NZ Marketing Magazine* 18, no. 5 (June 1999): 7.

14. See, for instance, Bruce Kogut and Harbir Singh, "The Effect of National Culture on the Choice of Entry Mode," *Journal of International Business Studies* 19 (1988), 411–432; Luigi Guiso, Paola Sapienza, and Luigi Zingales, "Cultural Biases in Economic Exchange," unpublished paper, University of Chicago, 2005; Jordan I. Siegel, Amir N. Licht, and Shalom H. Schwartz, "Egalitarianism and International Investment," working paper no. 120-2006, European Corporate Governance Institute (ECGI) Finance Research Paper Series, Brussels, 21 April 2006.

15. William P. Alford, *To Steal a Book Is an Elegant Offense: Intellectual Property Law in Chinese Civilization, Studies in East Asian Law* (Stanford, CA: Stanford University Press, 1995).

16. This section has benefited greatly from my joint work on China versus India with Thomas Hout of the Boston Consulting Group and the University of Hong Kong.

17. Thomas G. Rawski, "Beijing's Fuzzy Math," *Wall Street Journal* (Eastern edition), 22 April 2002, A18.

18. "Dim Sums," *The Economist,* 4 November 2006, 79–80.

19. "Extending India's Leadership in the Global IT and BPO Industries," NASSCOM-McKinsey Report, New Delhi, December 2005.

20. Raymond Hill and L. G. Thomas III, "Moths to a Flame: Social Proof, Reputation, and Status in the Overseas Electricity Bubble," mimeographed working paper, Goizueta Business School, Emory University, Atlanta, May 2005.

21. Donald J. Rousslang and Theodore To, "Domestic Trade and Transportation Costs as Barriers to International Trade," *Canadian Journal of Economics* 26, no. 1 (February 1993): 208–221.

22. For a more detailed description of the Star case, see Pankaj Ghemawat and Timothy J. Keohane, "Star TV in 1993," Case 9-701-012 (Boston: Harvard Business School, 2000; rev. 2005) and Pankaj Ghemawat, "Star TV in 2000," Case 9-706-418 (Boston: Harvard Business School, 2005); and for a more detailed analysis, see Pankaj Ghemawat, "Global Standardization vs. Localization: A Case Study and a Model," in *The Global Market: Developing a Strategy to Manage Across Borders,* ed. John A. Quelch and Rohit Deshpande (New York: Jossey-Bass, 2004), 115–145.

23. Rupert Murdoch, quoted in the *Times* (London), 2 September 1993, reprinted in *Los Angeles Times,* 13 February 1994; and, for instance, "Week in Review Desk," *New York Times,* 29 May 1994.

24. See, for example, Stephen Hymer, *The International Operations of National Firms* (Cambridge, MA: MIT Press, 1976); and Srilata Zaheer, "Overcoming the Liability of Foreignness," *Academy of Management Journal* 38, no. 2 (1995): 341–363.

25. Subramaniam Rangan and Metin Sengul, "Institutional Similarities and MNE Relative Performance Abroad: A Study of Foreign Multinationals in Six Host Markets," working paper, INSEAD, Cedex, France, October 2004.

26. For more details on the analysis that follows, see Pankaj Ghemawat, "Distance Still Matters: The Hard Reality of Global Expansion," *Harvard Business Review,* September 2001, 137–147.

27. The alert reader will note that I am supplementing (actually, dividing) the measures of market size or income that traditionally occupy the horizontal axis of country portfolio analysis planning grids with measures of distance.

28. Jeremy Grant, "Yum Claims KFC Growth Could Match McDonald's," *Financial Times,* 7 December 2005, 19.

Chapter 3: Global Value Creation: The ADDING Value Scorecard

1. Compare the most prominent writers in this vein: Christopher A. Bartlett and Sumantra Ghoshal, *Managing Across Borders: The Transnational Solution* (Boston: Harvard Business School Press, 1989). As they put it, "For all the companies we studied, the key challenge in responding to the demands of the 1980s was not to define a strategy, but to overcome the unidimensional organizational capabilities and management biases that stood in the way of building a new, more complex, and dynamic transnational posture." Just in case you didn't get it, the objectives and content of cross-border strategy—the why and the what—are supposed to be obvious, but organization (the how) is not. To me, this is placing the cart squarely before the horse, given the general acknowledgment, even by organizational scholars, that organizational structure, broadly defined, has to be contingent on strategy. For more discussion see chapter 7.

2. According to one recent study, 6 percent of the articles published between 1996 and 2000 in the top twenty academic management journals had international content and, of that subset, 6 percent focused on multinational enterprise strategies and policies. See Steve Werner, "Recent Developments in International Management Research: A Review of the Top 20 Management Journals," *Journal of Management* 28, no. 3 (2002): 277–306. To quote Werner himself, "Other than strategic alliances and entry mode strategies there is very little research on MNC strategies."

3. See C. Northcote Parkinson, *Parkinson's Law and other Studies in Administration* (Boston: Houghton Mifflin, 1956).

4. Raymond Hill and L. G. Thomas III, "Moths to a Flame: Social Proof, Reputation, and Status in the Overseas Electricity Bubble," mimeographed working paper, Goizueta Business School, Emory University, Atlanta, May 2005.

5. See, for instance, Steven Prokopy, "An Interview with Francisco Garza, Cemex's President—North American Region & Trading," *Cement Americas*, 1 July 2002, available at www.cementamericas.com/mag/cement_cemex_interview_francisco/.

6. For more—but not unmanageable—detail, see my strategy textbook, *Strategy and the Business Landscape*, 2nd ed. (Upper Saddle River, NJ: Prentice Hall, 2005), especially ch. 2 and 3.

7. See Michael E. Porter, *Competitive Strategy* (New York: Free Press, 1980).

8. See Michael E. Porter, *Competitive Advantage* (New York: Free Press, 1985); and Adam M. Brandenburger and Harborne W. Stuart Jr., "Value-Based Business Strategy," *Journal of Economics & Management Strategy* 5, no. 1 (1996): 5–24.

9. Christopher Hsee et al., "Preference Reversals Between Joint and Separate Evaluations of Options," *Psychological Bulletin* 125, no. 5 (1999): 576–590.

10. Janet Adamy, "McDonald's CEO's 'Plan to Win' Serves Up Well-Done Results," *Wall Street Journal Europe*, 5–7 January 2007, 8.

11. This point emerges from surveys that were conducted by Paul Verdin of the Solvay Business School of the University of Brussels and that he has been kind enough to share with me.

12. See, for instance, Richard E. Caves, *Multinational Enterprise and Economic Analysis*, 3rd ed. (Cambridge: Cambridge University Press, 2007), ch. 1.

13. Country-of-origin effects were discussed in a bit more detail in chapter 2.

14. Wendy M. Becker and Vanessa M. Freeman, "Going from Global Trends to Corporate Strategy," *McKinsey Quarterly* 3 (2006): 17–28.

15. For an application of the ADDING Value test to the DaimlerChrisler merger—which it fails—see my Web site, www.ghemawat.org.

16. Similar patterns show up over the last quarter century in terms of regional concentration, with the exception of West Europe, where initial concentration levels were particularly low and have since increased, albeit to levels that are still relatively low.

17. On this bias, see, for example, Timothy G. Bunnell and Neil M. Coe, "Spaces and Scales of Innovation," *Progress in Human Geography* 25, no. 4 (2001) 569–589.

18. The Shiseido example is drawn from Yves L. Doz, José Santos, and Peter Williamson, *From Global to Metanational: How Companies Win in the Knowledge Economy* (Boston: Harvard Business School Press, 2001), 65–67.

19. On sustainability, see the short discussion of barriers to imitation—one of the four threats to sustainability—in Pankaj Ghemawat, "Sustainable Advantage," *Harvard Business Review*, September–October 1986, 53–58. For a full-length, up-to-date treatment, see Pankaj Ghemawat, "Sustaining Superior Performance," in *Strategy and the Business Landscape*, 2nd ed. (Upper Saddle River, NJ: Prentice Hall, 2006), ch. 5. On judgment, see Pankaj Ghemawat, *Commitment* (New York: Free Press, 1991), ch. 7. And on creativity, see my Web site, www.ghemawat.org.

Chapter 4: Adaptation: Adjusting to Differences

1. See, for instance, evidence on how even "high-involvement exporters" tend to be insufficiently adaptive, in Douglas Dow, "Adaptation and Performance in Foreign Markets: Evidence of Systematic Under-Adaptation," *Journal of International Business Studies* 37 (2006): 212–226.

2. David Whitwam and Regina Fazio Maruca, "The Right Way to Go Global: An Interview with Whirlpool CEO David Whitwam," *Harvard Business Review*, March 1, 1994.

3. In addition to the academic research available on this industry, which has attracted particular attention in the is-versus-isn't globalizing debate ever since Ted Levitt's 1983 article on the globalization of markets, I have written an industry note on it as well as cases on two leading competitors and have interviewed the managers of two other leading competitors.

4. Actually, given the ambiguities in sizing up the market and relevant sales, this list of ten might better be thought of as ten of the top twelve competitors (including all the very largest ones) rather than strictly as the top ten.

5. Charles W. F. Baden-Fuller and John M. Stopford, "Globalization Frustrated: The Case of White Goods," *Strategic Management Journal* 12 (1991): 493–507.

6. John A. Quelch, quoted in Barnaby J. Feder, "For White Goods, a World Beckons," *New York Times*, 25 November 1997.

7. Conrad H. McGregor, "Electricity Around the World," World Standards Web site, http://users.pandora.be/worldstandards/electricity.htm.

8. Larry Davidson and Diego Agudelo, "The Globalization That Went Home: Changing World Trade Patterns Among the G7 from 1980 to 1997," unpublished paper, Indiana University Kelley School of Business Administration, Bloomington, IN, November 2004.

9. J. Rayner, "Lux Spoils Us for Choice," *Electrical and Radio Trading*, 4 March 1999, 6.

10. Another candidate for inclusion under the heading of externalization includes market-based controls, which in at least some settings have been demonstrated to lead to better performance than do microcontrols. See Srilata Zaheer, "Overcoming the Liability of Foreignness," *Academy of Management Journal* 38 (1995): 341–363.

11. Martin Lindstrom, private communication to author, November 24, 2006.

12. Ted Friedman, "The World of the World of Coca-Cola," *Communication Research* 19, no. 5 (October 1992): 642–662.

13. See Donald F. Hastings, "Lincoln Electric's Harsh Lessons from International Expansion," *Harvard Business Review*, May 1999, 163–178; and Ingmar Björkman and Charles Galunic, "Lincoln Electric in China," Case 499-021-1 (Paris: INSEAD, 1999).

14. Interview with former Lincoln Electric executive, February 26, 2007.

15. Kayla Yoon, "Jinro's Adaptation Strategy," paper prepared for International Strategy course, Harvard Business School, Boston, fall 2005; "Localizing the Product and the Company Is the Key to Success in the Japanese Market," *Business Update of Osaka* 1 (2003), available at www.ibo.or.jp/e/2003_1/index.html. Note that while the company has recently changed hands because of financial mismanagement and fraud, the Jinro brand continues to perform well in the marketplace.

16. In addition, Jinro's concentration on Japan and East-Southeast Asian markets—and on the Korean diaspora in the United States—reflects the complementary lever of focus and its heavy reliance on a Japanese distributor who later became a business partner reflects the lever of externalization, both of which will be discussed later on.

17. Simon Romero, "A Marketing Effort Falls Flat in Both Spanish and English," *New York Times*, 19 April 2004.

18. Warren Berger, "The Brains Behind Smart TV: How John Hendricks Is Helping Shape the Future of a More Intelligent World of Television," *Los Angeles Times*, 25 June 1995, magazine section 16.

19. Yasushi Ueki, "Export-Led Growth and Geographic Distribution of the Poultry Meat Industry in Brazil," Discussion Paper 67, Institute of Developing Economies, JETRO, Japan, August 2006.

20. Bruce Kogut and Harbir Singh, "The Effect of National Culture on the Choice of Entry Mode," *Journal of International Business Studies* 19 (1988): 411–432.

21. Recognition of some of these costs and risks is presumably part of the reason that, according to data compiled by the Securities Data Company, the number of cross-border joint ventures has fallen by as much as four-fifths since the mid-1990s, while cross-border mergers and acquisitions have surged.

22. The description that follows is based on Anton Gueth, Nelson Sims, and Roger Harrison, "Managing Alliances at Lilly," *IN VIVO* (Norwalk, CT: Windhover Information, Inc.), June 2001; telephone conversation with Dominic Palmer of Accenture, 7 December 2006.

23. Of course, it hasn't been all plain sailing. For a detailed discussion of a key alliance that nearly went sour but was successfully rehabilitated, see Leila Abboud, "How Eli Lilly's Monster Deal Faced Extinction—but Survived," *Wall Street Journal*, 27 April 2005.

24. Jeffrey L. Bradach, *Franchise Organizations* (Boston: Harvard Business School Press, 1998).

25. See, for instance, Eric von Hippel, *Democratizing Innovation* (Cambridge, MA: MIT Press, 2005).

26. Steve Hamm, "Linux Inc.," *BusinessWeek*, 31 January 2005, 60–68.

27. Erik Brynjolfsson, Yu (Jeffrey) Hu, and Michael D. Smith, "Consumer Surplus in the Digital Economy: Estimating the Value of Increased Product Variety at Online Booksellers" *Management Science* 49, no. 11 (November 2003).

28. Chris Anderson, *The Long Tail: Why the Future of Business Is Selling Less of More* (New York: Hyperion, 2006).

29. John Menzer, conversation with the author, 12 October 2004.

30. Martin Lindstrom, "Global Branding Versus Local Marketing," 23 November 2000, at www.clickz.com.

31. Jeremy Grant, "Golden Arches Bridge Local Tastes," *Financial Times*, 9 February 2006, 10.

32. Carliss Y. Baldwin and Kim B. Clark, *Design Rules: The Power of Modularity*, vol. 1 (Boston: Harvard Business School Press, 2000).

33. Pankaj Ghemawat, Long Nanyao, and Gregg Friedman, "Ericsson in China: Mobile Leadership," Case 9-700-012 (Boston: Harvard Business School, 2001; rev. 2004).

34. Nicolay Worren, Karl Moore, and Pablo Cardona, "Modularity, Strategic Flexibility, and Firm Performance: A Study of the Home Appliance Industry," *Strategic Management Journal* 23 (2002): 1123–1140.

35. Richard Waters, "Yahoo Under Pressure After Leak," *Financial Times*, 19 November 2006.

36. For some examples of innovations that involve melding knowledge from different parts of the world, see Yves Doz, José Santos, and Peter Williamson, *From Global to Metanational: How Companies Win in the Knowledge Economy* (Boston: Harvard Business School Press, 2001).

37. Roberto Vassolo, Guillermo Nicolás Perkins, and María Emilia Bianco, "Disney Latin America (A)," Case PE-C-083-IA-1-s, IAE (Buenos Aires, Argentina: Universidad Austral, March 2006).

38. James Murdoch and Bruce Churchill, telephone interview by author, 1 May 2001.

39. The first name sported by Starbucks stores was not Starbucks, but "Il Giornale," so one could make the case that Starbucks is actually Italian cultural imperialism at work, although in a transformed state. See Howard Schultz and Dori Jones Yang, *Pour Your Heart into It: How Starbucks Built a Company One Cup at a Time* (New York: Hyperion, 1997).

40. Sarah Schafer, "Microsoft's Cultural Revolution: How the Software Giant Is Rethinking the Way It Does Business in the World's Largest Market," *Newsweek*, 28 June 36.

41. Amyn Merchant and Benjamin Pinney, "Disposable Factories," *BCG Perspective* 424 (March 2006).

42. The Philips story is from Pankaj Ghemawat and Pedro Nueno, "Revitalizing Philips (A)," Case N9-702-474 (Boston: Harvard Business School, 2002); and Pankaj Ghemawat and Pedro Nueno, "Revitalizing Philips (B)," Case 9-703-502 (Boston: Harvard Business School, 2002).

43. See, for example, Charles Handy, "Balancing Corporate Power: A New Federalist Paper," *Harvard Business Review*, November–December 1992, 59–68.

44. Survey by the International Consortium of Executive Development Research, as reported in B. Dumaine, "Don't Be an Ugly-American Merger," *Fortune*, 16 October 1995, 225.

45. Thomas P. Murtha, Stefanie Ann Lenway, and Richard P. Bagozzi, "Global Mind-Sets and Cognitive Shift in a Complex Multinational Corporation," *Strategic Management Journal* 19, no. 2 (1998): 97–114.

46. See, for example, P. Christopher Earley and Elaine Mosakowski, "Cultural Intelligence," *Harvard Business Review*, October 2004, 139–146.

47. The description that follows is based on Samsung, *Samsung's New Management* (Seoul: Samsung Group, 1994); Youngsoo Kim, "Technological Capabilities and Samsung Electronics' International Production Network in East Asia," *Management Decision* 36, no. 8 (October 1998): 517–527; B. J. Lee and George Wehrfritz, "The Last Tycoon," *Newsweek* (international edition), 24 November 2003; and Martin Fackler, "Raising the Bar at Samsung," *New York Times*, 25 April 2006.

48. "Interbrand/*BusinessWeek* Ranking of the Top 100 Global Brands," *BusinessWeek*, 7 August 2006.

Chapter 5: Aggregation: Overcoming Differences

1. Robert J. Kramer, *Regional Headquarters: Roles and Organization*, (New York: The Conference Board, 2002).

2. John H Dunning, Masataka Fujita, and Nevena Yakova, "Some Macro-data on the Regionalisation/Globalisation Debate: A Comment on the Rugman/Verbeke Analysis," *Journal of International Business Studies* 38, no. 1 (January 2007): 177–199.

3. Susan E. Feinberg, "The Expansion and Location Patterns of U.S. Multinationals," unpublished working paper, Rutgers University, New Brunswick, NJ, 2005.

4. Alan Rugman and Alain Verbeke, "A Perspective on Regional and Global Strategies of Multinational Enterprises," *Journal of International Business Studies* 35, no. 1 (January 2004): 3–18.

5. These nine "tri-regional" companies were, in decreasing order of total sales revenues, IBM, Sony, Philips, Nokia, Intel, Canon, Coca-Cola, Flextronics, Christian Dior, and LVMH.

6. This quote is from http://www.toyota.co.jp/en/ir/library/annual/pdf/2003/president_interview_e.pdf.

7. For additional details on Dell's production network, see Kenneth L. Kraemer and Jason Dedrick, "Dell Computer: Organization of a Global Production Network," Center for Research on Information Technology and Organizations, University of California at Irvine, December 1, 2002; and Gary Fields, *Territories of Profit* (Palo Alto: CA: Stanford University Press, 2004).

8. Paul Verdin of Solvay Business School is one of those who recognizes the importance of focusing on regional strategy, rather than RHQs. See for example, Paul Verdin et al., "Regional Organizations: Beware of the Pitfalls," in *The Future of the Multinational Company*, ed. Julian Birkinshaw et al. (London: John Wiley, 2003).

9. Philippe Lasserre, "Regional Headquarters: The Spearhead for Asia Pacific Markets," *Long Range Planning* 29, no. 1 (1996): 30–37.

10. Another typology is provided in Hellmut Schütte, "Strategy and Organisation: Challenges for European MNCs in Asia," *European Management Journal* 15, no. 4 (1997): 436–445. Schütte divides RHQs into those directed at corporate headquarters in the sense of being concerned with strategy development and implementation—including Lasserre's scouting and strategic stimulation functions—and those directed at regional operations that try to enhance efficiency and effectiveness through coordination and pooling.

11. Michael J. Enright, "Regional Management Centers in the Asia-Pacific," *Management International Review,* Special Issue, 2005, 57–80.

12. Dell historically ensured that this kind of duplication didn't occur in development, where there are significant global economies of scale, by centralizing that function at headquarters in Austin, although it has begun to migrate certain development activities to Asia as well.

13. Department of Trade and Industry, as reported in the *Economist,* 4 November 2006, 113.

14. Nick Scheele, "It's a Small World After All—Or Is It?" in *The Global Market: Developing a Strategy to Manage Across Borders,* ed. John A. Quelch and Rohit Deshpande (San Francisco: Jossey Bass, 2004), 146–157, especially p. 150 for the quote.

15. For background on Ford and Ford 2000, see Douglas Brinkley, *Wheels for the World* (New York: Viking, 2003); as well as Scheele, ibid.

16. Karl Moore and Julian Birkinshaw, "Managing Knowledge in Global Service Firms: Centers of Excellence," *Academy of Management Executive* 12, no. 4 (1998): 81–92.

17. See, for instance, David B. Montgomery, George S. Yip, and Belen Villalonga, "Demand for and Use of Global Account Management," Marketing Science Institute Report 99-115 (Stanford, CA: Stanford Graduate School of Business, 1999); and David Arnold, Julian Birkinshaw, and Omar Toulan, "Implementing Global Account Management in Multinational Corporations," Marketing Science Institute Report 00-103 (Stanford, CA: Stanford Graduate School of Business, 2000).

18. Thomas Friedman, "Anyone, Anything, Anywhere," *New York Times,* 22 September 2006.

19. Eleanor Westney, "Geography as a Design Variable," in *The Future of the Multinational Company,* ed. Julian Birkinshaw et al. (London: John Wiley, 2003), 133.

Chapter 6: Arbitrage: Exploiting Differences

1. For details on the assumed cost savings and the results of the store checks, see Pankaj Ghemawat and Ken A. Mark, "Wal-Mart's International Expansion," Case N1-705-486 (Boston: Harvard Business School, rev. 2005), available on my Web site, www.ghemawat.org.

2. The Lego Group, "Company Profile 2004," available at www.lego.com/info/

pdf/compprofileeng.pdf; and Sarah Bridge, "Trouble in Legoland," *The Mail on Sunday,* 13 November 2004.

3. This belief is particularly entrenched in regard to capital, since most modern financial theory is predicated on the absence of arbitrage opportunities in financial markets, also referred to as the law of one price. But even in finance, one can think of conspicuous exceptions to this "law"; for example, American Depositary Receipts that trade at significantly different prices from the equity shares in other countries that underlie them.

4. Andrew Yeh, "Woman Breaks Mould to Top List of China's Richest People," *Financial Times,* 11 October 2006, 3.

5. Bumrungrad International, Bangkok, Web page, www.bumrungrad.com.

6. "Health Tourism," *Esquire,* August 2006, 63–64.

7. Louis Uchitelle, "Looking at Trade in a Social Context," *International Herald Tribune,* 30 January 2007, 12.

8. Haig Simonian, "Swiss Query Tax Deals for Super-Rich Foreigners," *Financial Times,* 30 January 2007, 3.

9. LAN Santander Investment Chile Conference, September 2006, available at www.lan.com/files/about_us/lanchile/santander.pdf.

10. Lynette Clemetson, "For Schooling, a Reverse Emigration to Africa," *New York Times,* 4 September 2003, available at www.nytimes.com/2003/09/04/education.

11. "Remittances Becoming More Entrenched: The Worldwide Cash Flow Continues to Grow," on Limits to Growth Web page, www.limitstogrowth.org/WEB-text/remittances.html; and "Moldova: Unprecedented Opportunities, Challenges Posed By $1.2 Billion Aid Package," *RadioFreeEurope/RadioLiberty Reports,* 5 January 2007, www.rferl.org/reports/pbureport.

12. Peter Czaga and Barbara Fliess, "Used Goods Trade: A Growth Opportunity," *OECD Observer,* April 2005, www.oecdobserver.org/news http://www.oecdobserver.org/news/fullstory.php/aid/1505/Used_goods_trade.html; and http://commercecan.ic.gc.ca/scdt/bizmap/interface2.nsf/vDownload/ISA_3745/$file/X_5392834.DOC.

13. For a more detailed examination of these issues, see Pankaj Ghemawat, "The Forgotten Strategy," *Harvard Business Review,* November 2003, 77. This section is drawn largely from that article.

14. Pankaj Ghemawat and Tarun Khanna, "Tricon Restaurants International: Globalization Re-examined," Case 700-030 (Boston: Harvard Business School, 1999).

15. Robert Plummer, "Brazil's Brahma Beer Goes Global," *BBC News,* 4 December 2005, available at http://news.bbc.co.uk/2/hi/business/4462914.stm.

16. Rick Krever from Deakin University, Melbourne, quoted in Kylie Morris, "Not Shaken, Not Stirred: Murdoch, Multinationals and Tax," ABC online, 2 November 2003, www.abc.net.au/news/features/tax/page2.htm.

17. For a very interesting overview, see Moises Naim, *Illicit: How Smugglers, Traffickers, and Copycats Are Hijacking the Global Economy* (New York: Doubleday, 2005).

18. "Attractions of Exile," *Financial Times,* 11 October 2006.

19. See, for instance, Jonathan Fahey, "This Is How to Run a Railroad," *Forbes,* 13 February 2006, 94–101.

20. This earnings breakdown is based on EBITDA—earnings before interest, taxes, depreciation, and amortization, and is for 2005–2006.

21. Michael Y. Yoshino and Anthony St. George, "Li & Fung (A): Beyond 'Filling in the Mosaic' 1995–1998," Case No. 9-398-092 (Boston: Harvard Business School, 1998).

22. Gene Grossman and Esteban Rossi-Hansberg, "The Rise of Offshoring: It's Not

Wine for Cloth Anymore," paper prepared for Federal Reserve Bank of Kansas City symposium, The New Economic Geography: Effects and Policy Implications, Jackson Hole, WY, 24–26 August 2006, available at www.princeton.edu/~grossman.

23. The calculations are based on Pankaj Ghemawat, Gustavo A. Herrero, and Luiz Felipe Monteiro, "Embraer: The Global Leader in Regional Jets," Case 701-006 (Boston: Harvard Business School, 2000); and Canadian payroll data.

24. "Chinese Jet Expects to Snare 60 Percent of Domestic Market," *China Post* (Taiwan), April 6, 2007.

25. Ashraf Dahod, "Starent Networks," presentation at the Cash Concours (Tewksbury, MA), 5 October 2006.

26. Arie Y. Lewin, Silvia Massini, and Carine Peeters, "From Offshoring to Globalization of Human Capital," unpublished draft, (Duke University, Durham, NC) January 2007.

27. The following section on Indian pharmaceuticals is based in part on unpublished research by J. Rajagopal and K. V. Anantharaman of the Global Life Sciences & Healthcare practice of Tata Consultancy Services (Bangalore, India), which I draw on here with their permission. Other sources used are cited below as appropriate.

28. "Billion Dollar Pills," *The Economist*, 27 January 2007, 61–63.

29. F. M. Scherer, quoted in Shereen El Feki, "A Survey of Pharmaceuticals," *The Economist*, 18 June 2005, 16.

30. Robert Langreth and Matthew Herper, "Storm Warnings," *Forbes*, 13 March 2006, 39.

31. See, for instance, Eva Edery, "Generics Size Up the Market Opportunity," March 2006, www.worldpharmaceuticals.net/pdfs/009_WPF009.pdf.

32. "Billion Dollar Pills."

33. Leila Abboud, "An Israeli Giant in Generic Drugs Faces New Rivals," *Wall Street Journal*, 28 October 2004.

34. Such opportunities are not confined to emerging markets. In late 2005, the U.S. government threatened to override the patents on treatments for avian flu if companies that controlled them did not expand U.S. production facilities.

35. For a description of Ranbaxy's basic strategy, which was set more than a decade ago, see Pankaj Ghemawat and Kazbi Kothavala, "Repositioning Ranbaxy," Case 9-796-181 (Boston: Harvard Business School, 1998).

36. Abraham Lustgarten, "Drug Testing Goes Offshore," *Fortune*, 8 August 2005, 67–72.

37. A less stringent regulatory environment is sometimes also cited as a source of advantage.

38. National Association of Software and Service Companies, "The IT Industry in India: Strategic Review, 2006" (New Delhi: NASSCOM, December 2005).

39. Andrew Jack, "Patently Unfair?" *Financial Times*, 22 November 2005, 21.

40. Amelia Gentleman, "Patent Rights Versus Drugs for Poor at Issue in India," *International Herald Tribune*, 30 January 2007, 10. For additional discussion of some of the tactics used by Big Pharma to discourage would-be imitators, see Pankaj Ghemawat, *Strategy and the Business Landscape* (Upper Saddle River, NJ: Pearson Prentice Hall, 2006), 100–103.

41. James Kanter, "Novartis Plans Lab in Shanghai," *International Herald Tribune*, 6 November 2006, 11.

42. Arie Y. Lewin and Carine Peeters, "The Top-Line Allure of Offshoring," *Harvard Business Review*, March 2006, 22–24.

43. For a detailed case study, see Pankaj Ghemawat, "GEN3 Partners: From Russia, with Rigor," on my Web site, www.ghemawat.org.

44. See "China Overtakes Japan for R&D," *Financial Times,* 4 December 2006, 1. I am grateful to Tom Hout for pointing out this interesting example.

45. Jim Hemerling and Thomas Bradtke, "The New Economics of Global Advantage: Not Just Lower Costs but Higher Returns on Capital" (Boston: Boston Consulting Group, December 2005).

46. The software comparisons are based on many years of work in that industry; the pharmaceutical comparisons are an extrapolation of earlier calculations in Rajesh Garg et al., "Four Opportunities in India's Pharmaceutical Market," *McKinsey Quarterly* 4 (1996): 132–145.

47. See Pankaj Ghemawat, "Tata Consultancy Services: Selling Certainty," case available on my Web site, www.ghemawat.org.

48. Minyuan Zhao, "Doing R&D in Countries with Weak IPR Protection: Can Corporate Management Substitute for Legal Institutions?" *Management Science* 52, no. 8 (2006): 1185–1199.

49. See Offshoring Research Network (ORN), https://offshoring.fuqua.duke.edu/community/index.jsp.

50. For the most exhaustive exegesis of the jackalope that I have found—which cites references dating back to the 1500s—see Chuck Holliday and Dan Japuntich, "Jackalope Fans, Take Note," updated 22 August 2005, ww2.lafayette.edu/~hollidac/jackalope.html.

Chapter 7: Managing Global Differences: The AAA Triangle

1. This literature essentially started with a discussion, nearly forty years ago, of the tension between pressures for unification within companies and for fragmentation that different national environments can create: see John Fayerweather, *International Business Management: A Conceptual Framework* (New York: McGraw-Hill, 1969). C. K. Prahalad and Yves L. Doz, in *The Multinational Mission: Balancing Local Demands and Global Vision* (New York: Free Press, 1987), elaborated on this tension as the widely cited trade-off between global integration and national responsiveness.

2. Until recently, the only aspect of arbitrage that had attracted much attention was the exploitation of international differences in knowledge. Compare Christopher A. Bartlett and Sumantra Ghoshal, *Managing Across Borders: The Transnational Solution* (Boston: Harvard Business School Press, 1989; 2nd ed. 1998). While such knowledge arbitrage is interesting, there is, as we have seen, *much* more to arbitrage in general.

3. For an excellent overview of this literature, see Richard E. Caves, *Multinational Enterprise and Economic Analysis,* 3rd ed. (Cambridge: Cambridge University Press, 2007).

4. See, for instance, Michael E. Porter, *Competitive Strategy* (New York: Free Press, 1980), ch. 2; and Michael E. Porter, *Competitive Advantage* (New York: Free Press, 1985), ch. 1.

5. For further discussion of the costs of conflict, compromise, and coordination—in a multibusiness context rather than a multigeographic one—see Pankaj Ghemawat and Jan W. Rivkin, "Choosing Corporate Scope," in *Strategy and the Business Landscape,* 2nd ed., by Pankaj Ghemawat (Englewood Cliffs, NJ: Prentice Hall, 2001).

6. Note that advertising-to-sales and R&D-to-sales ratios are the two most robust markers of the incidence of multinational companies, but that advertising economies

of scale still operate primarily at the local or regional level, whereas R&D is more likely to be characterized by global economies of scale or scope. Advertising-to-sales ratios, therefore, have affinities with adaptation, which is focused on local responsiveness, and R&D-to-sales ratios relate to aggregation, which is focused on international economies of scale or scope. And labor expenses-to-sales ratios are an obvious proxy for the prospects of labor arbitrage—although we should keep reminding ourselves that arbitrage encompasses a much wider array of international differences than simply labor costs. Thus, the oil companies, the largest global companies by many measures, built their worldwide operations around differences in the prices of raw materials.

7. All figures are for 2005, unless otherwise noted. The account is largely based on Pankaj Ghemawat, "Philips Medical Systems in 2005," Case 706-488 (Boston: Harvard Business School, 2006); D. Quinn Mills and Julian Kurz, "Siemens Medical Solutions: Strategic Turnaround," Case 703-494 (Boston: Harvard Business School, 2003); and Tarun Khanna and Elizabeth A. Raabe, "General Electric Healthcare, 2006," Case 706-478 (Boston: Harvard Business School, 2006).

8. Jeffrey R. Immelt, quoted in Thomas A. Stewart, "Growth As Process," *Harvard Business Review*, June 2006, 60–71.

9. Joon Knapen, "Philips Stakes Its Health on Medical Devices," *Dow Jones Newswires*, 9 June 2004.

10. This example and the discussion of Standard Oil are based on Mira Wilkins, ed., *The Growth of Multinationals* (Aldershot, England: Edward Elgar Publishing, 1991), 455.

11. This description is based on press releases from and articles about Cisco. See, in particular, "Cisco Chooses India As Site of Its Globalization Center and Names Wim Elfrink Chief Globalization Officer," 6 December 2006, http://newsroom.cisco.com/dlls/2006/ts_120606.html; and Rachel Konrad, "At Globalization Vanguard, Cisco Shifts Senior Executives to India's Tech Hub," Associated Press, 5 January 2007.

Chapter 8: Toward a Better Future: Getting Started

1. See Karl Polanyi, Conrad M. Arensberg, and Harry W. Pearson, eds., *Trade and Market in the Early Empires; Economies in History and Theory* (Glencoe, IL: Free Press, 1957); and Karl W. Deutsch and Alexander Eckstein, "National Industrialization and the Declining Share of the International Economic Sector, 1890–1959," *World Politics* 13 (1961): 267–299.

2. Heather Timmons, "Goldman Sachs Rediscovers Russia," *New York Times*, 3 February 2006.

3. Max H. Bazerman and Michael D. Watkins, *Predictable Surprises: The Disasters You Should Have Seen Coming and How to Prevent Them* (Boston: Harvard Business School Press, 2004).

4. For an even longer list, see the twenty-three core global risks discussed in World Economic Forum, *Global Risks 2007* (Davos, Switzerland: World Economic Forum, January 2007).

5. On the implications of a general liquidity crisis see, for instance, Niall Ferguson, "Sinking Globalization," *Foreign Affairs* 84, no. 2 (March–April 2005): 64–77.

6. Muhammad Yunus, Nobel lecture, Oslo, Norway, 10 December 2006, accessed at http://nobelprize.org/nobel_prizes/peace/laureates/2006/yunus-lecture-en.html.

7. Frank Luntz, *Words That Work: It's Not What You Say, It's What People Hear* (New York: Hyperion, 2007).

8. McKinsey Global Institute, "Offshoring: Is it a Win-Win Game?," (San

Francisco, August 2003), http://hei.unige.ch/~baldwin/ComparativeAdvantageMyths/
IsOffshoringWinWin_McKinsey.pdf.

9. Despite the steps being presented in a neat sequence, a global strategy audit
usually requires some back-and-forth iteration across them.

10. Compare the discussion and debunking of the belief that increasing global
integration leads to increasing global concentration, for example (chapters 1 and 3).

Selected Resources

Ghemawat, Pankaj. 2001. Distance Still Matters: The Hard Reality of Global Expansion. *Harvard Business Review*, September, 137–147.

———. 2003. The Forgotten Strategy. *Harvard Business Review*, November, 76–84.

———. 2003. *Getting Global Strategy Right*. Boston: Harvard Business School Publishing. Faculty Seminar CD.

———. 2003. Semiglobalization and International Business Strategy. *Journal of International Business Studies* 34 (2):138–152.

———. 2003. Strategy and the Business Landscape. Upper Saddle River, NJ: Prentice-Hall.

———. 2004. Global Standardization vs. Localization: A Case Study and a Model. In *The Global Market: Developing a Strategy to Manage across Borders*, ed. J. A. Quelch and R. Deshpande. San Francisco: Jossey-Bass.

———. 2004. The Growth Boosters. *Harvard Business Review*, July–August, 35–40.

———. 2005. Regional Strategies for Global Leadership. *Harvard Business Review*, December, 98–108.

———. 2006. Apocalypse Now? *Harvard Business Review* 84 (10):32.

———. 2007. Managing Differences: The Central Challenge of Global Strategy. *Harvard Business Review* 85 (3):58–68.

———. 2007. Why the World Isn't Flat. *Foreign Policy* (159):5–60.

Ghemawat, Pankaj, and Fariborz Ghadar. 2000. The Dubious Logic of Global Megamergers. *Harvard Business Review*, July–August, 64–72.

Index

About the Author

Pankaj Ghemawat is the Anselmo Rubiralta Professor of Global Strategy at IESE Business School and the Jaime and Josefina Chua Tiampo Professor of Business Administration (on leave) at the Harvard Business School.

Ghemawat's current teaching and research focus is on globalization and strategy. He has developed a thirty-session MBA course and written more than fifty case studies and articles on the topic, including "Regional Strategies for Global Leadership," which received the McKinsey Award for the best article published in the *Harvard Business Review* in 2005. Other journals in which he has recently published globalization-related articles include *Foreign Policy, Industrial and Corporate Change,* and the *Journal of International Business Studies.* He is one of HBS's ten bestselling case writers. He also serves as the Departmental Editor for Strategy at *Management Science.* Ghemawat is the author of several influential business and strategy books, including *Commitment, Games Businesses Play,* and *Strategy and the Business Landscape.*

Ghemawat earned his AB degree in Applied Mathematics from Harvard College, where he was elected to Phi Beta Kappa, and his PhD in Business Economics from Harvard University. He then worked as a consultant before joining the Harvard Business School faculty in 1983. In 1991, he was appointed the youngest full professor in HBS's history. He joined the IESE faculty in 2006. In 2007, Ghemawat was elected a fellow of the Academy of International Business.